MUSIC AND LAW

SOCIOLOGY OF CRIME, LAW AND DEVIANCE

Series Editor: Mathieu Deflem
Jeffrey T. Ulmer (Volumes 1–5)

Recent Volumes:

Volume 6: Ethnographies of Law and Social Control – Edited by Stacey Lee Burns, 2005

Volume 7: Sociological Theory and Criminological Research, Views from Europe and United States – Edited by Mathieu Deflem, 2006

Volume 8: Police Occupational Culture: New Debates and Directions – Edited by Megan O'Neill, Monique Marks and Anne-Marie Singh, 2007

Volume 9: Crime and Human Rights – Edited by Stephan Paramentier and Elmar Weitekamp, 2007

Volume 10: Surveillance and Governance: Crime Control and Beyond – Edited by Mathieu Deflem, 2008

Volume 11: Restorative Justice: From Theory to Practice – Edited by Holly Ventura Miller, 2008

Volume 12: Access to Justice – Edited by Rebecca Sandefur, 2009

Volume 13: Immigration, Crime and Justice – Edited by William F. McDonald, 2009

Volume 14: Popular Culture, Crime and Social Control – Edited by Mathieu Deflem, 2010

Volume 15: Social Control: Informal, Legal and Medical – Edited by James J. Chriss, 2010

Volume 16: Economic Crisis and Crime – Edited by Mathieu Deflem, 2011

Volume 17: Disasters, Hazards and Law – Edited by Mathieu Deflem, 2012

SOCIOLOGY OF CRIME, LAW AND DEVIANCE
VOLUME 18

MUSIC AND LAW

EDITED BY

MATHIEU DEFLEM
University of South Carolina, Columbia, USA

United Kingdom – North America – Japan
India – Malaysia – China

Emerald Group Publishing Limited
Howard House, Wagon Lane, Bingley BD16 1WA, UK

First edition 2013

British Library Cataloguing in Publication Data
A catalogue record for this book is available from the British Library

ISBN: 978-1-78350-036-9
ISSN: 1521-6136 (Series)

CONTENTS

PART II: POLITICS AND CULTURE

PART III: ILLEGALITY AND DEVIANCE

LIST OF CONTRIBUTORS

Heitor Alvelos	ID+ Institute of Research in Design, Media and Culture, University of Porto, UPTEC PINC, Portugal
Cecilia Blengino	Dipartimento d Giurisprudenza, Università degli Studi di Torino, Torino, Italy
Victor P. Corona	Department of Social Sciences, Fashion Institute of Technology, New York, NY, USA
Manuel Cuadrado-García	Departamento de Comercialización e Investigación de Mercados, Universitat de València, Valencia, Spain
Mitch Daschuk	Department of Sociology, University of Saskatchewan, Saskatoon, Canada
Mathieu Deflem	Department of Sociology, University of South Carolina, Columbia, SC, USA
Serona Elton	Department of Music, Media, and Industry, University of Miami, Coral Gables, FL, USA
Jon M. Garon	Northern Kentucky University Chase College of Law, Highland Heights, KY, USA
Sara Towe Horsfall	Department of Sociology, Texas Wesleyan University, Fort Worth, TX, USA
Juan D. Montoro-Pons	Departamento de Economía Aplicada, Universitat de València, Valencia, Spain
Cynthia R. Nielsen	Ethics Program, Villanova University, Wayne, PA, USA

James Popham	Department of Sociology, University of Saskatchewan, Saskatoon, Canda
Danwill D. Schwender	Foldenauer Law Group, APLC, San Diego, CA, USA
Jean-Marie Seca	Department of Sociology, UFR Connaissance de l'Homme, University of Lorraine, NANCY CEDEX, France
Masaya Takahashi	Department of Education, Saitama University, Saitama, Japan

INTRODUCTION: THE LAWS OF MUSIC

The chapters in this volume deal with a variety of issues concerning the relationships between music and law. The nexus of law and music can intellectually be approached within the social sciences from at least two angles, which can each and both usefully explore a wide number of interesting themes.

One, looking at law from the viewpoint music, the sociology of law and other social and behavioral disciplines focused on law and law-related phenomena can untangle social issues posed by music as a cultural expression in its relation to the social reality of law. In the sociology of law, by example, the relationship of law to culture has been of central concern since the development towards modern sociology (Deflem, 2008). Classical scholars such as Emile Durkheim and Max Weber, in their opposition to Marxian thought, devoted considerable attention to the continued relevance of culture vis-à-vis economic aspects of industrialization. In the move toward contemporary sociology, the cultural–idealist viewpoint of Talcott Parsons (1971) and other modern giants of sociological thought likewise accorded a central role to culture and especially sought to uncover its relationship to the need for normative integration. In the work of modernist scholars like Jürgen Habermas (1996) the relationship between values and norms becomes the central problem of the modern age, contemplating especially on the continued need for normative integration in the light of a drift towards hyper-multiculturalism.

Two, looking at music from the angle of law, intellectual refuge can be sought in the sociology of culture, in general, and the sociology of music, in particular (Roy & Dowd, 2010). Developing from the classic contributions in the sociology of music by the likes of Max Weber (1921) and Theodore Adorno (1976), the contemporary sociology of music has done much to advance our understanding of the important social dimensions as well as s sociological relevance of music as a relevant aspect of contemporary cultures (Roy & Dowd, 2010). Among the forces particular to be reckoned with – useful for settling the score, one could say, in the sociology of music – are aspects of power and market commodification (Dowd, 2002, 2003, 2004), technology (Dowd, 2005), racial and gender issues (Dowd & Blyler, 2002; Dowd, Liddle, & Blyler, 2005), career opportunities and constraints (Dowd & Kelly, 2012), and indeed law and legality, as the chapters in this volume show.

Needless to suggest then, the answer to a question on the sociology of music is easily answered as there is nothing sociological about music, while there is much sociologically relevant about music. And in analyzing this relevance not of the least importance is the role of law and legal regulation. In this day and age, in fact, the expansion of so-called entertainment law at the level of professional legal training stands as a prime expression of the heightened relevance of the legal dimensions of music, especially in the digital age. It is in the light of this contemporary relevance that the present work is situated.

The chapters in this volume are divided into three parts. In Part I, the main emphasis of the contributions is on the normative frameworks and sanctioning mechanisms that are applied to musical expressions in the contemporary world. Danwill David Schwender opens the book with a detailed account of some of the legal issues involved with the use of popular music at presidential campaigns in the United States. Schwender usefully demonstrates the relevance of copyright issues and how the courts deal therewith. The chapter by Serona Elton continues with exploring legal aspects of online piracy in the United States and elsewhere in the world. Elton argues that a graduated response can be most successful in addressing the problems at hand. Mitch Daschuk and James Popham devote their chapter to an analysis of the recording industry in guiding copyright policy. Their analysis is especially relevant in the light of technological changes affecting music today. Jon M. Garon, in the final chapter of Part I, centers on the consequences of legal issues for the creative and artistic side of music. Garon also suggests the practical consequences of his analysis for musicians and their counsel.

Part II of the book contains chapters that in various ways address issues of politics and culture. Jean-Marie Seca researches the main characteristics of the social construction of the policy of electro-amplified popular music in France. These musical forms, Seca shows, mediate between a deliberative rationalization of protest and a musicalization of revolt. Cynthia R. Nielsen next articulates an historically attuned model for the understanding of jazz. Nielsen's analysis affirms African-American musicians' artistic contributions to the shaping of modern jazz as a respected art form. In the context of Japan, Masaya Takahashi discusses cultural norms of traditional folk music. Takahashi argues that the practitioners of such music see the tracing of the roots of their work as an obligation. Heitor Alvelos focuses on pop music production in relation to a range of analogue sound artefacts. Alvelos shows how actual developments are confronted with an orthodoxy by media labels and distributors. Victor P. Corona's chapter researches prison depictions in fictional contexts of popular music, specifically concentrating on Elvis Presley, Michael Jackson, and Lady Gaga. Corona's analysis is significant by linking queer expression in this context in relation to some of the most iconic superstars in pop music.

The final part of this volume addresses deviance and other forms of illegalities involved with music. Sara Towe Horsfall develops a framework for understanding deviant genres of music. She identified the three important functions of social criticism, spreading the news, and public catharsis of exceptional events. Cecilia Blengino's chapter discusses the criminalization of sharing music on peer-to-peer networks, especially in the Italian situation. Blengino shows that treating the matter with the means of criminal law produces unintended consequences. Finally, Juan D. Montoro-Pons and Manuel Cuadrado-García offer a quantitative analysis, conducted in the context of Spain, concerning the effects of copyright infringement on recorded music purchases and live music attendance. The authors find positive effects of copyright infringement on both album purchases and live attendance. Collectively, the chapters here presented hope to show the reader much of what social-science research can offer in analyzing the connections between music and law.

Mathieu Deflem
Editor

REFERENCES

Adorno, T. W. (1976). *Introduction to the sociology of music*. New York, NY: Seabury Press.

Deflem, M. (2008). *Sociology of law: Visions of a scholarly tradition*. Cambridge, UK: Cambridge University Press.

Dowd, T. J. (2002). Culture and commodification: Structural power in the early U.S. recording industry. *International Journal of Sociology and Social Policy*, *22*, 106–140.

Dowd, T. J. (2003). Structural power and the construction of markets: The case of rhythm and blues. *Comparative Social Research*, *21*, 147–210.

Dowd, T. J. (2004). Concentration and diversity reconsidered: Production logics and the U.S. mainstream recording market, 1940–1990. *Social Forces*, *82*, 1411–1455.

Dowd, T. J. (2005). From 78s to mp3s: The embedded impact of technology in the market for prerecorded music. In J. Lampel, J. Shamsie & T. Lant (Eds.), *The business of culture: Emerging perspectives on entertainment, media and other industries* (pp. 205–224). Mahwah, NJ: Lawrence Erlbaum.

Dowd, T. J., & Blyler, M. (2002). Charting race: The success of black performers in the mainstream recording market, 1940–1990. *Poetics*, *30*, 87–110.

Dowd, T. J., & Kelly, K. J. (2012). Composing a career: The situation of living composers in the repertoires of US orchestras, 2005–2006. In C. Mathieu (Ed.), *Careers in creative industries* (pp. 210–233). London: Routledge.

Dowd, T. J., Liddle, K., & Blyler, M. (2005). Charting gender: The success of female acts in the U.S. mainstream recording market, 1940–1990. *Research in the Sociology of Organizations*, *23*, 81–123.

Habermas, J. (1996). *Between facts and norms: Contributions to a discourse theory of law and democracy*. Cambridge, MA: The MIT Press.

Parsons, T. (1971). *The system of modern societies*. Englewood Cliffs, NJ: Prentice Hall.

Roy, W. G., & Dowd, T. J. (2010). What is sociological about music? *Annual Review of Sociology*, *36*, 183–203.

Weber, M. (1921). *Die rationalen und soziologischen Grundlagen der Musik*. Tübingen: Mohr.

PART I
NORMS AND SANCTIONS

IF REAGAN PLAYED DISCO: ROCKING OUT AND SELLING OUT WITH THE TALKING HEADS OF POLITICAL CAMPAIGNS AND THEIR UNAUTHORIZED USE OF MUSIC

Danwill D. Schwender

ABSTRACT

Purpose – *This chapter explores the use of music and celebrity endorsements in political campaigns of the United States. It focuses on two aspects: (1) the legality of a political campaign's use of music at rallies and in advertisements without authorization from the owner of the musical work and (2) a review of the literature on the potential effect of the use of music in political campaigns on voter behavior.*

Design/methodology/approach – *A brief history of the use of music in political campaigns precedes an examination of the expansion of copyright law protection for music and the legal claims musicians may raise against the unauthorized use of music by political campaigns.*

Music and Law
Sociology of Crime, Law and Deviance, Volume 18, 3–36

ISSN: 1521-6136/doi:10.1108/S1521-6136(2013)0000018004

The chapter then reviews the potential effect of political campaigns' use of music and celebrity endorsements on voter behavior.

Findings – *A musician's primary legal protection falls under copyright law, but the courts disagree on whether the unauthorized use of music at political rallies and in political campaign advertisements results in copyright infringement. Social research suggests music and celebrity endorsements affect voter behavior with a likely greater effect on first-time voters.*

Originality/value of chapter – *This chapter introduces the complicated application of copyright law to the unauthorized use of musical works by political campaigns. Additionally, it notes the limited research on the effect of music and celebrity endorsements on voter behavior even as political campaigns increasingly target niche demographics with specific music selections to motivate voters to vote.*

Keywords: Music; political campaign; voter behavior; copyright

INTRODUCTION

If Reagan played disco,
he'd shoot it to shit.
You can't disco in Jack boots.
Born, born on a white horse,
he'd sing lame lyrics and
try to reach the working man.

"If Reagan Played Disco"
By The Minutemen (1982) (Album: Bean-Spill).

Music is a powerful force that can mobilize political and social change. Political campaigns have used music to motivate voters since the beginning of our republic – from George Washington's 1788 presidential campaign's, "God Save Great Washington" (a very simply reworded rendition of "God Save the King") to President Barack Obama's use of Al Green's "Let's Stay Together" in his 2012 presidential reelection campaign (ASCAP, 2013; Kasper & Schoening, 2012). Music provides a quick and easy tool for politicians to appeal to the emotions of the voting public and attempt to sway voters to vote their way (Brader, 2005). Sometimes, musicians have authorized the use, as with Mitt Romney's use of Kid Rock's hit "Born Free" which included Kid Rock singing at rallies and fund-raisers. But, other times they have not. Despite the unauthorized use of music to encourage a politician's supporters, copyright law provides little protection to musicians in this situation because the courts disagree on whether the unauthorized use of music by a political campaign is a commercial endeavor.

Commentators generally highlight the 1984 exchange between President Ronald Reagan and musician Bruce Springsteen as sounding the fighting bell between political campaigns and musical artists (Larson, 2009). In 1984, President Reagan's presidential reelection campaign decided Springsteen's song "Born in the U.S.A." would perfect the campaign's emotional appeal to voters. Springsteen's management, however, rebuffed the campaign's request to use the song. Although many now believe President Reagan actually played the song at a rally, he actually respected the artist's wishes. Nonetheless, President Reagan did reference Springsteen in a stump speech in New Jersey just days after Springsteen denied use of the song, stating: "All that we've done and all that we mean to do is to make this country freer still. America's future rests in a thousand dreams inside your hearts. It rests in the message of hope in songs of a man so many young Americans admire – New Jersey's own, Bruce Springsteen. And helping you make those dreams come true is what this job of mine is all about" (Reagan, 1984). Two days later, Springsteen raised his ideological differences with President Reagan at a concert in Pittsburgh stating, "Well, the President was mentioning my name in his speech the other day, and I kind of got to wondering what his favorite album of mine must've been, you know? I don't think it was the 'Nebraska' album … I don't think he's been listening to this one …." at which point Springsteen tore into his song "Johnny 99" about an unemployed autoworker who turns to murder (Dolan, 2012; Larson, 2009). The comments of both made headlines.

Subsequent campaigns have not been as courteous as was President Reagan. For example, the 2008 presidential campaign of John McCain and Sarah Palin received demands to stop playing the songs of the Wilson sisters, Jackson Browne, John Cougar Mellencamp, Van Halen, the Foo Fighters, Frankie Vallie, ABBA, Bon Jovi, Heart, and Gretchen Peters (Johnston, 2010; Rolling Stone, 2012). These unauthorized uses raise complicated legal issues. Do politician's need consent to use a song at a public rally? In a campaign video advertisement?

Unfortunately, these legal questions are not easily answered. Copyright law exists to protect artists, such as musicians. Copyright law currently protects two separate aspects of musical works: (1) the musical composition, i.e., the notes and lyrics, and (2) the sound recording, i.e., the recording of a performance of a musical composition. Among the rights granted is the right to publicly perform a work, but sound recordings do not have a public performance right outside of digital streaming. Therefore, to play a pre-recorded song at a public rally, a user need only obtain a license from the copyright owner of the musical composition. To play Jimi Hendrix's recording of "All Along the Watchtower," for example, would require permission from Bob Dylan, the song's composer, not Hendrix, the performer.

Political campaigns generally obtain a public performance license from a collective rights organization for use at rallies and conventions. To use a pre-recorded song in an advertisement, however, requires obtaining authorization from both the owner of the musical composition and the sound recording.

Copyright protection must also comply with the First Amendment right to free speech of the U.S. Constitution. The fair use doctrine accomplishes this by excluding from copyright infringement certain unauthorized uses of music for noncommercial, educational uses that do not affect the market for the music. Application of the fair use doctrine to uses by political campaigns remains murky because the courts disagree on whether a political campaign is a commercial or noncommercial endeavor. Therefore, musicians may have no remedy against politicians that use their work without authorization.

The prevalent use of music by political campaigns also raises several interesting social questions. Why do politicians choose particular artists and songs for use? Do voters perceive the use of music by a campaign as an endorsement of the song's author or performer? For example, President Reagan likely desired to use Springsteen's song to sway younger, working class, and New Jersey voters to vote for him. President Reagan's message, and reach, would have likely changed if he had played "Dance People" a 1984 disco hit by Finesse, or "Relax" a 1984 pop hit by Frankie Goes to Hollywood, a band with an openly gay member.

Though challenging to ascertain, modern political campaigns effectively use music with specific political focus to persuade niche demographics. In the political realm, most early commentators, and some contemporary researchers, believe political campaigns in general have minimal effect on an election's outcome (Bartels, 1993; Berelson, Lazarsfeld, & McPhee, 1954; Campbell, Converse, Miller, & Stokes, 1960; Finkel, 1993; Gelman & King, 1993; Markus, 1988). Current research, however, generally indicates that campaigns can affect election outcomes (Ansolabehere & Iyengar, 1995; Franklin, 1991; Holbrook, 1996; Jacobson, 1989; Shaw, 1999) and that music possesses the power to inspire, motivate, and energize a campaign and the voting public (Brader, 2005; Larson, 2009; Ridout & Searles, 2011; Weber, 2012). The direct and purposeful use of music by political campaigns warrants better protection for musical artists due to the prevalence of political campaigns in using music without permission. Thus, a change in the law is necessary. This chapter advocates for defining political campaigns as commercial endeavors and adding the right of sound recording artists to control use of their music by political campaigns.

After providing a brief history of the use of music in political campaigns, this chapter reviews the legal claims musicians often make against political campaigns for the unauthorized use of music. The chapter then discusses the benefits of the use of music to a politician's campaign followed by a short proposal for clarification and change in copyright law.

A BRIEF HISTORY OF THE USE OF MUSIC IN POLITICAL CAMPAIGNS

The form and manner in which politicians have used music in their campaigns has changed over time, but the core purpose has always been to motivate and energize a campaign and the voting public.

In the early stages of the republic, political campaigns selected music that spoke directly on a politician's personality and political views. These tunes were often completely original or satires of existing, popular songs. Some say William Henry Harrison's 1840 presidential campaign set the standard for singing as a campaign device with his theme song "Tippecanoe and Tyler Too" that sang his praises and denigrated the incumbent President Martin Van Buren (Kasper & Schoening, 2012). Campaigners and citizens would sing these campaign theme songs at conventions and beer halls as a way to spread the campaign's message, rally support, and "reinforce the mainstream relevance of the candidate" (Larson, 2009, p. 5).

As radio, phonographs, and film entered the homes of Americans, music grew in popularity, as did its impact on popular culture. Eventually, political campaigns began choosing songs "for their appeal to the largest bloc of voters, often from a popular film or musical that a majority would recognize" (Larson, 2009, p. 10). The campaigns, however, generally continued to reword the songs to portray the candidate as in tune with the dominant narrative of the time. Dwight Eisenhower, for example, used "I Like Ike" adapted from the 1950 Broadway hit "Call Me Madam" in his 1953 presidential campaign.

By the late 1960s, political campaigns began using music to target particular voting blocs (Kasper & Schoening, 2012). In George Wallace's 1968 and 1972 political campaigns, Wallace used exclusively country music in an attempt to appeal to lower middle class whites across the nation, but particularly in the South. Wallace believed targeting these individual demographics could capture enough votes to win the election. With Wallace's campaign, "the race for the political niche market" began (Larson, 2009, p. 15). This targeting quickly expanded to all demographics. In 1976, Gerald Ford's presidential campaign recorded his theme song, "I'm Feeling Good About America," in several styles, including choral, rock, marching band, and Latin-themed versions.

By the 1980 presidential campaigns, national politicians rarely used music to explain their platform or identity (Kasper & Schoening, 2012). Instead, political campaigns simply played popular songs at political rallies and incorporated the music, as originally written and performed, into their television and Internet video advertisements. As a result, political campaigns ceased educating voters through music. Campaign music now consists solely as a tool to spur voters' emotions and to motivate specific demographics. In the 1988 campaign, for instance, the candidates sought to inspire patriotism. George H. W. Bush's campaign used the Woody Guthrie folk tune "This Land Is Your Land" and Michael Dukakis's campaign employed the Neil Diamond song "America." As an example of demographic targeting, Bill Clinton's 1992 campaign targeted the baby boomers with Fleetwood Macs "Don't Stop" and George W. Bush's 2000 presidential campaign attempted to appeal to blue-collar workers with Billy Ray Cyrus's "We the People." For Hillary Clinton's 2008 presidential campaign, Clinton posted a YouTube video in which she provided a list of songs and asked viewers to vote for her campaign theme song. In the video she stated, "I want to know what you're thinking on one of the most important questions of this campaign" (Newman, 2007). She issued a subsequent video that included the top five songs voted on by YouTube viewers plus the top five songs written in by YouTube viewers. The public viewed each of Clinton's videos more than 900,000 times, and she garnered more than 100,000 votes in the first round of musical selections.

In addition to choosing a campaign theme song, today's political campaigns also vary the musical selections and rotate play lists depending on the desired response or demographic of the day's political rally (Kasper & Schoening, 2012). Interestingly, one commentator notes that this divided playlist corresponds with a national political narrative that is also temporary and varied in order to appeal to any demographic at any time (Larson, 2009). As a result, political campaigns now consider their music themes and play lists early in the preparatory stages of running for office.

Beyond the enthusiasm and motivational appeal of music, the use of music can also lead to the perception of celebrity endorsement by the musician of the song in support of the politician who used the music (Kasper & Schoening, 2012, p. 187). As with music, politicians have bolstered their campaigns through entertainment celebrity endorsements at least as far back as the film stars Al Jolson and Mary Pickford, who voiced support for Warren Harding's 1920 campaign (Garthwaite & Moore, 2012; Kamins, 1989). The combination of using unmodified popular songs and the media attention from a celebrity endorsement led to the growing trend of celebrity musicians endorsing politicians and assisting with campaigns. The first most notable example was Frank Sinatra singing President John F. Kennedy's campaign theme song "High Hopes" on the campaign trail and at large fund-raisers for President Kennedy. President Kennedy's shrewd media understanding likely marked the onset of political campaigns' heavy use of popular culture (Garthwaite & Moore, 2012; Larson, 2009).

Celebrity involvement in political campaigns has continued to grow. The presidential elections of 2004, 2008, and 2012 included a variety of media figures including actors, entertainers, and athletes in campaign ads, at political rallies, and at special fund-raising events – each aimed at encouraging the populace to vote. Sometimes, celebrities remain politically neutral, as with the Rock-the-Vote campaign, endorsed by such notable musical celebrities as Madonna, Snoop Dogg, Fall Out Boy, and Jacob Dylan, to encourage young citizens to vote in general. Sometimes, celebrities direct their endorsement at a specific candidate – Jay-Z and Bob Dylan endorsed President Obama in 2012 and Ted Nugent and Taylor Hicks endorsed presidential candidate Mitt Romney in 2012 (Woods & Herbst, 2007). Other times, celebrities aim at a particular demographic, such as Bruce Springsteen's "Vote for Change" Tour through several battleground states. Obviously, politicians hope celebrities can motivate their fans to vote and to vote a certain way, volunteer, and donate money to the campaigns (Brubaker, 2011; Jackson & Darrow, 2005). As a result, celebrity endorsements are now a necessity for political candidates. The Republican National Committee's ("RNC") 2013 Growth and Opportunity Project Report highlights this need. The report reassessed the republican campaign strategy and recommended the establishment of "an RNC Celebrity Task

Force of personalities in the entertainment industry to host events for the RNC and allow donors to participate in entertainment events as a way to attract younger voters" (Barbour, Bradshaw, Fleischer, Fonalledas, & McCall, 2013). Quite simply, when a celebrity endorses a politician or political cause, people take notice, including the media, the policy-makers, and the voting public, and political campaigns gain their most desired items: media attention and fund-raising ability (Brubaker, 2011).

Political campaigns generally use music in two ways: public performances at rallies and incorporation into audiovisual advertisements for television and the Internet. In 2008, the Republican National Convention and the Democratic National Convention each reached nearly 50 percent of U. S. households and both played music throughout the events for dramatic affect as speakers entered and exited the stage and during down times as entertainment for the viewers (Nielsen, 2008). The 2012 presidential election alone accounted for over $2.6 billion spent. Between June and October 21, 2012, over 900,000 advertisements appeared on television, radio, and the internet for the presidential election at a cost of over $900,000 (The Week Staff, 2012). Over 80 percent of campaign ads in the 1999–2000 election season contained music (Brader, 2006, p. 157).

Politicians have routinely used music in political campaigns without first obtaining permission. When a musician disagrees with such use, the musician generally sends a letter asking the politician to stop using of the music based on claims of copyright infringement and false endorsement. If this fails, the remaining option is to file a lawsuit. As discussed below, however, the outcome of such a lawsuit remains questionable.

MUSICIANS LACK ADEQUATE PROTECTION AGAINST THE UNAUTHORIZED USE OF MUSIC BY POLITICIANS

> I was pretty upset by [the ad], the damage had already been done by it being out there. People that I knew had seen [the ad] so it had gotten around. It's about copyright and about the fact that it does imply that I would have licensed it and endorsed him and whatever he stands for.
>
> – David Byrne, Talking Heads singer commenting on Charlie Christ's use of the song "Road to Nowhere" in a campaign advertisement without authorization (Kreps, 2010).

> We don't like people going behind our backs, using our music without asking, and we don't like the Romney campaign.

> – Brian Aubert, singer & guitarist for Silversun Pickups, commenting on Mitt Romney's 2012 presidential campaign's use of the song "Panic Switch," even though Romney's campaign had obtained a blanket license to publicly perform the song (Rolling Stone, 2012).

People comply with laws for various reasons, but, in general, four factors shape human behavior: the law, the market, the physical constraints of the surrounding architecture, and social norms (Lessig, 1998, 1999b; Schultz, 2007). Of these, the market and architecture have little influence on the use of music in political campaigns. Collective rights organizations offer blanket licenses to perform songs at rallies creating an affordable and simple market. Similarly, the market has long provided the ability to obtain individual licenses from the copyright owners for use of music in a political advertisement with costs varying on popularity of song choice and the value of such use to the copyright owner. As for architectural limitations, musicians may be able to track unauthorized uses with some form of digital watermark, but to prevent use entirely is extremely difficult. To obtain the desired behavior of politician's respecting the rights of musical authors, therefore, requires persuasive social norms or adequate legal remedies.

Social Norms

Social norms are "pattern[s] of rationally governed behavior, instantiated in a group, maintained by acts of conformity" (Hetcher, 2004). Social norms act in much the same way as laws and control behavior through social approval or disapproval. The social group, rather than the government authority, rewards and punishes their members "either by withholding or conferring signs of group status and respect, or more directly by channeling material resources toward or away from particular members" (Tyler, 1990). Social norms are the predominant influence on one's behavior and can support or supplant a law (Ellickson, 1991; Hart, 1961; Lessig, 1998, 1999a; Levin, 2002; Posner, 2000; Schultz, 2007).

The long history of music use by political campaigns has created a social acceptance of music in political campaigns and has failed to raise sufficient concern over whether such use was authorized. Over the last few decades, political campaigns have made headlines many times for receiving musicians' requests to stop the use of their music. Examples are plentiful, as mentioned previously. At least one of these demands resulted in a lawsuit. Jackson Browne sued presidential candidate John McCain and his political campaign in 2008 for unauthorized use of Browne's song "Running on

Empty." The suit settled out of court and included a public apology and a pledge: "We apologize that a portion of the Jackson Browne song *Running on Empty* was used without permission ... The ORP, RNC and Senator McCain pledge in future election campaigns to respect and uphold the rights of artists and to obtain permissions and/or licenses for copyrighted works where appropriate" (Kreps, 2010).

The risk of bad publicity from a cease and desist letter or lawsuit, and prior pledges to respect copyright protections of music, apparently falls short of inhibiting political campaigns from using music without consent from the owners. In the 2010 U.S. Senate election in Florida, Charlie Crist, a well-known republican governor of Florida, used the Talking Head's song "Road to Nowhere" in an online campaign video without authorization – the result, David Byrne sued Crist for $1,000,000 (Kreps, 2010). The case settled out of court and the settlement included a public apology video from Crist published on YouTube (Crist, 2011).

Perhaps these requests to stop unauthorized uses are too little and too late to prevent politicians from capitalizing on the initial rush of enthusiasm enjoyed from their political rally playlists and advertisements, especially in situations where the musician is unlikely to authorize the use. In other words, social norms currently lack persuasion in this context.

The expansion of copyright law to protect various rights of musical works also calls into question the unauthorized use of music by politicians. As discussed below, however, the law fails to protect musicians from the unauthorized use of music by political campaigns. The next sub-sections will discuss the status of the law and attempt to clarify when and how musicians can stop politicians from using their music.

Copyright Law

A musician's claim of copyright infringement against a political campaign is not straightforward. First, copyright law for music evolved slowly in the United States and, by some accounts, remains incomplete. Additionally, the use of music by a political campaign raises freedom of speech issues that may exclude such use from a copyright infringement claim under the doctrine of fair use.

The Constitution of the United States grants Congress the power "To ... promote the Progress of Science and useful Arts, by securing for limited Times to Authors and Inventors the exclusive Right to their respective Writings and Discoveries" (U.S. Constitution, 1787). Congress utilized this power to create the Copyright Act. The Copyright Act grants limited property rights to the author of original, creative works fixed in a tangible medium (Copyright Act, 1976). These rights are limited in scope and time. Works under today's Copyright Act generally enjoy the exclusive right to reproduce, distribute, make derivative works, and perform and display the work publicly for the period of time of the life of the author plus 70 years. Upon expiration of the copyright term, the works enter the public domain.

Congress's first copyright law issued in 1790, however, only protected an author's right to print and reprint books, maps, charts, and pamphlets and did not include music, which at the time consisted primarily of sheet music and live performances (Act of April 10, 1790). Thus, the early political campaigns in America operated clear and free from copyright restrictions on their musical selections.

The courts eventually interpreted literary works to include sheet music in 1829, which Congress codified in 1831, but only for a musical composer's reproduction and distribution rights (Clayton v. Stone, 1829; Act of Feb. 3, 1831). Congress did not grant musical composers public performance rights until 1897 and the 1909 Act limited this right to performances engaged in for-profit only – meaning only those performances for which an entrance fee was charged to hear the performance (Act of Jan. 6, 1897; Act of Mar. 4, 1909; Litman, 1987). In addition to this limitation, the public performance right proved worthless to copyright owners because of the high transactional cost of licensing works and collecting fees by a single copyright owner for public performances across the country (Loren, 2003). Nearly 20 years later, copyright owners created the first collective rights organization, the American Society of Composers, Authors, and Publishers (ASCAP) to license thousands of musical compositions under a blanket public performance license, thus reducing the transaction costs. ASCAP also began demanding licensing fees from business owners who used music as background ambiance, such as restaurants and hotels, despite the narrow legal protection of for-profit uses. The courts upheld this expanded right in 1917 stating, "If music did not pay, it would be given up. If it pays, it pays out of the public's pocket. Whether it pays or not, the purpose of employing it is profit, and that is enough" (Herbert v. Shanley, 1917).

In 1976, Congress reworded the for-profit limitation on the public performance of musical compositions and essentially provided a limited right in certain nonprofit public performances. (Copyright Act, 1976). As Congress explained at the time,

> The line between commercial and "nonprofit" organizations is increasingly difficult to draw. Many "non-profit" organizations are highly subsidized and capable of paying royalties, and the widespread public exploitation of copyrighted works by public broadcasters and other noncommercial organizations is likely to grow. In addition to these trends, it is worth noting that performances and displays are continuing to supplant markets for printed copies and that in the future a broad "not for profit" exemption could not only hurt authors but could dry up their incentive to write. (Performance Royalty, 1975)

The late 1960s and early 1970s witnessed an invasion of sound recordings into the homes of Americans, but Congress did nothing to protect this new distribution form. In the absence of a national law, individual states passed antipiracy and other laws to protect producers of sound recordings from unauthorized duplication and sale of recordings (Jaszi & Lewis, 2009; Sparkman, 1974). Federal copyright law eventually followed suit and protected the distribution and duplication of sound recordings in 1971, but a right to the public performance of a sound recording remained elusive (Act of Oct. 15, 1971). At this point, sound recordings were the only copyrighted work not granted a federal right of public performance.

As personal computers and high-speed Internet connections reached many of the households in the United States, the potential for digital piracy of sound recordings forced Congress to enact the Digital Performance Right in Sound Recordings Act of 1995. This Act added the right to perform a sound recording publicly by means of a "digital audio transmission" only.

As stated in the Introduction, the Copyright Act now protects two separate, exclusive layers of a musical recording. Authors of the underlying musical composition, i.e., the written notes and lyrics of a song, may document their musical compositions in sheet music, performances, broadcasts, and recordings. An owner of a copyrighted musical composition has the exclusive rights to reproduce and distribute the work, prepare derivative works, and to perform and display the work publicly, with some exceptions. Artists of the sound recording, i.e., the performance of the musical composition by a recording artist that is fixed onto a record, tape, compact disc, or digital file, enjoy the exclusive rights to reproduce and distribute the recordings, prepare derivative works, and perform publicly by means of a digital audio transmission only (Nimmer & Nimmer, 2012).

Because of the massive and varying uses of music in the modern world, administering licenses, obtaining licenses, and collecting royalties would be daunting if handled by each individual artist. Thus, many artists sell or license their works to a company that can control the exploitation of the work, such as registering for a copyright, promoting the work, collecting royalties, and often providing an advance payment. Ownership, and thus enforcement, of the copyright in a musical composition and sound recording are subject to the contractual relationship between the creators and the publishing companies and record labels creating an array of ownership possibilities.

Most copyright owners of musical compositions assign their rights to publicly perform their works to one of the three collective rights organizations in the United States: American Society of Composers, Authors and Publishers (ASCAP), Broadcast Music, Inc. (BMI), and SESAC, Inc. (originally the Society of European Stage Authors and Composers).[1] These organizations collect royalties on performances and distribute them to the copyright owners. When performances can be tracked, as in radio plays, the royalty goes directly to the owner. When performances cannot be tracked, such as in restaurants and stores, the organizations instead issue blanket licenses to the locations and allocate the revenues among songs likely to have been performed based on statistical analysis.

Thus, to perform music at a political rally, a politician need only acquire a license from the copyright holder of the musical composition. Many large concert halls, typical venues for large political campaign rallies, already have a blanket license in place – though these licenses sometimes exclude campaign events and conventions. Political campaigns can also purchase their own blanket license for use throughout the country to protect them at venues that may not have a proper license in place, or whose license may exclude political events. Obtaining these licenses does not require direct permission from the songwriter or the performer or the individual copyright holder as they have already assigned the right to the collective rights organization.

To use a musical work in an audiovisual advertisement requires a synchronization license (to synchronize the music in time to a video) from the owner of the musical composition and, if an existing recording of the song is used, a master recording license from the owner of the sound recording is required. Users normally obtain these licenses directly from the copyright owners, which are generally the publishing company for the musical composition and the record label for the sound recording.

Without these licenses, a campaign risks a possible lawsuit for copyright infringement. Copyright infringement requires a showing of ownership of a valid copyright and copying of the constituent elements of the work that are original. To prove copying requires evidence of access to the copyrighted work and a substantial similarity of the copied work to the original work (Feist Publications, Inc., v. Rural Telephone Service Co., 1991). On its face, a political campaign's public performance of a previously recorded song at a rally or in a political advertisement without a license constitutes infringement.

Fair Use

The courts, however, weigh the exclusive right of a copyright owner against the public's interest in dissemination of information affecting areas of universal concern under the U.S. Constitution's First Amendment protection of free speech and the ability of new artists to transform prior works into new, original ones. Application of the fair use doctrine (codified in the Copyright Act) accomplishes this balancing (Campbell v. Acuff-Rose Music, Inc., 1994; Copyright Act, 1976; Harper & Row, Publishers, Inc. v. Nation Enterprises, 1985; Sony Corp. of America v. Universal City Studios, Inc., 1984). The Copyright Act identifies four nonexclusive factors to consider in determining whether use of a copyright protected work is fair in light of the objectives of copyright to promote the progress of science and the useful arts: (1) the purpose and character of the contested use; (2) the nature of the copyrighted use; (3) the amount and substantiality of the copyrighted work used; and (4) the effect of the contested use on the potential market for the original work (Copyright Act, 1976).

When a political campaign performs a song at a rally or incorporates a song into an advertisement, the second, third, and fourth fair use factors generally weigh in favor of the copyright owner. Under the second factor, original works of music are at the core of copyright. Political campaigns usually use complete, unaltered songs at political rallies and political campaign ads tend to use a significant portion of the original works, placing the third factor in favor of copyright owners. The fourth factor also tends to weigh in favor of the copyright owner because the unauthorized use denies copyright owners the ability to license the work for a fee. Therefore, the fair use analysis of unauthorized use of music by political campaigns hinges on the first factor.

The first factor asks whether unauthorized use is of a commercial nature or is for nonprofit educational purposes, such as "criticism, comment, news reporting, teaching (including multiple copies for classroom use), scholarship, or research" (Copyright Act, 1976). This allows teachers to copy, play, and distribute works to teach and news outlets to reprint portions of a work for criticism or as items of public interest without fear of liability for copyright infringement. Parody is also included in the first factor. Parody is a form of social and literary criticism, in which a new work comments on an original work by using pieces of the original work. Satire, on the other hand, does not receive as much protection. Satire uses an original work to comment on something other than the original work. Satirical uses may be protected, however, if they are significantly transformative. This means the use transformed the original to a point that the subsequent work does not fall under the copyright owner's right to make derivative works (Cariou v. Prince, 2013).

Because the majority of cases settle out of court, only a few cases have reviewed copyright infringement claims against a political campaign's unauthorized use of music. The results are mixed.

In *Keep Thompson Governor Committee v. Citizens for Gallen Committee* (1978), Governor Thompson's reelection campaign purchased all rights, title, and interest to the song and recordings of "Live Free or Die" written and recorded by Great American Music Machine, Inc. The opposing campaign for Hugh Gallen created a 60 second radio advertisement that included 15 seconds of the three-minute long recorded song "Live Free or Die." Governor Thompson's campaign sued for copyright infringement. In applying the fair use doctrine, the court found the use to be noncommercial in nature as part of the political campaign's message implicating the freedom of expression and that the use did not affect the song's potential market or value. Therefore, the court found Hugh Gallen's political campaign did not infringe on the copyright of "Live Free or Die."

In *Browne v. McCain* (2009), the Ohio Republican Party released a political video on behalf of presidential candidate John McCain's and the Republican National Committee's 2008 campaign. The video incorporated a portion of Jackson Browne's song "Running on Empty." The case settled out of court, but in declining to rule on the issue of fair use on a motion to dismiss the complaint, the court stated: "The mere fact that Plaintiff's claim is based on Defendants' use of his copyrighted work in a political campaign does not bar Plaintiff's claim as a matter of law." Thus, this court declined to rule on the issue at such an early stage of the litigation, but indicated the mere fact a political campaign used the music may not warrant a finding of fair use.

In *Henley v. DeVore* (2010), musician Don Henley of the band The Eagles claimed that politician Charles DeVore infringed on his copyrighted songs "The Boys of Summer" and "All She Wants to Do Is Dance." DeVore's campaign created two political advertisements featuring the songs "The Hope of November" and "All She Wants to Do Is Tax," which were rewritten to the tunes of Henley's songs. One song heckled President Obama and the naiveté and subsequent disappointment of his supporters and the other song criticized American foreign policy in Latin America in the 1980s. Although one of the songs constituted a parody of sorts, the court held that "DeVore ... stood to gain publicity and campaign donations from their use of Henley's music" and, therefore, " 'profited' from their use by gaining an advantage without having to pay customary licensing fees to the Plaintiffs." Therefore, this court found DeVore infringed on Henley's copyrights.

A number of related cases have ruled on the issue outside of a musical use, but also only offer split decisions.[2] As can be seen from the existing case law, the outcome of a finding of fair use hangs on the determination of whether the court deems a political campaign as a commercial or noncommercial endeavor and in this regard, the courts are inconsistent in their rulings.

The purpose of fair use is to protect free speech and allow for the dissemination of information that is of public interest. Political campaigns most often use music to motivate and energize its base and increase the amount of money donated to the campaign rather than to make some political comment on society or the music itself. Moreover, political campaigns bring in large sums of money for advertising purposes in particular and are able to pay licensing fees. This form of use is more analogous to a business that plays music in the background to create a particular ambiance in an effort to increase sales than it is to use in a classroom or a news program regarding a particular musician.

In sum, sound recording artists are unable to bring a suit for the unauthorized public performance of their songs by a political campaign because no copyright right exists to prohibit such use and the application of copyright law to musical compositions remains unclear due to the disagreement over whether a political campaign is a commercial endeavor. As a result, musicians often claim use of their music creates a false endorsement of the politician that violates their trademark rights and rights to publicity. These claims, however, also generally fail to protect musicians, as discussed below.

Trademark

Adding to the sting of a politician's unlicensed use of a song without payment, musicians also endure the perception they have endorsed a politician with whom they may not agree. In Henley v. DeVore (2010), for example, Don Henley of The Eagles provided evidence that 48 percent of viewers believed Henley endorsed DeVore's political campaign due to the use of Henley's songs in DeVore's political advertisements. The perception of certain political endorsements can adversely affect a musician's public image and sales market, as seen by the demise of the Dixie Chicks, a country music band that spoke poorly of President George W. Bush angering their fan base. Thus, musical artists often bring claims of false endorsement under trademark law or right of publicity laws for the unauthorized use of their music.

Trademark law protects symbols, elements, or devices used to identify a product in the marketplace and to prevent confusion as to its source. The federal trademark act, the Lanham Act, prohibits the use of false designations of origin, false descriptions, and false representations in the advertising and sale of goods and services. This protection can extend to music, as with the sound of Microsoft's Windows operating system when it begins or a celebrity's distinctive voice. Similarly, many state laws exist to protect one's right to publicity. Thus, celebrities can own rights in their identity or persona and in their distinctive attributes, such as a singer's voice (Waits v. Frito-Lay, Inc., 1992). These claims face significant obstacles against a political campaign's unauthorized use of music.

First, the courts generally refuse to apply trademark law or state law claims for unfair competition in situations more appropriately covered by federal copyright law. To determine whether copyright law preempts these claims, courts review the nature of the work in question and the rights claimed in that work under state law (Copyright Act, 1976). Courts usually find claims grounded solely in the copying of a protected expression, such as music, preempted by copyright law (Harper & Row, Publishers, Inc. v. Nation Enterprises, 1980). In other words, trademark law does not protect a musical composition or sound recording as its own trademark because copyright law protects an artist's right in a musician's creative work (EMI Catalogue Partnership v. Hill, Holliday, Connors, Cosmopulos, Inc., 2000; McCarthy, 2012). Therefore, a false endorsement claim only arises from the use of an imitator. When a political campaign uses an exact copy of a recorded song, copyright law preempts a claim for false endorsement (Henley v. DeVore, 2010; Oliveira v. Frito-Lay, Inc., 2001).

Second, in instances of direct copying of a song by a voice imitator, the courts apply the standard likelihood of consumer confusion test to determine trademark infringement.[3] Under this test, however, the use of a song must create a likelihood of confusion as to the performance of the song, not the endorsement of the politician. In Henley v. DeVore (2010), for example, DeVore used a Don Henley imitator to re-record songs by The Eagles, but the court found no reasonable jury could mistake the imitator's voice for Don Henley's voice. The use of a better imitator, however, could make this a viable remedy against political campaigns that create parodies or satires of songs.

Additionally, as with claims of copyright infringement, some trademark claims may require determination of whether speech by a political campaign is commercial or noncommercial. The Lanham Act applies only to uses in connection with the sale of goods or services in interstate commerce, but there is no exemption for noncommercial uses of a trademark under standard trademark infringement claims. Thus, the courts have generally found the Lanham Act covers use of trademarks by political campaigns (United We Stand America, Inc. v. United We Stand, America New York, Inc., 1997; MGM-Pathe Communications Co. v. Pink Panther Patrol, 1991; Browne v. McCaine, 2009a). However, the Federal Trademark Dilution Act (1996), which protect against the use of marks that impair the goodwill and value of a famous mark and lessen the famous mark's ability to identify and distinguish goods or services regardless of competition or likelihood of confusion, specifically exempts noncommercial uses of a mark from its coverage. As Congress stated, the Trademark Dilution Act "should not be read in any way to limit political speech, consumer or editorial comment, parodies, satires, or other constitutionally protected material" (S. 1883, 1989). The Congress also stated, "Political advertising and promotion is political speech, and therefore not encompassed by the [Lanham Act's] term 'commercial'" (134 Cong. Rec. H. 1297, 1989). Despite the courts' split on the determination of whether a political campaign is noncommercial under copyright law, the courts have generally agreed with Congress and have excluded political speech from claims of trademark dilution (American Family Life Insurance Co. v. Hagan, et al., 2002; Mastercard Int'l Inc. v. Nader 2000 Primary Comm., Inc., 2004).

In short, the use of a performance by a political campaign does not violate any trademark right of the performer. As such, trademark claims will only protect musicians from the unauthorized use of their music by a political campaign if the politician uses a voice imitator. Unfortunately, this narrow protection does not assist most musicians because modern political campaigns generally use songs as originally recorded.

Right of Publicity

Many states have introduced laws to protect the misappropriation of celebrities' rights of privacy. For example, California Civil Code section 3344 provides for a cause of action when "any person ... knowingly uses another's name, voice, signature, photograph, or likeness, in any manner, ... for purposes of advertising ... or soliciting purchases of, ... goods or services ... without such person's prior consent ...." These laws vary in scope state by state – potentially limiting any relief to musicians depending on which state's law applies to each particular claim. Moreover, many of these laws explicitly exempt political uses. The California statute above states consent is not required for uses "in connection with ... any political campaign ...." Where an express exemption does not exist, the courts again weigh whether a political campaign is noncommercial in nature to determine whether the First Amendment protects such use – resulting in the same mixed bag of decisions as copyright infringement claims. Of course, any use of a pre-recorded song also raises copyright law's preemption doctrine. As a result, musicians' rights to publicity offer limited remedies.

In summary, copyright law remains the most promising protection for musicians against the unauthorized use of their music by political campaigns. But, the law requires clarifications and changes to offer better protection – as discussed further in the Conclusion.

Regardless of the legal ramifications of a political campaign's unauthorized use of music, a nagging question remains as to what extent such use affects voters. The next section discusses the research on the effect of music on voter behavior.

MUSIC ENERGIZES POLITICAL CAMPAIGNS AND PERSUADES VOTERS

Research substantially supports that music and celebrity endorsements have a powerful effect on consumer purchasing behavior (Agrawal & Kamakura, 1995; Butler, Cowan, & Nilsson, 2005; Dholakia & Sternthal, 1977; Mathur, Mathur, and Ragan, 1997; Ohanian, 1991). Examining changes in voter behavior due to a campaign's use of music, however, proves more difficult than distinguishing between a shopper's choice of Nike or Adidas shoes. Voter behavior consists of more than the final vote placed. Voter behavior also includes overall voter turnout, campaign contributions, and campaign volunteer assistance. Testing voter behavior requires an experiment that can isolate the seemingly trivial use of music from the onslaught of actual content in political ads and speeches on social and policy issues that can affect voters' choices.

Further complicating the research is the third person effect theory, which indicates individuals overestimate the influence of persuasive mass communication on others as compared to themselves (Brubaker, 2011; Davison, 1983). As the social distance increases so too does the perceived persuasive impact of a message (Brubaker, 2011; Meirick, 2004). In other words, Republicans viewing an anti-republican ad would see the smallest effect on themselves, a larger effect on other Republicans, and the largest effect on Democrats. Perhaps because of these hurdles, little research exists on the effect of music on voter behavior.

Early research found political campaigns in general may have a minimal effect on election outcomes (Bartels, 1993; Berelson et al., 1954; Campbell et al., 1960; Finkel, 1993; Gelman & King, 1993; Markus, 1988). Instead, the early research indicates that a voter's choice is a product of partisan identification, the economy, views on the incumbent party, and the social characteristic of the voter – all of which are in place prior to a political campaign. As party identification levels lowered among the electorate and campaigns continued to grow in size and expenditure, research on voter behavior renewed.

Current research, benefitted by the increased data availability of the Internet age, generally indicates that campaigns can affect election outcomes. Campaign rallies and advertisements engage, mobilize, and educate voters, especially the politically unsophisticated, and music substantially assists in this regard (Ansolabehere & Iyengar, 1995; Brader, 2005; Franklin, 1991; Franz, Freedman, Goldstein, & Ridout, 2007; Holbrook, 1996; Jacobson, 1989; Larson, 2009; Ridout & Searles, 2011; Shaw, 1999; Weber, 2012). Obviously, music and the related celebrity endorsements also assist in fund-raising and successful political outcomes are generally associated with the campaign of greatest spending (Garthwaite & Moore, 2012; Levitt, 1994).

Music can produce intense emotional response and research suggests, "cueing emotions with images and music can dramatically influence responses to campaign ads" (Brader, 2005, p. 389; see also Blood & Zatorre, 2001; Brader, 2006; Marcus, Neuman, & MacKuen, 2000; Ridout & Searles, 2011; Weber, 2012). Political ads commonly appeal to one of two emotions: enthusiasm or fear. "Enthusiasm is a reaction to signals that have positive implications for a person's goals (i.e., things are going well).

It reinforces commitment to those goals and strengthens the motivation to act or stay involved" (Brader, 2005, p. 390). "[F]ear is a reaction to threat. Fear breaks a person out of routines, directs attention to relevant portions of the environment, and activates thinking about alternative courses of action." (Brader, 2005, p. 390). Ads attempting to raise enthusiasm generally use uplifting or patriotic music and ads seeking a fear response tend to use tense discordant music or none at all. In step with this research, political campaigns paint their messages with imagery and music aimed at voters' emotions. In recent years, nearly three quarters of campaign ads placed an emotional appeal over a logical appeal (Brader, 2006).

Professor Ted Brader has conducted extensive research on emotional appeals in campaign advertisements and found that "enthusiasm appeals greatly improve the motivational power of political ads" (Brader, 2005, p. 394). His research reveals several effects of emotional appeals on voter behavior: an increase on a person's preference for the same candidate, thus solidifying preexisting preferences, an increase on a voter's reliance on prior beliefs, an increase on a voter's interest in the campaign, and an increase on the willingness to vote. In short, a voter's enthusiasm strongly motivates a potential voter to vote.

As for cuing fear, "there is no evidence from [Professor Brader's] experiment to suggest that ads can stimulate interest or voting by appealing to fear" (Brader, 2005, p. 399). Fear appeals do, however, improve recall of related news, provoke information seeking, and thereby may cause changes in political choice (Brader, 2005; Marcus et al., 2000).

Music can be especially effective in this regard because music has the ability to elicit emotional responses while allowing the observer to focus attention on the accompanying speech or video (Brader, 2005, 2006).

Celebrity endorsements affect voters similar to enthusiasm appeals. As noted earlier, extensive research documents the persuasive effect of celebrity endorsements on consumer behavior. Celebrity endorsement of political campaigns may also affect voters in a number of ways. Some research has noted that celebrity endorsements increase the perceived trustworthiness of the source of information thereby increasing the level of agreement with certain ideas – termed by some as "source credibility" (Dholakia & Sternthal, 1977; Hovland & Weiss, 1952; Jackson & Darrow, 2005; McCracken, 1989; Mueller, 1973; Page, Shapiro, & Dempsey, 1987; Sternthal, Dholakia, & Leavitt, 1978). Other research has noted that the physical attractiveness of the endorser may also influence a message's effectiveness – termed by some as "source attractiveness" (Baker & Churchill, 1977; Jackson & Darrow, 2005; Kahle & Homer, 1985; McGuire, 1985). A third theory incorporates the characteristics of the celebrity and their interaction with the product being sold (a politician in this case) – termed "meaning transfer theory" (Jackson & Darrow, 2005; McCracken, 1989). Professor Grant McCracken argues that a celebrity's social status, class, gender, age, personality, and lifestyle type all lend meaning and vary the effectiveness of an endorsement. This "meaning" transfers from the celebrity to the product and then from the product to the consumer. Regardless of the theory, the research supports the premise that voters rely on celebrities for part of their political education (Brubaker, 2011; Marks & Fischer, 2002) and viewers may perceive use of a musician's work as an endorsement of the politician (Henley v. DeVore, 2010). To the contrary, however, some research indicates that while celebrity endorsements may affect voter turnout, such endorsements may have little effect on voter choice of candidate (Woods & Herbst, 2007; Pease & Brewer, 2008).

Further research indicates that celebrity endorsements can "strengthen support among those already predisposed toward a position" and may effectively "strengthen support among their followers, mobilize voters, and raise funds" (McCracken, 1989, p. 314; see also Jackson & Darrow, 2005; Zaller & Feldman, 1992. But compare Ekant, Becirovic, & Martin, 2010). Results also show that celebrity endorsements may "make unpopular causes, candidates, or ideas slightly more palatable" (Jackson & Darrow, 2005, pp. 94–95). Add to this the expansive media reach of celebrities and it is easy to understand why political campaigns seek endorsements from entertainment stars in hopes of convincing the celebrity's fans to support, and vote for, the endorsed politician (Brubaker, 2011; Payne, Hanlon, & Tworney, 2007).

Again, these appeals are likely more effective on first time voters, who may be seeking a familiar knowledge source (Jackson & Darrow, 2005; Jackson & Jesse, 2008; MediaVest USA, 2004; Rosenberg, 2004; Woods & Herbst, 2007). Also notable is that if the endorsement does not elicit an actual vote, it may still act as a stepping-stone into politics for young citizens. If young citizens attend a political event/concert because their favorite musician is playing, they might stay to take part in the associated political activity (Brubaker, 2011). This connection, however, also has its detractors who claim any actual impact is minimal at best (Hoover & Orr, 2007).

During the 2008 presidential campaign, for example, almost 70 percent of Americans claim Oprah Winfrey's endorsement of a presidential candidate would not influence their vote, yet 60 percent of Americans believed Winfrey's endorsement of presidential candidate Barack Obama would help his candidacy (Brubaker, 2011; Pew Research Center, 2007). An interesting paper that reviewed the effect of Winfrey's endorsement of Obama in 2008 reveals the potential effect of celebrity endorsements. Winfrey's book club has notoriously skyrocketed sales of endorsed books – Leo Tolstoy's "Anna Karenina" (1877) and Gabriel Garcia Marquez's "Love in the Time of Cholera" (2007) both increased sales over 100 percent immediately after Winfrey's endorsement. Professors Craig Garthwaite and Timothy J. Moore sought to find whether a similar effect occurred with Barrack Obama. Their results indicate that Winfrey's endorsement of Obama increased the number of votes Obama received in the Democratic presidential primary by 1,015,559 votes, increased the amount of contributions made to Obama's campaign, and increased voter turnout by 2,196,300 voters (Garthwaite & Moore, 2012). Separate polling showed similar results (Andelman, 2007; Bosman, 2007; Garthwaite & Moore, 2012; Halloran, 2007; Pew Research Center, 2007). Although Oprah Winfrey is likely a large-scale example, the results show the effect of celebrity endorsements. Less known celebrities may have smaller, but similar, impacts – especially when viewed within their own niche market of fans. In the end, even a small impact may be enough to change the outcome in closely held elections.

The potential impact of music and the perception of a musician's celebrity endorsement on political campaigns and voter behavior require a clear legal outcome on the unauthorized use of music by political campaigns.

CONCLUSION

The ever expanding cyber-culture, which allows everyday citizens to easily appropriate and share songs and pictures from others for use in their own quasi-personal way, reflects a contradiction between a strong association and love for music and the limited, fleeting value placed on that music. No one seems to care whether musicians earn money for their product, and yet artists still seem wary of the career damaging "sell-out" to commercial ad campaigns. This concern probably increases with the risk of a perceived association of their music to a political ideology with which they disagree.

Surprisingly, the expected social control inherent in the negative publicity from a musician's public request that a politician cease use of particular songs offers little assistance. Perhaps research that indicated voters would flee from politicians associated with such public demand letters could change politician's attitudes. But, if the results prove negligible, then politicians may find the benefits of unauthorized use outweigh the risks of bad publicity – as they seem to now.

Absent a social norm to control politicians' behavior, improvement of musicians' legal remedies is necessary. The legal landscape currently offers questionable protection because of the split of authority on whether a political campaign is a noncommercial endeavor excluded from infringement under the fair use doctrine and the glaring omission of a public performance right for sound recording artists. Therefore, improved protection requires two main changes to the law: (1) clarification that a political campaign's use of music is not part of the politician's noncommercial, political speech, but a commercial marketing tool used to increase campaign funds, volunteer assistance, and votes; and (2) a legal provision granting rights to sound recording artists against unwanted public performances of their works by political campaigns.

The fair use doctrine balances copyright protection with free speech. Political speech is a fundamental First Amendment activity integral to our operation of government. Many commentators agree that the fair use doctrine should not cover all political campaign uses (Bilasz, 2010; Cursio, 2011; Desai, 2001; Henslee, 2009; Gunderson, 1993; Schacter, 2011; Vahdani, 2011/2012). Arguably, use of music by a political campaign is not political speech, but rather a valuable marketing tool used to motivate voters to vote, donate, and volunteer. The use at a rally generally provides no educational purpose and offers no criticism, comment, or review. Music at a political rally is not making a political comment on society or criticizing the music itself. This form of use is more analogous to a business that plays music in the background to create a particular ambiance in an effort to increase sales than it is to teach citizens or offer comments of national interest regarding a particular musician. Additionally, political campaigns raise large sums of money for advertising and regularly pay for advertisement spots and video production; they are particularly well situated to pay licensing fees too. Certainly, a Bruce Springsteen concert does not rise to the level of political speech because he tours in battleground states or opens for a politician's stump speech. Therefore, a finding that all political campaigns operate under fair use due to noncommercial status stretches the fair use doctrine too far.[4]

The answer is to place a limit on the fair use exception for political campaigns. Any new rule must avoid labeling all political speech as commercial and allow for some use of music in direct political appeals. Presidential candidate John McCain's use of "Running on Empty" to comment on Obama's energy policy provides an example. Although this use may form political speech, use of Jackson Browne's song is unnecessary to make the statement (though it likely enhances the impact) (Cursio, 2011; Schacter, 2011). Additionally, it is a satirical use and not a parody in that it comments on Obama, not the song or Jackson Browne. As such, it should receive less protection under the First Amendment than parody and far less protection than pure political speech, such as a McCain speech on Obama's energy policy.

Several scholars have recommended various changes to the law to limit the fair use doctrine (Bilasz, 2010; Desai, 2001; Henslee, 2009; Schacter, 2011. But compare Rumfelt, 2006). One suggests excluding political events from the rights granted to collective rights organizations or allowing musicians to remove their works from the blanket licenses (Bilasz, 2010). Another suggests creating a new substantive approval right for musical artists in political campaigns (Schacter, 2011). Professor Henslee recommends enumerating specific fair uses by statute for only news reporting, teaching, scholarship, and research with a statutory compulsory licensing scheme in place for artists creating new works with the old (Henslee, 2009).

An unlikely solution of granting musicians moral rights (the right to integrity and the right to attribution currently enjoyed only by the fine arts) has also been offered (Bilasz, 2010; Desai, 2001). With these rights, musicians could arguably claim a political use disparages their work and thereby stop the use. The United States has historically shied away from moral rights.

Each solution above retains the difficult weighing of commercial versus noncommercial uses, and political campaigns claim to operate for noncommercial, educational purposes. Thus, a better solution may be to offer a statutory definition of commercial or to delineate between use of music as political speech and use of music as entertainment regardless of the commercial setting of the user. Of course, all of the above solutions would increase the transaction costs for political campaigns, but may offer better protection to musicians.

The second aspect requires expansion of copyright to include the public performance of sound recordings. This seems especially important given the likelihood viewers probably associate the musical performer of a song at a political rally over the author of the underlying musical composition. Numerous commentators have discussed this solution and noted the difficulty of passing such a law given the extensive lobbying of the broadcasters (DelNero, 2004; Wolke, 2005). Therefore, a narrow right should be granted – limited to public performances by political campaigns, or even government election campaigns. This would require a clear definition of political campaigns (Bilasz, 2010).

Forcing political campaigns to obtain authorization to use each song individually would also assist campaigns from inappropriately using songs that are out of line with their political rhetoric or ideology. Often the separation of an artist's intent and context of the song varies with the political campaign's desired emotional and motivational application. For example, Silversun Pickups asked Mitt Romney's 2012 presidential campaign to stop playing its song "Panic Switch" at campaign events and noted the irony of the song's content compared to the political use stating: "We were very close to just letting this go because the irony was too good. While he is inadvertently playing a song that describes his whole campaign, we doubt that 'Panic Switch' really sends the message he intends" (Rolling Stone, 2012). Similarly, the musician's political ideology often differs from the politician using the musician's music, which could harm the musician's marketability. As an example, country stations across the United States stopped playing songs by the Dixie Chicks in 2003 following reports that lead singer Natalie Maines commented on President Bush and said she was "ashamed the president of the United States is from Texas" (Reuters, 2003).

In the end, politicians need to respect the law, but more importantly in this context, artists and politicians need clarification of the law.

NOTES

1. These three collective rights organizations together represent the public performance rights for over 97 percent of U.S. musical compositions, e.g., BMI represents approximately 600,000 songwriters, composers, and music publishers in the United States and around the world and about 7.5 million compositions, and processes almost 100 billion copyright transactions annually. For the public performance right in digital sound recordings, SoundExchange provides collective rights organization to copyright owners.

2. In *Long v. Ballantine*, 1998 U.S. Dist. LEXIS 7813; 1998 WL 35156025 (E.D. N. Car., March 25, 1998), mayoral candidate Patrick Ballantine used a photograph of his opponent Mayor Donald Betz in a campaign advertisement which the court found infringed the photographers copyright.

In *Mastercard Int'l Inc. v. Nader 2000 Primary Comm., Inc.*, 70 U.S.P.Q.2D (BNA) 1046 (S.D.N.Y. 2004), presidential candidate Ralph Nader's campaign created a satirical advertisement implying that candidates of the two major political parties were for sale for cash and beholden to special interests using the premise of Mastercard's Priceless Advertisement campaign series. The court found in favor of Nader's campaign because the political nature of the use created a noncommercial use and the use was a parody and transformative. The court stated "Even assuming the Nader Ad caused greater contributions to be made to his political campaign, this would not be enough to deem Ralph Nader's Ad 'commercial.'"

In *American Family Life Insurance Co. v. Hagan, et al.*, 266 F. Supp. 2d 682 (N. D. Ohio 2002), a candidate running for Governor in Ohio against the incumbent Governor Robert Taft created an advertisement that used a white duck quacking "TaftQuack" with Governor Taft's head sitting on the body mimicking the insurance company's Aflac advertisements. The court found no infringement because defendants' solicitation of contributions, and the resulting making of contributions, "is much more than merely a commercial transaction. Indeed, this exchange is properly classified not as a commercial transaction at all, but completely noncommercial, political speech."

In *Worldwide Church of God v. Phila. Church of God, Inc.*, 227 F.3d 1110 (9th Cir. 2000), the court held a church's copying and distribution of a copyrighted religious text infringement because "monetary gain is not the sole criterion, particularly in a setting where profit is ill-measured in dollars." The court found that the church stood to gain parishioners through the unlicensed use of the copyrighted work and therefore unquestionably profited by taking it at no cost and distributing it to new members who tithe part of their income to the church. This advantage is profiting from the copying of the text.

3. Courts weigh a number of factors in determining the likelihood of consumer confusion, which generally include: (1) The similarity or dissimilarity of the marks in their entireties as to appearance, sound, connotation, and commercial impression. (2) The similarity or dissimilarity and nature of the goods or services as described in an application or registration or in connection with which a prior mark is in use. (3) The similarity or dissimilarity of established, likely-to-continue trade channels. (4) The conditions under which and buyers to whom sales are made, i. e., "impulse" vs. careful, sophisticated purchasing. (5) The fame of the prior mark (sales, advertising, length of use). (6) The number and nature of similar marks in use on similar goods. (7) The nature and extent of any actual confusion. (8) The length of time during and conditions under which there has been concurrent use without evidence of actual confusion. (9) The variety of goods on which a mark is or is not used (house mark, "family" mark, product mark). (10) The market interface between applicant and the owner of a prior mark. (11) The extent to which applicant has a right to exclude others from use of its mark on its goods. (12) The extent of potential confusion, i.e., whether de minimus or substantial. (13) Any other established fact probative of the effect of use.

The courts apply a different test in the context of expressive works that incorporate a trademark. (*Mattel, Inc. v. MCA Records, Inc.*, 2002). In claims that raise First Amendment issues, such as expressive uses of a celebrity's identity, courts apply the "artistic relevance" test. Under this test, no trademark violation is found unless the use of the mark has no artistic relevance to the underlying work whatsoever, or if it has some artistic relevance, unless it explicitly misleads as to the source or content of the work. In *Brown v. McCain* (2009), the court did not apply this test because no artistic expression by McCain had been established.

4. Some commentators disagree with limiting fair use. (Babiskin, 1994; Bisceglia, 1987; Patry & Perlmutter, 1993).

ACKNOWLEDGMENTS

The author thanks Stacey Bergeson and Amanda Andersen for their constant curiosity and rock n' roll knowledge. All errors are the author's own.

REFERENCES

Agrawal, J., & Kamakura, W. A. (1995). The economic worth of celebrity endorsers: An event study analysis. *Journal of Marketing*, *59*, 56–62.

Andelman, D. A. (2007). Celebrity power? *Forbes.com*. Oct. 7. Retrieved from http://www.forbes.com/2007/10/17/forbes-tracker-celebs-oped-cx_daa_1017celebs.html

Ansolabehere, S., & Iyengar, S. (1995). *Going negative: How political advertisements shrink and polarize the electorate*. New York, NY: Free Press.

ASCAP. (2013). *Political campaign music use*. Retrieved from http://www.ascap.com/~/media/Files/Pdf/advocacy-legislation/ASCAP_Political_Campaign_Music_Use_02022012.pdf

Babiskin, L. M. (1994). Oh, pretty parody: Campbell v. Acuff-Rose Music, Inc. *Harvard Journal of Law & Technology*, *8*, 193–229.

Baker, M. J., & Churchill, G. A. (1977). The impact of physically attractive models on advertising evaluations. *Journal of Marketing Research*, *14*(4), 538–555.

Barbour, B., Bradshaw, S., Fleischer, A., Fonalledas, Z., & McCall, G. (2013). Grand Ole Party. *Growth and Opportunity Project Report*. Retrieved from http://online.wsj.com/public/resources/documents/RNCreport03182013.pdf

Bartels, L. M. (1993). Messages received: The political impact of media exposure. *American Political Science Review*, *87*(2), 267–285.

Berelson, B., Lazarsfeld, P., & McPhee, W. (1954). *Voting: A study of opinion formation in a presidential campaign*. Chicago: Univesity of Chicago Press.

Bilasz, L. M. (2010). Note: Copyrights, campaigns, and the collective administration of performance rights: A call to end blanket licensing of political events. *Cardozo Law Review*, *32*, 305–336.

Bisceglia, J. (1987). Parody and copyright protection: Turning the balancing act into a juggling act. In ASCAP. *Copyright Law Symposium*, *34*, 1–34.

Blood, A. J., & Zatorre, R. J. (2001). Intensely pleasurable responses to music correlate with activity in brain regions implicated in reward and emotion. PNAS, 98(20). Retrieved from www.pnas.org/cgi/doi/0.1073/pnas.191355898

Bosman, J. (2007). The Oprah factor and Obama. *New York Times*, Sep. 11, A22.

Brader, T. (2005). Striking a responsive chord: How political ads motivate and persuade voters by appealing to emotions. *American Journal of Political Science*, *49*(2), 338–405.

Brader, T. (2006). *Campaigning for hearts and minds: How emotional appeals in political ads work*. Chicago: University of Chicago Press.

Brubaker, J. (2011). It doesn't affect my vote: Third-person effects of celebrity endorsements on college voters in the 2004 and 2008 presidential elections. *American Communication Journal*, *13*(2), 4–22.

Butler, R. J., Cowan, B. W., & Nilsson, S. (2005). From obscurity to bestseller: Examining the impact of Oprah's book club selections. *Publishing Research Quarterly*, *20*(3), 23–34.

Campbell, A., Converse, P., Miller, W., & Stokes, D. (1960). *The American voter*. New York, NY: John Wiley.

Crist, C. (2011). *Charlie Crist official apology to David Byrne for copyright infringement*. Retrieved from http://www.youtube.com/watch?v=s4k13LmlcUE

Cursio, M. J. (2011). Comment: Born to be used in the USA: An alternative avenue for evaluating politicians' unauthorized use of original musical performances on the campaign trail. *Villanova Sports & Entertainment Law Journal*, *18*, 317–373.

Davison, W. P. (1983). The third-person effect in communication. *Public Opinion Quarterly*, *47*, 1–15.

DelNero, M. S. (2004). Long overdue? An exploration of the status and merit of a general public performance right in sound recordings. *Vanderbilt Journal of Entertainment Law & Practice*, *6*, 181–212.

Desai, R. (2001). Article: Music licensing, performance rights societies, and moral rights for music: A need in the current U.S. music licensing scheme and a way to provide moral rights. *University of Baltimore Intellectual Property Law Journal*, *10*, 1–23.

Dholakia, R. R., & Sternthal, B. (1977). Highly credible sources: Persuasive facilitators or persuasive liabilities? *Journal of Consumer Research*, *3*(4), 223–232.

Dolan, M. (2012). *Bruce Springsteen and the promise of rock 'n' roll*. New York, NY: W.W. Norton & Co. Inc.

Ekant, V., Becirovic, I., & Martin, B. (2010). If Kate voted conservative would you? The role of celebrity endorsements in political party advertising. *European Journal of Marketing*, *44*(3/4), 436–450.

Ellickson, R. C. (1991). *Order without law: How neighbors settle disputes*. Cambridge, MA: Harvard University Press.

Finkel, S. F. (1993). Reexamining the 'minimal effects' model in recent presidential campaigns. *Journal of Politics*, *55*(1), 1–21.

Franklin, C. H. (1991). Eschewing obfuscation? Campaigns and the perception of U.S. Senate incumbents. *American Political Science Review*, *85*(4), 1193–1214.

Franz, M. M., Freedman, P. B., Goldstein, K. M., & Ridout, T. N. (2007). *Campaign advertising and American democracy*. Philadelphia, PA: Temple University Press.

Garthwaite, C., & Moore, T. J. (2012). Can celebrity endorsements affect political outcomes? Evidence from the 2008 US democratic presidential primary. *Journal of Law, Economics, and Organization*, *29*(2), 355–384.

Gelman, A., & King, G. (1993). Why are American presidential election polls so variable when votes are so predictable. *British Journal of Political Science*, *23*(4), 409–451.

Gunderson, E. (1993). Every little thing I do (incurs legal liability): Unauthorized use of popular music in presidential campaigns. *Loyola of Los Angeles Entertainment Law Review*, *14*(5), 137–172.

Halloran, L. (2007). Oprah lends her magic to Obama's run: How the 'O' factor lures cash and – maybe – women's votes. *U.S. News & World Report*, Dec. 10, *143*(20), 18–18.

Hart, H. L. A. (1961). *The concept of law* (3rd ed. 2012). Oxford, UK: Oxford University Press.

Henslee, W. (2009). You can't always get what you want, but if you try sometimes you caan steal it and call if fair use: A proposal to abolish the fair use defense for music. *Catholic University Law Review*, *58*, 663–700.

Hetcher, S. A. (2004). *Norms in a wired world*. Cambridge, UK: Cambridge University Press.

Holbrook, T. M. (1996). *Do campaigns matter?* Thousand Oaks, CA: Sage Publications, Inc.

Hoover, M., & Orr, S. (2007). Youth political engagement: Why rock the vote hits the wrong note. In D. M. Shea & J. C. Green (Eds.), *Fountain of youth: Strategies and tactics for mobilizing America's young voters*: Lanham, MD: Rowman & Littlefield.

Hovland, C. I., & Weiss, W. (1952). The influence of source credibility on communication effectiveness. *Public Opinion Quarterly*, *15*(4), 635–650.

Jackson, D. J., & Darrow, T. I. A. (2005). The influence of celebrity endorsements on young adults' political opinions. *The Harvard International Journal of Press/Politics*, *10*(3), 80–98.

Jackson, D., & Jesse, N. (2008). *Celebrity politics and young adults' political beliefs in the United Kingdom*. Presented at the annual meeting of the MPSA Annual National Conference, Palmer House Hotel, Hilton, Chicago, IL. April 3. Retrieved from http://citation.allacademic.com/meta/p266657_index.html

Jacobson, G. C. (1989). Strategic politicians and the dynamics of U.S. House elections, 1946–1986. *American Political Science Review*, *83*(3), 773–794.

Jaszi, P., & Lewis, N. (2009). *Protection for pre-1972 sound recordings under state law and its impact on use by nonprofit institutions: A 10-state analysis*. Retrieved from www.loc.gov/rr/record/nrpb/pub146.pdf

Johnston, D. C. (2010). The singer did not approve this message: Analyzing the unauthorized use of copyrighted music in political advertisements in Jackson Browne v. John McCain. *Cardozo Arts & Entertainment Law Journal*, *27*, 687–708.

Kahle, L. R., & Homer, P. M. (1985). Physical attractiveness of celebrity endorsers: A social adaptation perspective. *Journal of Consumer Research*, *11*(4), 954–961.

Kamins, M. A. (1989). Celebrity and non-celebrity advertising in a two sided context. *Journal of Advertising Research*, *29*, 34–42.

Kasper, E. T., & Schoening, B. S. (2012). *Don't stop thinking about the music: The politics of songs and musicians in presidential campaigns*. Lanham, MD: Lexington Books.

Kreps, D. (2010). David Byrne sues Florida governor Charlie Christ for $1 million: Talking head leader sues over unauthorized use of music in Republican Senate campaign. *Rolling Stone*, May 24. Retrieved from http://www.rollingstone.com/music/news/david-byrne-sues-florida-governor-charlie-christ-for-1-million-20100524

Larson, J. (2009). American tune: Postwar campaign songs in a changing nation. *Journal of Popular Culture*, *42*(1), 3–26.

Lessig, L. (1998). The new Chicago school. *Journal of Legal Studies*, *27*, 661–691.

Lessig, L. (1999a). *Code and other laws of cyberspace*: New York, NY: Basic Books.

Lessig, L. (1999b). The law of the horse: What cyberlaw might teach. *Harvard Law Review*, *113*, 501–549.

Levin, D. B. (2002). Building social norms on the internet. *Yale Journal of Law & Technology*, *4*, 97–138.

Levitt, S. (1994). Using repeat challengers to estimate the effect of campaign spending on election outcomes in the U.S. House. *Journal of Political Economy*, *102*, 777–798.

Litman, J. (1987). Copyright, compromise, and legislative history. *Cornell Law Review*, *72*, 857–904.

Loren, L. P. (2003). Untangling the web of music copyrights. *Case Western Reserve Law Review*, *53*, 673–722.

Marcus, G. E., Neuman, W. R., & MacKuen, M. (2000). *Affective intelligence and political judgment*. Chicago: University of Chicago Press.

Marks, M. P., & Fischer, Z. M. (2002). The king's new bodies: Simulating consent in the age of celebrity. *New Political Science*, *24*(3), 371–394.

Markus, G. B. (1988). The impact of personal and national economic conditions on the presidential vote: A pooled cross-sectional analysis. *American Journal of Political Science*, *32*(1), 137–154.

Marquez, G. G. (2007). *Love in the time of cholera*. New York, NY: Vintage.

Mathur, L. K., Mathur, I., & Ragan, N. (1997). The wealth effects associated with a celebrity endorser: The Michael Jordan phenomenon. *Journal of Advertising Research*, *37*, 67–73.

McCarthy, J. (1998–2013). *McCarthy on trademarks and unfair competition* (4th ed.). Deerfield, IL: Clark Boardman Callaghan.

McCracken, G. (1989). Who is the celebrity endorser? Cultural foundations of the endorsement process. *Journal of Consumer Research*, *16*(3), 310–321.

McGuire, W. J. (1985). Attitudes and attitude change. In G. Lindzey & E. Aronson (Eds.), *The handbook of social psychology* (3rd ed.), New York, NY: Random House.

MediaVest USA. (2004). *Word to presidential hopefuls: Celebrities on campaign trail reach young voters*. Retrieved from http://www.mediavestww.com/news/download/Celeb_Politics_20040825.pdf

Meirick, P. C. (2004). Topic-relevant reference groups and dimensions of distance: Political advertising and first- and third-person effects. *Communication Research*, *31*, 234–255.

Mueller, J. (1973). *War, presidents, and public opinion*. New York, NY: Wiley.

Newman, A. A. (2007). A theme song for Clinton: 'I'm a Believer' vs. 'Cold as Ice'. *New York Times*, June 4. Retrieved from http://www.nytimes.com/2007/06/04/business/media/04song.html?pagewanted = print

Nielsen. (2008). Nielsen examines TV viewers to the political conventions. Sept. Retrieved from http://blog.nielsen.com/newswire/wp-content/uploads/2008/09/2008_convention_tvr_final.pdf

Nimmer, M. B., & Nimmer, D. (1976–2012). *Nimmer on copyright: A treatise on the law of literary, musical and artistic property, and the protection of ideas*. New York, NY: M. Bender.

Ohanian, R. (1991). The impact of celebrity spokespersons' perceived image on consumers' intention to purchase. *Journal of Advertising Research*, *31*(1), 46–54.

Page, B. I., Shapiro, R. Y., & Dempsey, G. R. (1987). What moves public opinion? *American Political Science Review*, *81*(1), 23–43.

Patry, W. F., & Perlmutter, S. (1993). Fair use misconstrued: Profit, presumptions, and parody. *Cardozo Arts & Entertainment Law Journal*, *11*, 667–719.

Payne, J. G., Hanlon, J. P., & Tworney, D. P. (2007). Celebrity spectacle influence on young voters in the 2004 presidential campaign. *American Behavioral Scientist*, *50*, 1239–1246.

Pease, A., & Brewer, P. R. (2008). The Oprah factor: The effects of a celebrity endorsement in a presidential primary campaign. *The International Journal of Press/Politics*, *13*(4), 386–400.

Pew Research Center. (2007). *The Oprah factor and campaign 2008: Do political endorsements matter?* Pew Research Center Report. Wash. DC: Pew Research Center. Retrieved from www.people-press.org/2007/09/20/the-oprah-factor-ad-campaign-2008/

Posner, E. A. (2000). *Law and social norms*. Cambridge, MA: First Harvard University Press.

Reagan, R. (1984). *Remarks at a Reagan-Bush Rally in Hammonton, New Jersey*. Sep. 19. Retrieved from http://www.reagan.utexas.edu/archives/speeches/1984/91984c.htm

Reuters. (2003). Dixie Chicks pulled from air after bashing Bush. *Cnn.com*. Mar. 14. Retrieved from http://www.cnn.com/2003/SHOWBIZ/Music/03/14/dixie.chicks.reut/

Ridout, T. N., & Searles, K. (2011). It's my campaign I'll cry if I want to: How and when campaigns use emotional appeals. *Political Psychology*, *32*(3), 439–458.

Rolling Stone. (2012). Silversun Pickups tell Romney to stop using 'Panic Switch' GOP hopeful is 'using a song that describes his whole campaign,' singer Brian Aubert says. *Rolling Stone*. Aug. 16. Retrieved from http://www.rollingstone.com/music/news/silversun-pickups-tells-romney-to-stop-using-panic-switch-20120816

Rosenberg, Y. (2004). Lost youth. *American Demographics*, *26*(2), 17–19.

Rumfelt, E. H. (2006). Comment: Political speech: Priceless – Mastercard v. Nader and the intersection of intellectual property and free speech. *Emory Law Journal*, *55*, 389–421.

Schacter, S. (2011). Note: The barracuda lacuna: Music, political campaigns, and the First Amendment. *Georgetown Law Journal*, *99*, 571–604.

Schultz, M. F. (2007). Copynorms: Copyright law and social norms. In P. K. Yu (Ed.), *Intellectual property and information wealth: Issues and practices in the digital age* (*Vol. 1*, 201–236). Westport, CT: Praeger Publishers.

Shaw, D. R. (1999). The effect of TV ads and candidate appearances on statewide presidential votes, 1988–1996. *American Political Science Review*, *93*(2), 345–361.

Sparkman, S. L. (1974). Tape Pirates: The New "Buck"-aneer$. *Copyright Law Symposium*, *21*, 98–119.

Sternthal, B., Dholakia, R., & Leavitt, C. (1978). The persuasive effect of source credibility: Tests of cognitive response. *Journal of Consumer Research*, *4*(4), 252–60.

The Week Staff. (2012). Presidential ad spending: By the numbers: The Wesleyan Media Project confirms that the 2012 battle between President Obama and Mitt Romney is the most expensive presidential campaign ever. *The Week*, Oct. 25. Retrieved from http://theweek.com/article/index/235448/presidential-ad-spending-by-the-numbers

Tolstoy, L. (1877). *Anna Karenina*. The Russian Messenger.

Tyler, T. R. (1990). *Why people obey the law*. New Haven, CT: Yale University Press.

Vahdani, M. (2011/2012). Selection from the grammy foundation entertainment law initiative 2010 writing competition: Running on empty: The problem with politicians and stealing (music). *Loyola Los Angeles Entertainment Law Review*, *32*, 75–86.

Weber, C. (2012). Emotions, campaigns, and political participation. *Political Research Quarterly*, *66*(2), 414–428.

Wolke, K. M. (2005). Some catching up to do: How the United States, in refusing to fully sign on to the WPPT's public performance right in sound recordings, fell behind the protections of artists' rights recognized elsewhere in this increasingly global music community. *Vanderbilt Journal of Entertainment Law & Practice*, *7*, 411–412.

Woods, N. T., & Herbst, K. C. (2007). Political star power and political parties: Does celebrity endorsement win first–time votes? *Journal of Political Marketing*, *6*(2/3), 141–158.

Zaller, J., & Feldman, S. (1992). A simple theory of the survey response: Answering questions versus revealing preferences. *American Journal of Political Science*, *36*(3), 579–616.

LEGAL CITATIONS

Act of April 10, 1790. Patent Act of 1790, ch. 7, 1 Stat. 109-12.

Act of Dec. 31, 1974, Pub. L. No. 93-573, 88 Stat. 1873.

Act of Feb. 3, 1831, 4 Stat. 36.

Act of Jan. 6, 1897, ch. 4, 29 Stat. 481-82, amended by Act of Mar. 4, 1909, ch. 320, § 25, 35 Stat. 1081.

Act of Mar. 4, 1909, ch. 320, § 1(e), 35 Stat. 1075.

Act of Oct. 15, 1971, Pub. L. No. 92-140, 85 Stat. 391 (effective Feb. 15, 1972).

American Famiy Life Insurance Co. v. Hagan, et al., 266 F. Supp. 2d 682 (N.D. Ohio 2002).

Brown v. McCain, 611 F. Supp. 2d 1073 (C.D. Cal. 2009a).

Browne v. McCain, 612 F. Supp. 2d 1125 (C.D. Cal. 2009b).

California Civil Code section 3344 (2013). Stats. 1971 ch 1595 § 1, amended, Stats. 1984 ch 1704 § 2.

Campbell v. Acuff-Rose Music, Inc., 510 U.S. 569 (1994).

Cariou v. Prince, 2013 U.S. App. LEXIS 8380, 106 U.S.P.Q.2D (BNA) 1497, 2013 WL 1760521 (2d Cir. April 25, 2013).

Clayton v. Stone, 5 F. Cas. 999, 1000-01 (Cir. Ct. S.D.N.Y. 1829).

Convention for the Protection of Producers of Phonograms Against Unauthorized Duplication of Their Phonograms, art. 2, Oct. 29, 1971, 25 U.S.T. 309, 866 U.N.T.S. 67.

Copyright Act of 1976. 17 U.S.C. §§ 101-1332.

Digital Performance Right in Sound Recordings Act of 1995, Pub. L. No. 104-39, § 2, 109 Stat. 336, codified as amended at 17 U.S.C. § 106(6) (2000).
EMI Catalogue Partnership v. Hill, Holliday, Connors, Cosmopulos Inc., 2000 U.S. App. LEXIS 30761 (2nd Cir. Sept. 15, 2000).
Federal Trademark Dilution Act, 15 U.S.C. § 1125(c) (1996), amended by, Trademark Dilution Revision Act of 2006 (2006).
Feist Publications, Inc. v. Rural Telephone Service Co., 499 U.S. 340 (1991).
Goldstein v. California, 412 U.S. 546 (1973).
H.R. Rep. No. 92-487. (1971). Reprinted in 1971 U.S.C.C.A.N. 1566, 1570.
H.R. Rep. No. 94-1476. (1976). 94th Cong., 2d Sess. 65. Reprinted in 1976 U.S.C.C.A.N. 5659, 5679.
Harper & Row, Publishers, Inc. v. Nations Enterprises, 501 F. Supp. 848 (S.D.N.Y. 1980), aff'd 723 F.2d 195 (2d Cir. 1983), reversed on other grounds, 471 U.S. 539 (1985).
Henley v. DeVore, 733 F. Supp. 2d 1144 (C.D. Cal. 2010).
Herbert v. Shanley, 242 U.S. 591 (1917).
Keep Thomson Governor Committee v. Citizens for Gallen Committee, 457 F. Supp. 957 (D.N.H. 1978).
Lanham Act, Trademark Act of 1946, 15 U.S.C. § 1051 et seq.
Long v. Ballantine, 1998 U.S. Dist. LEXIS 7813, 1998 WL 35156025 (E.D.N.C. 1998).
Mastercard International Inc. v. Nader 2000 Primary Committee Inc., 2004 U.S. Dist. LEXIS 3644 (S.D.N.Y. Mar. 8, 2004).
Mattel, Inc. v. MCA Records, Inc., 296 F.3d 894 (9th Cir. 2002).
MGM-Pathe Communications Co. v. Pink Panther Patrol, 774 F. Supp. 869 (S.D.N.Y. 1991).
New.Net, Inc. v. Lavasoft, 356 F. Supp. 2d 1090 (C.D. Cal. 2004).
Oliveira v. Frito-Lay, Inc., 251 F.3d 56 (2d Cir. 2001).
Performance Royalty: Hearings on S. 1111 Before the Subcomm. on Patents, Trademarks, and Copyright of the Senate Comm. on the Judiciary, 94th Cong., 5 (1975).
S. 1883, 101st Cong., 1st Sess., 135 Cong. Rec. 1207, 1217 (April 13, 1989).
Sony Corporation of America v. Universal City Studios, Inc., 464 U.S. 417 (1984).
Sound Recordings Act of 1971, Act of Oct. 15, 1971, Pub. L. No. 92-140, 85 Stat. 391 (1971).
United States Constitution (1787).
United We Stand America, Inc. v. United We Stand, America New York, Inc., 128 F.3d 8 (2d Cir. 1997).
Waits v. Frito-Lay, Inc., 978 F.2d 1093 (1992), cert. denied, 506 U.S. 1080 (1993).
Wojnarowicz v. American Family Association, 745 F. Supp. 130 (S.D.N.Y. 1990).
Worldwide Church of God v. Philadelphia Church of God, Inc., 227 F.3d 1110 (9th Cir. 2000).

MUSICAL CITATIONS

Byrne, D., Frantz, C., Harrison, J., & Weymouth, T. (Talking Heads). (1985). Road to Nowhere. Little Creatures. Warner Brothers.
Berlin, I. (1950). Call Me Madam.
Berlin, I. (1950, 1952). I Like Ike.
Cyrus, B. R. (2000). We the people. Southern Rain for Monument.

Diamond, N. (1980). America. The Jazz Singer. Capitol Records.
Finesse. (written by Nichols, B. & King, F.N.). (1984). Dance People. PMP Records.
Frankie Goes to Hollywood. (written by Gill, P., Johnson, H., Nash, B., & O'Toole, M.) (1983) Relax. ZTT Records.
Gardner, R. K. (1976). I'm feeling good about America.
God Save Great Washington. (1786). Philadelphia Continental Journal.
Green, A. (1971). Let's Stay Together. Let's Stay Together. High Records.
Guthrie, W. (1940). This land is your land. Ludlow Music.
Hendrix, J. (written by Dylan, B.) (1968). All Along the Watchtower. Reprise Records.
Kid Rock. (written by Ritchie, R. J. & Young, M.). (2010). Born Free. Atlantic Records.
McVie, C. (Fleetwood Mac). 1977. Don't stop. Rumours. Warner Brothers.
Ross, A. C. (1840). Tippacanoe and Tyler Too.
Silversun Pickups. (2009). Panic switch. Swoon. Dangerbird.
Sinatra, F. (Van Heusen, J. (music) & Cahn, S. (lyrics)) (1959). High Hopes. All the Way. Capitol Records.
Springsteen, B. (1984). Born in the U.S.A. Born in the U.S.A. Columbia Records.
The Minutemen. (1982). If Reagan Played Disco. Bean-Spill. Thermidor Records.
Unknown (attributed Bull, J. 1619). God Save the King.

GRADUATED RESPONSES TO ONLINE PIRACY: APPROACHES TAKEN IN THE UNITED STATES AND AROUND THE WORLD

Serona Elton

ABSTRACT

Purpose – *In this chapter, I explore the graduated response approach to combatting online piracy, and examine the different ways in which this approach has been implemented in the United States and around the world.*

Design/methodology/approach – *I discuss the legal, political, and industrial origins and current state of the graduated response programs in each country.*

Findings – *Overall, the most successfully launched graduated response programs have been the ones where a single entity is overseeing the program implementation, and the code of conduct has been well articulated.*

Music and Law
Sociology of Crime, Law and Deviance, Volume 18, 37–58

ISSN: 1521-6136/doi:10.1108/S1521-6136(2013)0000018005

Originality/value of chapter – *Few scholars have examined the processes leading up to the implementation of graduated response programs and the mechanics of how they work in practice. This chapter does this by looking, chronologically, at the developments in each country as well as the choreography of its notice process.*

Keywords: Copyright; infringement; graduated; piracy; three-strikes; online

INTRODUCTION

Online piracy is a huge threat to all of the copyright industries. The copyright industries are described in the World Intellectual Property Organization (WIPO) 2012 study on the Economic Contribution of Copyright-Based Industries as "industries which are dependent on copyright and related rights protection" (p. 1). These industries include music, as well as motion picture, press and literature, software, and others (WIPO, 2012). Online piracy refers to the sharing of content, such as recorded music, movies, ebooks and computer programs, in violation of copyright laws (i.e., illegally), via the Internet. According to a recent *New York Times* editorial, online piracy is "growing by leaps and bounds" (Porter, 2012). The article cites a powerful statistic from Cisco Systems' Visual Networking Index, indicating that over one-fourth of all Internet traffic is generated by the use of peer-to-peer and cyberlocker sites, and most of the activity involves illegal file sharing (Porter, 2012). A study by Stephen Siwek at the Institute for Policy Innovation (2007) indicates that the annual losses relating to sound recordings alone number around USD 12.5 billion. However, the economic losses resulting from online piracy are difficult to quantify precisely. The U.S. Government Accounting Office (GAO) has indicated that this is due to the illicit nature of the activity and the reliance on assumptions to estimate what purchasing activities consumers would engage in if they were not obtaining the goods illegally. However, the GAO did find that the problem is sizeable and concerning (GAO, 2010). Even some critics of the various economic studies which have attempted to quantify the size of the problem agree that, through the eyes of the copyright industries, it is seen a serious problem worthy of significant effort and attention (Sanchez, 2012). Efforts to combat online piracy in the United States have been underway since the late 1990s. Some approaches have proven more successful than others. One of the more recent approaches is the so-called graduated response which involves rights holders, and Internet service providers (ISPs) and their subscribers.

EARLY HISTORY OF ONLINE PIRACY

The technological seeds of online piracy today were planted as early as 1988. In 1988, the Motion Picture Experts Group (MPEG) was created as a working group of the International Standards Organization (ISO) and International Electrotechnical Commission (IEC), for the purpose of developing standards for digital audio and video compression. Within the MPEG, a sub-group focused on audio was formed. After just over four years of work, the MPEG-1 standard was published around the beginning of 1993. Within the MPEG-1 standard, Audio Layer 3 was the ability to "compress high quality audio CD data by a factor of 12 while maintaining a high quality audio sound" (MPEG, 1993). This form of compression became known as MP3. In 1996, electronics giant Philips, demonstrated its audio MPEG technology at the Consumer Electronics Show, and by 1997 unauthorized MP3 copies of recordings were popping up on fan created websites. An article about this new phenomenon, which appeared in the music industry trade publication, *Billboard,* contained several important statements which foretold of events to come, to wit, "[m]ore conflicts over copyright violations on websites are likely to arise as the industry aims to protect copyrighted material on the Internet" and, "[m]ajor entertainment companies that choose to crack down on fan-created sites may find themselves with a public relations nightmare" (Atwood, 1997). The record companies, owners of the copyrights in the sound recordings which were being illegally shared, were slowly starting to realize that they had a major problem brewing. That same year, the music industry took what it considered its first collective legal action to stop Internet piracy, bringing suit against the operators of three different Internet sites, all of which supported the sharing of unauthorized MP3 files (Don, 1997).

Concern over this new problem within the music industry continued to grow and consume more attention. Industry conferences, such as the 1998 Webnoize conference, held panel sessions dedicated to the topic, such as the one titled "MP3s: Friend or Foe" (Reece, 1998a). The 1998 *Billboard* article titled "Industry Grapples with MP3 Dilemma" warned that Pandora's digital box had been opened and that "no amount of policing pirate Web sites will force the lid shut" (Reece, 1998b, p.80). The article's author also pointed out, insightfully, that "[i]ronically, the CD format that revived and invigorated a stalled music industry may be responsible for its greatest future worries," referencing the fact that every professionally manufactured CD had become, in effect, a digital master from which an unlimited number of MP3 files could be created (Reece, 1998b, p. 80). In a short amount of time, a large number of websites sprang up to offer illegal MP3 files of popular music. A *New York Times* article published in 2000 said that *MP3* was as popular a search term in Internet searches as *sex* (Walker, 2000).

In 1998, the Digital Millennium Copyright Act (DMCA) was passed in the US, which made numerous amendments to the existing copyright law in order to address digital technologies. One of the components of the law, which plays a major role in the fight against online piracy, was the establishment of a safe harbor from copyright infringement liability for online service providers, which includes ISPs as well as website operators and others, so long as they comply with the conditions of the law. Without such a safe harbor, online service providers may be found liable for copyright infringement based on the actions of their users or subscribers, under the theories of vicarious and/or contributory liability. These theories of liability hold that those who assist and facilitate copyright infringement should be held responsible for their actions in the same way that the party who actually commits the infringement is. Section 512(i)(1)(A) of the DMCA requires ISPs to maintain a policy for "the termination in appropriate circumstances of subscribers and account holders of the service provider's system or network who are repeat infringers."

LOOKING BACK: WEBSITE OPERATORS AND FILE-SHARING INDIVIDUALS

A series of highly publicized lawsuits followed the first collective legal action taken by the music industry to stop Internet piracy in 1997. During this initial phase of fighting Internet piracy, the music industry focused on stopping the operators of websites and services which enabled the sharing of unauthorized MP3 files. The key question raised in these lawsuits was whether or not the operators could be held vicariously and/or contributorily liable for the unauthorized peer-to-peer sharing of MP3 files that was taking place on their services.

In August 1999, a new software client called Napster became available via the Internet. Napster users were able to download the software for free and install it on their computers. The software enabled the central Napster server to identify the MP3 files which existed on each of the users computers. When a user wanted to find an MP3 file of a particular recording, they would initiate a search of Napster's central server index, find an instance of that recording on another Napster user's computer, and click on the file to download it from the computer where the file was stored. In December 1999, the Recording Industry Association of America (RIAA), the trade association representing the major record labels, on behalf of its members, brought suit against Napster. The case was considered the first time a company was sued for trafficking in unauthorized music (Holland, 1999). The lawsuit alleged that Napster was guilty of copyright infringement, under the theories of contributory and vicarious liability. In March 2000, the *New York Times* ran a cover story titled "Potent Software Escalates Music Industry's Jitters," describing Napster and how prevalent its use had become, including diagrams of how the system worked. The article quoted the RIAA as saying it "has no plans to prosecute individual users of Napster, though copyright experts say the industry would have a very strong case" and that doing so would be counterproductive (Harmon, 2000, p. C6). The article confirmed that not only the music industry, but also the television and film industry, had growing concerns about whether or not the Internet would undermine the control of copyright holders. After a few court decisions and appeals in the case, Napster ultimately had to block access by its users to recordings owned by the record companies that the RIAA represented, which resulted in Napster shutting down its service in July 2001.

Once Napster stopped working, its more than 50 million users went looking for alternative ways to share files (Richtel, 2001). The music industry pursued lawsuits against each of the new peer-to-peer services that popped up, including Kazaa, Morpheus, Grokster, Aimster, LimeWire and MegaUpload. New technical protocols for sharing files became more popular, such as BitTorrent, and operators of services moved overseas where some copyright laws treat secondary liability for infringement differently than the United States laws. Lawsuits have been filed in many countries around the world, including Finland, Hong Kong, Sweden, and New Zealand. Some of these have been civil suits initiated by the copyright owners, while others have been criminal cases brought by the governments. In the Grokster case, once the file sharing service ceased operating, the following text appeared on the site, at the URL http://grokster.com/, and remains there today:

> The United States Supreme Court unanimously confirmed that using this service to trade copyrighted material is illegal. Copying copyrighted motion picture and music files using unauthorized peer-to-peer services is illegal and is prosecuted by copyright

> owners. There are legal services for downloading music and movies. This service is not one of them. YOUR IP ADDRESS IS XX.XX.XXX.XX AND HAS BEEN LOGGED. Don't think you can't get caught. You are not anonymous.

This got the attention of peer-to-peer service users who mistakenly thought their actions could not be tracked.

In 2003, the RIAA filed suit against 261 individuals who had been using peer-to-peer sites to illegally trade music files (Kravets, 2010). In these cases, unlike those brought against the operators of the peer-to-peer services, the individuals' actions were alleged to have directly infringed the rights of the copyright owners. Individuals were identified via their Internet Protocol (IP) address, which is the unique identifier assigned to a device participating in a computer network. The identification process involved the John Doe subpoena process. The copyright owner, or their representative, uses a variety of means, including automated or manual searches of file sharing sites, to identify the IP addresses associated with the sharing of large numbers of their recordings. With the IP address, the copyright owner can readily find, through the American Registry for Internet Numbers (ARIN), which entity owns the IP address. This is typically the ISP, such as a cable or telephone company. In 2003, the process involved the RIAA sending subpoenas to ISPs to obtain the identity which corresponded to the IP address before the RIAA actually filed the copyright infringement lawsuit. At the beginning of 2004, this legal process changed, requiring the RIAA to file a suit against the John Doe before issuing the subpoena to find out their identity. That year, the RIAA announced that it had brought suit against an additional 532 individuals. Defendants in these suits were typically given the opportunity to settle the suit by paying the RIAA USD 3000, although that figure varied depending on the number of infringements. The RIAA was widely criticized for its approach in going after individuals. Despite the fact that the RIAA had no way of knowing the identity of a particular IP address until the legal proceeding was already underway, it was often characterized as a bully going after 12-year olds and grandmothers. While most of these lawsuits resulted in settlements, a few highly publicized trials took place, including one against Jammie Thomas-Rasset and another against Joel Tenenbaum, both of which resulted in judgments against the defendants for more than USD 200,000 and USD 675,000, respectively. In December 2008, the RIAA, after bringing more than 35,000 suits, announced the end of its approach to suing individual file sharers, saying that it was going to focus instead on working with the ISPs to disconnect the Internet access of repeat infringers (Kravets, 2009).

TODAY: INTERNET SERVICE PROVIDERS AND ACCESS

Pursuing legal action against the operators of websites and services that encourage peer-to-peer sharing of unauthorized copies of music is often described as being analogous to the arcade game, Whac-A-Mole, such that for every site that ceases to operate, a new one pops up. Pursuing legal action against individuals who share unauthorized music files proved to be a public relations nightmare for the music industry, and didn't achieve the deterrent effect that had been hoped for. In searching for a more effective means to combat online piracy, the music industry shifted its focus to how websites which encourage peer-to-peer sharing are accessed. This latest phase of the fight to stop online piracy has a number of different components to it, including the seizing of Internet domains and so-called graduated responses to continued infringement by individuals.

In 2010, the Department of Homeland Security's Immigration and Customs Enforcement branch (ICE) began a major crackdown on websites promoting copyright infringement and dealing in counterfeit goods. This crack down involved the government taking over control of a number of domains and replacing the websites that they previously mapped to with a warning page. The warning page reads:

> This domain name has been seized by ICE – Homeland Security Investigations, pursuant to a seizure warrant issued by a United States District Court under the authority of 18 U.S.C. §§ 981 and 2323. Willful copyright infringement is a federal crime that carries penalties for first time offenders of up to five years in federal prison, a $250,000 fine, forfeiture and restitution (17 U.S.C. § 506, 18 U.S.C. § 2319). Intentionally and knowingly trafficking in counterfeit goods is a federal crime that carries penalties for first time offenders of up to ten years in federal prison, a $2,000,000 fine, forfeiture and restitution (18 U.S.C. § 2320).

The United States government controls all of the .com and .net domains, as well as those ending in .org, .cc, and several others. Other countries control their own top-level domains, such as .uk for the United Kingdom and .fr for France. The enforcement initiative falls under an umbrella of activities overseen by the National Intellectual Property Rights Coordination Center (IPR Center), a U.S. government task force which focuses on combating intellectual property theft. Similar efforts have been launched in other countries, such as Italy and Denmark. One of the most notable international seizures was of the Pirate Bay website, which began with a Swedish domain (.se). After getting wind of the imminent seizure of its domain by Swedish authorities, it quickly moved its website to a .gl domain in Greenland where it was then also seized, then to a .is domain in Iceland, then, fearing what the Icelanders would do, finally settling with a .sx domain in Sint Maarten in the Caribbean. The Pirate Bay's outrageous effort to evade intellectual property law serves as a good example of the challenges that are faced when seeking to enforce intellectual property rights in the international arena.

In 2007, France became the first country to seriously consider implementing a graduated response to the infringing actions of individual file sharers. The broad concept, which has been implemented differently in various countries, involves an escalating series of consequences each time an individual is caught engaging in illegal file sharing. The response is therefore graduated in that it gradually increases. The theory behind it is that once an individual realizes that they have been caught, and is made aware of the consequences, they will stop the behavior. This approach differs from the one in which individual filer sharers were sued for copyright infringement as the first step in an attempt to curtail their efforts in that there are numerous warnings given, many of which involve an educational component. The graduated response approach has been implemented in numerous countries, and has become one of the primary ways that online piracy is being combatted today. In some countries, the approach had been codified into law, while in others it has been implemented as a result of voluntary agreements between rights holders and ISPs. How an ISP is defined also differs somewhat from country to country, and some graduated response programs exclude certain ISPs, such as governments or schools, and those with fewer subscribers than a specified threshold. In most cases, the ISP is not monitoring peer-to-peer use by its subscribers. Rather, copyright owners must use a variety of measures, including anonymously venturing onto the peer-to-peer websites, and using third party monitoring companies, such as Dtechnet, to detect the illegal sharing. In almost all of the cases, the graduated response program is paired with an educational initiative to make the public more aware of copyright law, and an effort to expand the number and awareness of legal digital music services and retailers. Critics of the approach tend to focus on two main arguments. One is that access to the Internet is a fundamental right, which is tied closely to free speech, and therefore should not be restrained in any way. The other is that there is not sufficient due process involved in the approach, to wit, the typical appeals process puts the burden of proving that the access or sharing was permissible on the subscriber, which looks like a guilty-until-proven-innocent schema. Proponents of the approach often cite studies which show that most people sharing music illegally would stop if they received a notice from their ISP.

GRADUATED RESPONSES: APPROACHES AROUND THE WORLD

France

In 2001, the European Parliament and Council enacted the European Copyright Directive, which was designed to harmonize some aspects of copyright law across the different countries in the European Union. Each Member State of the European Union was required to implement the directive into their own national law. In 2006, the French enacted DADVSI, which is an acronym for the French title, *Loi sur le Droit d'Auteur et les Droits Voisins dans la Société de l'Information,* or the law on authors' rights and related rights in the information society. Parts of the law were designed to address illegal peer-to-peer sharing of copyrighted works, and in many ways it is similar to the U.S. Digital Millennium Copyright Act. The law was considered highly controversial and went through a complicated and protracted political process. It prohibited certain acts, such as taking the action "to edit, place at the public's disposal or communicate to the public, voluntarily and under any form, a means destined to place non-authorized works at the disposal of the public," or "voluntarily incit[ing], including through advertisement, such use," making them punishable by up to three years imprisonment and a fine of up to EUR 300,000. The law also provided for establishing an independent commission to oversee the implementation of portions of the law. The commission was created and called ARMT, which is an acronym for the French title, *Autorité de Régulation des Mesures Techniques*, or authority for the regulation of technical measures, otherwise known as digital rights management (DRM). DRM is a type of technical measure which controls the use of digital content. ARMT focused primarily on regulating DRM, rather than on the peer-to-peer sharing. In 2007, at the request of the French Minister of Culture, a task force was created, called the Olivenne Commission, to explore sanctions for illegal file sharing. The commission's work resulted in a Memorandum of Understanding (MoU) between rights holders and ISPs to experiment with new ways to address illegal file sharing. The recommendations of the Olivenne Commission lead to the enactment of another law, in May 2009, designed to supplement DADSVI, called the Creation and Internet Law, which expanded and renamed the ARMT commission. The new name became HADOPI, which is an acronym for the French name of the authority, *Haute Autorité pour la diffusion des œuvres et la protection des droits sur internet or* High Authority for the dissemination of works and protection of rights on the Internet.[1] Because HADOPI puts in place a three-level graduated response to illegal file sharing, it is often referred to as a *three strikes law*. In June 2009, part of the HADOPI law was declared unconstitutional because it would have allowed a non-governmental body to impose a sanction. A revised version of the law was approved in October 2009, and HADOPI first began sending notices in October 2010.

The first step in the graduated response procedure followed by HADOPI involves a copyright owner providing an IP address to HADOPI, HADOPI obtaining the IP address owner's contact information from their ISP, and the Commission for the Protection of Rights sending the subscriber a warning via email. The warning informs the subscriber of the allegations, and the existence of legal alternatives available in the market. If a second infringement is detected within the six month period following the warning, a certified letter, requiring acknowledgement of receipt, is sent to the subscriber with similar information as that found in the first email warning. The subscriber is then monitored for an additional period of one year. If a third infringement is detected during that period, they are sent another letter informing them that their actions are subject to criminal prosecution. The Commission may also decide to refer the case to a criminal prosecutor. The subscriber may find themselves in court, subject to a fine of up to EUR 1500, and to a court order disconnecting their Internet access for a period of up to one month. Throughout the entire process, a subscriber may challenge the notices by contacting HADOPI.

By the end of 2012, HADOPI had sent over a million first warnings, over 100,000 second warnings, and 340 third warnings. Of the 14 cases referred to a criminal prosecutor, judgments were reached in only three of them, with only one of them resulting in a fine of EUR 150. A study was released in March 2012 by HADOPI, analyzing the effects of its warning system, and it found a steady decline in use of illegal peer-to-peer sharing in France since the warnings went into effect, and that 71% of Internet users surveyed said they would stop downloading illegal content if they received a warning from HADOPI. The results of HADOPI's efforts have been viewed differently by different groups. Rights holders generally view its efforts as a success, as demonstrated by the drastic reduction in the number of Internet subscribers making it to the second and third warning levels. Others argue that a cost-benefit analysis of the effort, which includes the cost of maintaining the sizeable staff of HADOPI, indicates that it should cease operations. Determining whether or not HADOPI has been successful at accomplishing its mission involves not only analyzing the impact of its activities to stop illegal file sharing, but also at how well it has accomplished its other goals, such as increasing the number of legal content offerings in France, and regulating the use of DRM technology. In May 2013, the report of a government-commissioned panel, referred to as the Lescure report, named after the person who led the panel, was published, reporting on the efforts against online piracy. It recommends numerous actions, including shutting down HADOPI and handing over the policing of online piracy to the *Conseil supérieur de l'audiovisuel* (CSA), the agency that regulates electronic media in France. Part of its proposal includes replacing the three-strikes approach with automated fines that would kick in after two warnings, which start at around EUR 60 and escalate for repeat offenders. It remains to be seen what actions, if any, will be taken in response to the Lescure report.

South Korea

In July 2009, South Korea enacted amendments to their copyright law that addressed online piracy. One section of the law gave the Minister of Culture, Sports and Tourism the right to order Online Service Providers (OSPs) to (a) issue warnings to subscribers who are transmitting illegal reproductions, and (b) suspend the accounts of infringers who had received at least three warnings. In November 2010, the Internet accounts of eleven subscribers were ordered suspended, which is considered the first instance, globally, of someone losing their Internet access because of their illegal file sharing activities. Another section of the law created the Korean Copyright Commission (KCC) and gave it the power to recommend that OSPs send warnings, delete the illegally copied materials, and/or suspend subscriber accounts.[2] Compliance with the recommendations of the KCC is voluntary; however, if not complied with, the KCC may request that the Minister of Culture issue an order requiring the suspension. While the law does not require the KCC to utilize a three warning approach before making a suspension recommendation, that is the process currently specified in the Commission's bylaws. Some have argued that South Korea enacted the copyright law amendments, such as the graduated response provision, because of pressure from the United States and the European Union, which required increased protection of intellectual property in the trade agreements they each entered into with South Korea. In 2009, South Korea was removed from the United States Trade Representative's piracy watch list for the first time in 20 years.

The process is outlined in the Enforcement Decree of the Copyright Act, issued in February 2010, and begins with the KCC monitoring illegal file sharing activity on its own. When it detects illegal activity, it sends the subscriber a warning. A process whereby a subscriber can challenge the allegations is also established by the decree. Under the law, the penalties are a one month suspension of Internet access for a first suspension, which comes after three warnings, between one and three months for a second suspension, and between three and six months for a third or subsequent suspension.

During the first year of operation after the law went into effect, the KCC recommended that warnings be sent to 32,878 subscribers. Thirty-one subscribers had their accounts suspended by their OSPs for less than one month, which was the recommendation of the KCC. There were very few instances of an OSP declining to follow the KCC recommendation. By early 2013, according to the press, over 450,000 warnings had been sent and 380 user accounts had been shut down. In early 2013, Korea's National Human Rights Commission recommended the law be reexamined because it may violate constitutional rights. Around the same time, a member of the Korean National Assembly, Congressman Choi Jae-cheon, put forth a proposal to repeal the graduated response portion of the law. He argues that the law violates due process and is inefficient from an economic perspective, imposing a punishment that is disproportionate to the crime. Proponents of the law argue that it has been very effective at curtailing illegal file sharing, and has helped to support the growth of the legitimate digital music business in South Korea.

New Zealand

In 2008, New Zealand passed the Copyright (New Technologies) Amendment Act, to address copyright in the digital world. A specific section of the act, labeled Internet Service Provider Liability, required Internet service providers to have a policy for terminating the accounts of repeat infringers. There was significant public outcry against how broadly Internet service providers were defined in the law and how the provision was to be implemented. Public protests were staged and, for a period of time, New Zealand Internet users changed their avatars to black squares to express their disdain for the particular section of the law. The implementation of the section was postponed until it was announced that it would be removed from the law and redrafted. In April 2011, a new law was passed, titled the Copyright (Infringing File Sharing) Amendment Act, which repealed the prior section. The new law established a graduated response approach, and replaced the term Internet Service Provider with Internet Protocol Address Provider (IPAP) to exclude schools and government departments that provide Internet access, but are not traditional ISPs.[3]

The first step in the graduated response process in New Zealand involves a copyright owner providing an IP address to the IPAP. The IPAP then sends the subscriber a *detection* notice, informing the subscriber of the allegations and informing them that what they have done is illegal. If a second infringement occurs within the 28 days from when the detection notice was received, a *warning* notice is sent, which says the same things as the detection notice, but makes clear that it is a second notice. If a third infringement occurs within the 28 days following when the warning notice was received, an *enforcement* notice is sent. The copyright owner can bring the subscriber before the Copyright Tribunal, and seek damages from the subscriber of up to NZD 15,000. It is not until the process gets to the Copyright Tribunal phase that the identity of the subscriber is revealed to the copyright owner. The subscriber can challenge the notices all throughout the process. While the 2011 Act contemplates the suspension of a repeat offender's Internet connection, that portion of the act can only be activated by an Order in Council, a form of legislation, which has not yet taken place. The Commerce Minister has stated that it will not be activated unless the existing process is unsuccessful.

In early 2013, the first case where the Copyright Tribunal assessed a fine after the graduated response protocol had been followed was decided, resulting in a fine of NZD 616.57. A short time after came the second case, resulting in a fine of NZD 557. By that time, the Recording Industry Association of New Zealand (RIANZ) had requested that around 6,000 notices be sent by IPAPs, and 11 subscribers had been forwarded to the Copyright Tribunal. Currently, the copyright owner must pay a NZD 25 fee for each notice they want issued, and the fee is designed to pay for the costs that the IPAP incurs in administering the notice. The RIANZ have argued that the fee is too high, particularly given that they are dealing with issuing thousands of notices, and are asking for it to be lowered to NZD 2. The IPAPs have argued that the fee is too low and it not adequately covering their administrative costs related to the notice program. In September 2012, after conducting a review, the Minister of Commerce recommended not changing the current fee. Proponents of the program, such as the RIANZ, say that there has been a significant decrease in the volume of peer-to-peer traffic since its implementation.

The United Kingdom

A government commissioned report published in 2006, called the Gowers Review of Intellectual Property, highlighted the damage being caused to the creative communities in the United Kingdom by illegal file sharing. It called for rights holders and ISPs to work together to create a set of best practices which would change attitudes and behavior with respect to illegal file sharing. Further, it said that if the two groups cannot reach agreement on the practices, the government should intervene and establish a statutory protocol. The trade associations for the music and film industries, six of the leading ISPs, and the government, came together and entered into a Memorandum of Understanding (MoU) in July 2008. The goal of the MoU was to achieve a significant reduction in illegal peer-to-peer activity within a two- to three-year time period. Each ISP was to put in place a three-month trial to send notifications to 1,000 subscribers per week, and the results were to be analyzed to determine how to move forward. The ISPs and rights holders were to craft a Code of Practice, which would be facilitated by Ofcom, the independent regulator for the U.K. communications industry. Despite much effort, the rights holders and ISPs were not able to reach an agreement over the practices. At the same time, the government was considering the results of several other commissioned studies on how intellectual property law supported innovation and growth in the digital realm. Another such study, published in June 2009, titled the Digital Britain Report, outlined the United Kingdom's strategic vision for its role in the digital economy. The report included a section which addressed protecting and rewarding creativity, which recommended that Ofcom be required to place obligations on ISPs to (a) notify alleged infringers that their conduct is illegal, and (b) collect information on repeat offenders which can be, subject to a court order, turned over to a copyright owner so that they may pursue individual legal action against the infringer. If, after 12 months from initial implementation, these two approaches do not prove effective in reducing illegal peer-to-peer sharing, then Ofcom would be able to direct the ISPs to implement a series of other steps, including blocking particular URLs, and capping subscriber bandwidth. However, the report did not recommend the penalty of having a subscriber lose their Internet access.

In April 2010, the United Kingdom passed the Digital Economy Act, which was based heavily on the Digital Britain Report, as well as the Gowers Review and MoU. Unlike the Digital Britain Report, the act included the penalty of losing one's Internet access for repeat infringement.

This additional remedy was included at the urging of the Secretary of State, Lord Mandelson, who some argue was swayed by lobbyists from the content communities such as music and film. The law could not be implemented until Ofcom set forth a code of practice, which would explain how the law would be implemented in detail. A draft code of practice has to go through a number of stages before it becomes law, to wit, a period where public comments on it are solicited, a review by the European Commission to ensure that it does not pose any potential barriers to trade, the approval of the Secretary of State, and then the approval of Parliament. The initial draft of the code was published in May 2010. However, before the end of the public comment period, in July 2010, two of the largest ISPs in the UK, BT, and TalkTalk sought a judicial review of the law on a number of grounds, including that it breached European Law. The High Court decided in April 2011 in favor of the law, and BT and TalkTalk appealed the decision. During the time period while the law was under judicial review, its implementation was put on hold. In March 2012, the appeals court dismissed the appeal, clearing the way for the law to be implemented. In June 2012, a revised draft of the code was put forth by Ofcom. Given time for the stages of review it must pass through, and given the time that will be needed in order to prepare for implementation, including establishing an appeals framework, the first warning notices will likely go out in early 2014.[4]

The first step in the graduated response process involves a copyright owner sending the ISP a Copyright Infringement Report, which includes the IP address associated with the illegal file sharing. The ISP then sends a warning notice to the subscriber, on paper, via first class mail. If the subscriber is issued three warnings within a 12-month period, their name is to be placed on the ISPs Copyright Infringer List. Copyright holders are allowed to ask for a copy of the list once a month. The list does not contain any identifying information about the subscribers other than their IP addresses. However, if a copyright owner sees that a subscriber has received three or more warnings within the 12-month period, they may go into court to seek an order requiring the ISP to reveal the identity of the subscriber, and then pursue legal action directly against the subscriber. A subscriber who has received a warning notice may appeal the notice at any stage throughout the process. There are costs involved with the process. Copyright owners must pay a fee that is meant, in the aggregate, to cover all of the costs incurred by Ofcom for administering the program, the majority of the costs incurred by operating an appeals body, and 75% of the cost that the ISPs incur for administering the program. Subscribers must pay a fee of GBP 20 to challenge the warnings, but the money is refunded if their challenge is successful.

Ireland

In 2008, the Irish Recorded Music Association (IRMA), on behalf of its member record companies, sued Eircom, the largest ISP in Ireland. The suit alleged that Eircom failed to remove copyright infringing material from its systems, and failed to put in place measures to combat piracy. In February 2009, the parties decided to settle the case, resulting in an agreement where Eircom agreed to put in place a graduated response program, which would ultimately disconnect a subscriber's Internet access after repeated warnings. The agreement was reviewed by the court and the graduated response process was found to be lawful. The agreement also required IRMA to do all that it could to put in place a similar agreement with Eircom's competitors. After the other ISPs declined to voluntarily agree to implement the same program, IRMA sued one of them, seeking to force their hand. In October 2010, the court found that laws to suspend Internet access for illegal file sharers were not enforceable under the present law in Ireland, which, the court pointed out, meant that Ireland was not in compliance with its obligations under European law. Specifically, Irish law was not in line with the European Directive, 2001/29/EC, Article 8(3), which provides that an injunction may be sought by a rights holder who is affected by an infringing activity. However, since the graduated response program in place at Eircom was the result of an agreement, rather than a law, the court decision did not stop the program's implementation. The same month, due to a technical glitch, Eircom mistakenly sent out warnings to 300 subscribers who were not at fault. This got the attention of the Office of the Data Protection Commissioner (ODPC), which decided to launch an investigation to determine if the program was violating data protection laws. In December 2011, the ODPC issued an enforcement notice banning Eircom from operating their graduated response program, which temporarily shut the program down. In July 2012, a court overturned the ban, and the program re-started.[5] In February 2012, an amendment to the Irish copyright law was enacted to remedy Ireland's non-compliance with European law, which paved the way for IRMA to once again pursue voluntary agreements with or legal action against the other ISPs.

The first step in the graduated response process involves a copyright owner sending the ISP notice regarding a specific IP address engaged in illegal file sharing. The ISP then contacts the subscriber, in writing, as well as by telephone and browser pop-up windows, to let them know that their IP address has been detected as infringing copyright, that such acts are illegal, and where they can find legal alternatives. If the subscriber continues to engage in the illegal behavior, they are sent a second warning letter, making it clear that if they continue, their Internet access will be suspended for a period of seven days. If the subscriber continues the same behavior, their Internet access is suspended for the seven day period. If the subscriber still continues to engage in the illegal behavior, their Internet access is suspended for a period of 12 months.

Taiwan

In May 2009 Taiwan passed an amendment to its Copyright Act, which created a liability safe harbor for ISPs, so long as they comply with a number of different requirements. Among the requirements, the ISPs had to inform subscribers of their copyright protection policy, and let them know that, in the case of repeat infringements of three times or more, the ISP will terminate the subscribers Internet access in whole or in part. The Taiwan Intellectual Property Office (TIPO) would be overseeing the implementation. TIPO, after a period of consulting with rights holders and ISPs, prepared Regulations Governing Implementations of Limitations on Liability for Internet Service Providers, which were promulgated in November 2009.[6] A 2013 a report on Taiwan by the International Intellectual Property Alliance (IIPA), an alliance of trade associations representing US-based copyright industries, drew attention to the fact that, despite being enacted four years prior, the law had not yet been implemented as the regulations only addressed the proper notice and counter-notice process, and did not set out the process regarding how ISPs should implement the law. The report urged further work by the rights holders, ISPs, and TIPO to reach agreement on a Code of Conduct. The report refers to a 2012 meeting which was held on the subject, but only resulted in an agreement by one ISP to test out a proposed process for a limited time period. Although the US Trade Representative removed Taiwan from the list of countries that do not sufficiently protect intellectual property in January 2009, the IIPA has indicated that its failure to implement its graduated response law remains an important issue to be watched closely.

While the graduated response process has yet to be ironed out, the first step involves a copyright owner sending the ISP notice regarding a specific

IP address engaged in illegal file sharing. The ISP then sends a warning to the subscriber. If the subscriber is warned three or more times, their Internet access is somehow restricted, although the specifics of the restriction are yet to be determined. The ISP is not required to provide the identity of the subscriber to the copyright owner unless the subscriber files a counter-notice, claiming they have a right to access the content. Once the copyright owner knows the identity of the subscriber, in addition to whatever actions the ISP might take with respect to restricting Internet access, the copyright owner is also free to pursue a direct legal action against the subscriber for infringement.

Other Countries

A number of other countries, such as Australia, Belgium, Colombia, and Spain, have considered a graduated response program, but thus far have decided not to implement one. In 2009, the European Parliament voted against keeping a three-strike policy within a telecommunication reform legislation, because it found that including it would restrict the fundamental rights and freedoms of users, without affording them an opportunity to be heard before a judicial authority. In June 2011, more than 40 nations, including the United States, signed a statement made by Sweden to the United Nations Human Rights Counsel condemning three-strike laws against online copyright infringers as violating human rights. Neither France nor the United Kingdom signed the statement. New Zealand did sign the statement, despite having its own graduated response law, although the portion of its law which allowed for restricting Internet access was not activated at the time, nor has it been thus far.

GRADUATED RESPONSES: THE UNITED STATES APPROACH

As early as December 2003, the RIAA sent letters to the 50 largest ISPs in the United States, asking them to voluntarily notify their subscribers who are involved in file sharing over peer-to-peer networks that their activity is illegal. This letter came right at the time when the RIAA lost a lawsuit arguing that it had the power to send ISPs subpoenas for the identity information corresponding to IP addresses, without first needing to file a legal action against those John Doe subscribers. The court disagreed, which resulted in the RIAA changing its process to first bring suit against the John Doe subscriber before issuing a subpoena to learn their identity. As already discussed, the RIAA program of pursing legal action against individual file sharers continued from 2003 until late 2008, when the RIAA announced that it was going to cease filing new actions against individuals, and instead seek cooperation from ISPs. In a hearing in May 2008, in front of the US House of Representatives, Subcommittee on Telecommunications and the Internet, Committee on Energy and Commerce, on the then proposed Internet Freedom Preservation Act of 2008, Mitch Bainwol, the RIAA CEO, testified that the industry was engaged in discussions with a number of ISPs about ways to address the illegal piracy issue, including a graduated response approach, among others. In the months that followed, the RIAA, as well as leaders from the movie and television industries, worked with New York Governor Andrew Cuomo to craft an agreement with the ISPs.

In January 2009, it was reported in the press that AT&T and Comcast, two of the largest ISPs in the United States, were amongst the group of ISPs working with the RIAA on a solution. In March 2009, AT&T announced that it would begin implementing, on a trial basis, a notification program. Two additional ISPs, Comcast and Cox, also confirmed they were exploring working with the RIAA on a new program, although they had been forwarding infringement notices to their subscribers for years. In July 2011, over two years later, the Memorandum of Understanding (MoU) was finally announced. Parties to it included numerous trade associations from the entertainment industry, as well as their members, such as the RIAA, the Motion Picture Association of America (MPAA), the Independent Film & Television Alliance (IFTA), the American Association of Independent Music (A2IM), and five ISPs, AT&T, Cablevision, Comcast, Time Warner Cable, and Verizon. It is worth mentioning that Cox chose not to sign the MoU, and instead maintains its own graduated response protocol, which involves Internet restrictions and potentially, after more than 10 notices, termination of the subscriber's Internet access. The MoU established a six step Copyright Alert System (CAS), which is a common framework of best practices, and created the Center for Copyright Information (CCI), to support implementation of the program.[7] In a White House blog post the same month, Victoria Espinel, the United States Intellectual Property Enforcement Coordinator, commended the entertainment industry and ISPs for reaching the agreement, and stated the Administration would continue to pursue solutions to the problems posed by online piracy. In order to give the ISPs time to develop their infrastructure to implement the system, the first notices under the new program were not expected to be sent out until the second quarter of 2012. In September 2011, the CCI was formed, and in April 2012, an Executive Director was appointed at the CCI, its advisory board was established, which included members from the consumer and privacy protection groups, and it announced that it had entered into an agreement with the American Arbitration Association to implement an independent review process. After numerous delays, said to be the result of those involved wanting to ensure that the program was consumer-friendly and remained true to the MoU, the CCI said in October 2012 that the program would be launching within several weeks. Unfortunately, hurricane Sandy hit the east coast of the United States in October which affected the CCI final testing schedules. In February 2013, the Copyright Alert System was officially launched. In May 2013, the press reported that the CCI had somehow lost its status as an official corporation due to a likely paperwork mishap, however, that was quickly remedied and the CCI continues to operate as before.

The first step in the CAS process involves a copyright owner providing an IP address to one of the participating ISPs. The ISP then notifies the subscriber associated with the IP address, via email and/or other technologies such as in-browser alters, that their account was involved in sharing copyrighted content over a peer-to-peer network. The notice, which is meant to be educational in nature, also includes information about how they can prevent this from occurring again, such as securing their wireless Internet connection with a password, and where they can legally access or purchase digital music. The second time an alert is sent, the notice is essentially the same as the first. The third and fourth alerts require the subscriber to acknowledge that they have received the alert and pledge to stop the unlawful activity. If a fifth and sixth alert are sent, mitigation measures will be utilized, such as requiring a subscriber to take a copyright tutorial, or reducing their Internet speed significantly for several days. If no further alerts are sent within a 12-month period, the number of strikes against the subscriber is reset to zero. If a subscriber's activity warrants alerts beyond the sixth alert, they are considered to be the type of infringer who falls outside of the scope of the CAS, and no further alerts will be sent. A copyright owner's ability to pursue legal action against an individual infringer is not affected by the CAS process, and that may be the recourse a copyright owner seeks with respect to hard-core infringers. A subscriber who has received three or more alerts may appeal the alerts, based on six different grounds, to an independent arbiter, but they have to pay a USD 35 fee to do so. The fee is refunded if their appeal is successful, and if they are not able to afford it, it can be waived. The goal of the fee is to prevent frivolous appeals. Unlike some three-strikes programs in other countries, a subscriber's Internet connection will not be suspended or terminated, nor will they incur a fine or criminal penalty.

CONCLUSION

The graduated response approach and its implementation is a changing area of law, policy, and industry. As with any attempt to curtain online piracy, there will be proponents and critics of the approach. As results of studies on the effectiveness of graduated responses continue to be reviewed, and other factors influence the digital music marketplace, the approach may be refined, more widely embraced, or abandoned.[8]

NOTES

1. For more information on the French graduated response program, visit the HADOPI website at the URL http://www.hadopi.fr/
2. For more information on the Korean Copyright Commission, visit their English-language site at the URL http://eng.copyright.or.kr/
3. For more information on the implementation of the New Zealand graduated response program, visit their website at the URL http://www.med.govt.nz/business/intellectual-property/pdf-docs-library/copyright/notice-process
4. For more information on the United Kingdom graduated response program, visit their website at the URL http://stakeholders.ofcom.org.uk/internet/terms-of-reference
5. For more information on the Irish graduated response program, visit the Eircom website at the URL http://www.eircom.net/notification/legalmusic/intro, and the IRMA website at the URL http://www.irma.ie/piracy_faq.htm#grc
6. For more information on the Taiwanese graduated response program, visit the TIPO website at the URL http://www.tipo.gov.tw/en/AllInOne_Show.aspx?path=2557&guid=26944d88-de19-4d63-b89f-864d2bdb2dac&lang=en-us
7. For more information on the United States graduated response program, visit the CCI website at the URL http://www.copyrightinformation.org/
8. For updates on the development of graduated response programs around the world, visit the WIPO website in the section for Internet Intermediaries and Creative Content (URL http://www.wipo.int/copyright/en/internet_intermediaries/index.html) and visit the Global Censorship Chokepoints website at the URL https://globalchokepoints.org/countries/

REFERENCES

Atwood, B. (1997). Oasis in c' right dispute with fans' web sites. *Billboard, 109*(21), 3.

Don, J. (1997). Downloading songs subject of RIAA suit. *Billboard, 109*(25), 3, 83.

GAO (2010). *Intellectual property: Observations on efforts to quantify the economic effects of counterfeit and pirated goods*. Washington, DC: United States Government Accountability Office.

Harmon, A. (2000, Mar 07). Potent software escalates music industry's jitters. *New York Times*, p. A1, C6.

Holland, B. (1999). RIAA sues MP3 search site. *Billboard, 111*(51), 9.

Kravets, D. (2009). RIAA seeks up to $150,000 a song in file sharing trial. *Wired*. July 30. Retrieved from http://www.wired.com/threatlevel/2009/07/riaa-jugular/

Kravets, D. (2010). Copyright lawsuits plummet in aftermath of RIAA campaign. *Wired*. May 18. Retrieved from http://www.wired.com/threatlevel/2010/05/riaa-bump/

MPEG. (1993). *ISO/IEC 11172, Coding of moving pictures and associated audio at up to about 1.5 Mbit/s*. Geneva, Switzerland: Author.

Porter, E. (2012, February 4). The perpetual war: pirates and creators. *New York Times*, p. SR10.

Reece, D. (1998a). Conference call. *Billboard, 110*(45), 88.

Reece, D. (1998b). Industry grapples with MP3 dilemma. *Billboard, 110*(29), 1, 80.

Richtel, M. (2001, Jul 20). With Napster down, its audience fans out. *New York Times*, p. A1, C2.

Sanchez, J. (2012). SOPA, Internet regulation, and the economics of piracy. *Ars Technica*, January 18. Retrieved from http://arstechnica.com/tech-policy/2012/01/internet-regulation-and-the-economics-of-piracy/

Siwek, S. (2007). *The true cost of sound recording piracy to the U.S. economy*. Lewisville, TX: The Institute for Policy Innovation. Retrieved from http://www.ipi.org/ipi_issues/detail/the-true-cost-of-sound-recording-piracy-to-the-us-economy

Walker, R. (2000, April 23). Between rock and a hard drive. *New York Times*, p. SM74.

WIPO. (2012). *WIPO study on the economic contribution of the copyright industries*. Geneva, Switzerland: Author.

MUSIC IDENTITIES, INDIVIDUALIZATION, AND OWNERSHIP SHIFTS: EMPOWERING A LITIGIOUS PARADIGM OF COPYRIGHT PROTECTION

Mitch Daschuk and James Popham

ABSTRACT

Purpose – *The purpose of this chapter is to relate to the reader how overlapping advancements in technology and the diffusion of popular music into the habitus of listeners have provided the framework for an instrumental rationalization of litigious approaches to copyright protection by their owners. Namely, the personalization of music, which has evolved with the aid of technological advancements, has privatized music consumption, thus establishing socio-legal parameters that limit consumption to an individual action.*

Design/methodology/approach – *We discuss the concepts of habitus and taste, communality in music ownership, communicative action, and*

Music and Law
Sociology of Crime, Law and Deviance, Volume 18, 59–78

ISSN: 1521-6136/doi:10.1108/S1521-6136(2013)0000018006

technology-driven consumption as they relate to the instrumental rationalization of industry-led governance structures defining music ownership rights. These arguments are supported in part by a consideration of historic examples of tension and responding legal actions.

Findings – *The primary outcome from this chapter is to illustrate the extent to which the recording industry has traditionally held a role in guiding copyright policy. The chapter concludes by illustrating the current legitimation crises encountered by the recording industry and policy makers as consumers abandon traditional ownership paradigms en masse.*

Originality/value of chapter – *The technologies associated with the Internet and music consumption continue to evolve. This chapter highlights the differing interests in controlling music interests, and casts light on how agency has influenced structural developments central to copyright.*

Keywords: Downloading; music piracy; copyright; litigation; lifeworld

INTRODUCTION

> For instance, I'm walking down the street and I see some beautiful girl walking along … and I she's got these white things coming out of her ears and I'm going, that poor girl: she's listening to real crap. And I go, it's so easy to fix that … People don't have MP3 listening parties. They have vinyl listening parties, a vinyl evening at my place. (Neil Young, interviewed by John Stewart on The Daily Show, November 29, 2012)

In 2001 the music industry changed. Apple Inc., a corporation hitherto known for quirky computer products and desperately holding on to a 4% share of the PC market, began marketing a personal electronic device that was capable of storing and playing 5GB worth of compressed audio files. Apple Inc. timed the initial release of the iPod to coincide with the holiday season, selling more than 125,000 units by January 2002, and another 475,000 through the remainder of Apple's fiscal year (Apple Inc., 2013).

The original iPod was a well thought-out device: it could store 1,000 songs, equivalent to about 50 audio-formatted compact discs; it had an internal, rechargeable battery that lasted 10 hours; it had a functional and easy-to-use interface including a backlit, multiple line LCD; and a freely distributed software package, known as iTunes, was developed by Apple, which made compressed audio file management simple. In the press the iPod was well received, at least as a new technological trinket, but early reviewers balked at the $399 price tag – after all, devices with similar capabilities went for half the price. A product report by the trusted tech media website Wired suggested that it was a nice but underwhelming device (Quigley, 2010).

Where Apple first broke ground for its eventual domination of the personal music device sector was with its presentation of the iPod. Along with its fresh stainless steel and white enamelled finish, Apple successfully implemented two strategies to get the word out: earbuds (brand language marketing) and a sleek advertising campaign (Reppel, Szmigin, & Gruber, 2006). As the iPod grew in popularity the white earbuds that accompanied the product became ubiquitous. Larréché (2008) explains that this sort of branding kicked off a perpetually motivated campaign, noting that

> How many white earbuds have you seen in the last week? Those tell-tale cables disappearing into a barely discernible bulge in the wearer's jacket were plugged into an iPod. Even if you don't own one you almost certainly know someone who does. It is the defining consumer item of the decade: 141 million units sold and counting. (p. 24)

Paired with the earbuds, Apple kicked off a marketing campaign that contrasted silhouetted dancers against bright colors and set to relatively unknown popular music tracks. The anonymity of both the dancer and music implied to the consumer that their music enjoyment could be taken to new realms – they could be dancer, and they could be discovering this new music. This tack harbored a deeply personal connection between the listener and their music (Cooper, 2009).

At about the same time another start-up technology was emerging. Napster, a file-sharing service designed by a young amateur computer programmer named Shawn Fanning, was designed to streamline the process of sharing music files between peers over a campus network. Within a few months of distributing 30 copies of Napster to online connections in early 1998, nearly 15,000 people were using it (without any marketing). By July 2000 nearly 20 million users had registered. As Steve Knopper (2009) puts it, Napster brought the music industry to its knees.

Despite its success, there turned out to be serious flaws in Napster's design. For example, users' file lists were stored on a centralized server that was owned and operated by the business. These flaws became a lynchpin for several major lawsuits against the nascent organization. Record producers, represented by the Recording Industry Association of America (RIAA), was confronted with a new technology that had figuratively thrown their rights to reproduction and distribution out of the window; and rather than capitalizing on new shifts in consumption behavior, the RIAA called upon decades of established legal precedent to reinforce their control over the music marketplace (Knopper, 2009).

Furthermore, the RIAA was able to call on significant artists within the recording community to support their fight against Napster. The Artists Against Piracy campaign, launched in 2000, saw 70 musicians including notable acts like Alanis Morissette, Blink-182, and Garth Brooks spoke up against online music swapping. These campaigns presented an artist-oriented image of piracy and suggested that ongoing, unauthorized copying of music stripped artists of their ability to work creatively. The slogan "If a song means a lot to you imagine what it means to us" seemed to suggest that the value of music was related to its profitability, rather than its impact on the listener (Borland, 2000).

One of the most infamous examples of artists fighting against Napster at the behest of record producers was Metallica. An earlier pioneer in the genre of thrash metal, Metallica had gained significant fame based on their lyrics against dogma and the military-industrial complex (James, 2009). Yet, by 2000 they were deeply seated in a lawsuit against Napster, making claims that

> Metallica is suing Napster because we felt that someone had to address this important artistic issue and we have always been known for taking a leadership role in the fight for artists' rights … Why is it all of a sudden OK to get music for free? Why should music be free, when it costs artists money to record and produce it? (James, 2009, p. 159)

Whereas the technological innovation of the iPod had encouraged music fans to share their music communally and expand the capacity to distribute it to any connected individuals, the organizations that traditionally hold power within the music industry had sought to contract these capacities to copyright holders as dictated by rigid legal frameworks.

SOCIOLOGICAL THEORY AND POPULAR MUSIC

The purpose of this chapter is to relate to the reader how overlapping advancements in technology and the diffusion of popular music into the habitus of listeners have provided the framework for an instrumental rationalization of litigious approaches to copyright protection by their owners. Namely, the personalization of music (i.e., establishing a sense of "ownership" in the listener for particular types of popular music relative to their identity), which has evolved with the aid of technological advancements (e.g., distributable forms of reproduction that do not require mass-airing), has privatized music consumption thus establishing socio-legal parameters that limit consumption to an individual action. The examples given above of the success of the iPod and the RIAA's Napster campaigns illustrate these overlapping phenomena: digital mediums provide opportunity for music collections to be deeply personal (and personalized), and the individualistic socio-legal stance contends that these collections must always be legitimate (i.e., purchasing the rights to consume).

This chapter does not contend that the concurrence of these phenomena is intentional, nor that excessive collusion between any bodies has occurred in order to establish the defined environs. Rather, we argue that co-occurring advancements have dictated a pathway to an industry-oriented instrumental rationality regarding copyright. We believe this posture has concentrated legal power into the hands of economic institutions that are functionally independent of individual relationships, allowing them to harness steering media and colonize the lifeworld with definitions of legitimate consumption that match their interests.

There are four underlying assumptions that make the basis for this argument. First, we adhere to Lessig's (2004) identification of popular culture as a collective process that relates to all elements of its production – the founders, recorders, transformers, and collectors. In sharing this perspective we assume that music and its circulation is not an inherently mechanical system of creation–production–distribution but rather an organic outcome of communicative action. Second, we align with arguments that technology plays a significant role in the production of musical taste, such as those presented by Avdeeff (2012). From this standpoint we assume that technological innovation has been the catalyst for consumption behaviours and ultimately the source for steering media used by the intellectual property system. Our third assumption is that, up to the time of the Napster lawsuits, the intellectual property system had not encountered legitimation crises; that is, consumers were under-aware of systematic biases against their role in music and its circulation. In taking this stance we assume that the "intrusion of technocratic controls" (Burkart, 2010) was enabled in part through inaction or paralysis of the individuals it affected. Fourth, we hold that within the context of this argument the state, as policy maker, is the accepted authority on the rightfulness and wrongfulness of a given action. Thus, with this in mind we assume the instrumental rationalization thrusts the power to legitimize action into the hands of those who direct the state.

Taste and Music

Critical analyses of art and its implications frequently point to social interpretations of its meaning (both esthetically and theoretically) as a foundation for understanding its relationship with society. Gazing at art with a critical-social lens reveals that the catalyst for its production is as much a function of structural social mechanisms as it is the creativity of agency. As such, the impact of artistic creation on the consumer (i.e., its emotional impact), and in turn the impact of its consumption on future creation, is more a function of the actor's verstehen than the esthetic of the artifact. At the basis of this creation–consumption cycle are "systems of durable, transposable dispositions," called habitus by Bourdieu (1990).

Habitus is at once an objective and structural culmination of individual's historic interactions with social elements (i.e., lifestyle limitations affected by cultural capital); and simultaneously, habitus is a subjective process that is actively steered and adapted by the individual (i.e., emulating and reproducing lifestyles relative to their cultural capital). Bourdieu's (1990) argument is that each individual's habitus establishes a set of robust "conditionings," which are reflexive of their cultural capital and dictate their disposition toward social artifacts and decision-making processes.

These conditionings are articulated as taste: a discrete set of preferences that dictate an individual's standing on items or settings. Furthermore, taste is extended beyond the individuals to groups via symbolic violence and dismissiveness directed toward competing interests – that items or activities beyond the financial or social reach of actors within a segment of the population are dismissed as superfluous while items or activities that are well below the actor's means are considered low brow (Bourdieu, 2010). This posturing, thus, cements the social rituals that define individuals' class and status, and serves to reproduce the social order. Popular music is an expressive form of cultural capital that empowers the actor to identify their social standing and present their tastes through symbolic representation. Viewed within this context of this chapter, the reader might consider the experiential qualities of life encountered by African Americans in impoverished areas of Los Angeles during the early 1980s and their relationship with the thematic areas expressed in early gangsta rap as an illustrative example of habitus and taste in action.

Bourdieu's identification of taste and its relevance to historic cultural experience relates to our first assumption, namely that individual's personalization of music is a process of enculturation that connects deeply with their historic social experiences. While this may seem an overly insidious remark, it aligns well with our intention to identify the personalization of music, and the control thereof, as a vessel by which instrumental rationalization has empowered intellectual property owners to establish a litigious paradigm of copyright enforcement.

Communality

Salient to this discussion is a consideration of the catalysts for popular music creation. Successful popular music is built upon the foundation of the triumphs and failures of past artists; those who succeed inform future creative avenues, while those who fail identify creative dead ends (Hesmondhalgh, 1999). This perspective echoes the conditioning process of taste: art (as an expressive form of popular culture) is built upon the collective histories of taste relative to the ongoing dialectic between communication and expression, relative to the medium, its multitude of genres and sub-genres, and its targeted audiences. In the case of popular music, this argument places significant portions of its creation in the hands of the consumers through democratic processes of vicarious reinforcement (Bandura, Ross, & Ross, 1963). This is the "Read/Write" (RW) culture defined by Lessig (2008):

> … ordinary citizens "read" their culture by listening to it or by reading representations of it (e.g., musical scores). This reading, however, is not enough. Instead, they (or at least the "young people of the day") add to the culture they read by creating and re-creating the culture around them. (p. 28)

The significance of the RW culture is that it views each point in cultural production as a culmination of past creativity – technologies, tastes, and esthetics are continually revised or "remixed" to adapt to current trends in taste. The logical continuation of this point is that creativity would be stifled without the free use of these developments. Imagine for a moment how the history of rock n' roll might have played out had Sunrise Records patented power chords (and enforced these patents) in the 1950s. The purpose of this argument, then, is that culture is free because it belongs to no one and everyone simultaneously:

> Creators … are always and at all times building upon the creativity that went before and that surrounds them now. That building is always and everywhere at least partially done without permission and without compensating the original creator. No society, free or controlled, has ever demanded that every use be paid for … Instead, every society has left a certain bit of its culture free for the taking – free societies more fully than unfree, perhaps, but all societies to some degree. (Lessig, 2004, p. 29)

Lessig's take on "Free Culture" explains that popular music is an organic and persistent cultural artifact rather than a commodity with a distinct creation point. By extension, ownership of cultural artifacts such as popular music is an artificially constructed concept.

Communicative Action

These assumptions are largely reliant on discourse ethics and their role in social evolution as outlined by Jurgen Habermas. A central idea in Habermas' sociological perspective is the macro-structural concept of the lifeworld: various domains of social life are constructed through shared meanings and concepts representative of normative cultural practice. Habermas describes the lifeworld as a platform for action, wherein it minimizes the risk of communicative disagreements by providing individual actors with a foundation of shared meaning. When new concepts are introduced that ameliorate understanding they are added to the lifeworld, thus redirecting and slowly changing reality. In turn, the lifeworld establishes a horizon or boundary of individual perspectives tthat designates a movable but omnipresent limit to actors' perspectives (Habermas, 1996).

Furthermore, Habermas argues that meaning is ascribed to human interaction as a result of coercive attempts by communicators onto interlocutors – for instance the intellectual property system interacting with society – and that the communication of these systems is enabled to a greater or lesser extent by the efficiency of the communicator, as well as the level of subjective understanding between communicators. The end goals of these relations are to develop a shared statement of validity; however, the shaping of these statements reflects the imbalance of power between actors – people or institutions seek to establish their perspective as the accepted meaning for any given action (Finlayson, 2005).

The significance of Habermas' theories relative to the arguments herein is the connection between his premises of communicative action with intellectual property systems and the dereliction of the collective nature of music in policy direction. For Habermas, legitimacy is a product of the communication and acceptance of validity statements, which then become the truth and carry the burden of meaning. As an implied expert acting under the premises of instrumental rationalism, the State has the capacity to reinforce their ideas as valid or truthful. Habermas' concern is that the steering media of money and power have achieved disproportionate validity, in part through the influence of political institutions, and have become deeply embedded in the lifeworld (Habermas, 1996).

As supportive components of governing bodies there is significant reason to believe that money and power have become steering mechanisms for society, no longer supporting lifeworlds but rather defining them. For Habermas, money and power form a media, which is used to reach a new consensus on lifeworld, rather than traditional social processes. Because of the power associated with money in Western society, the state has adapted procedural laws to lead cultural direction according to the institutions with the greatest access to wealth. In terms of policy on controlling the distribution of popular music, the interested copyright holders have the upper hand.

Technological Interplay

Before approaching the process through which music-consumption became enmeshed in Western processes of identity construction, it is first important to appreciate how music's technological reproducibility in and of itself popularized new processes of individualized self-building. Toward the close of the 19th century, the American sociologist Thorstein Veblen (1934) noted a process whereby cultural processes involved in the development of group identity (primarily based along considerations of class standing) began to give way to those better attuned to the production of individual identities. Whereas Veblen suggests that members of a shared social class formerly utilized their free time to engage in practices meant to demonstrate and reinforce their collective social standing – a practice termed "conspicuous leisure" – he perceived of a shift whereby individuals now strove to demonstrate and reinforce their individualistic identities through "conspicuous consumption." Notes Veblen, as "the consumption of [consumer] goods is an evidence of wealth, it becomes honorific; and conversely, the failure to consume in due quantity and quality becomes a mark of inferiority and demerit" (1934, p. 74). Although Veblen's primary focus was on noting the manner in which the procurement of items such as automobiles and fashion accessories came to be repurposed as a means of broadcasting status, evolutions in the technological reproducibility of artistic forms would soon also allow for the procurement of artistic goods to assume a similar function.

As recording technologies ushered musical forms into that which Benjamin (2008) described as the "age of technological reproducibility," consumers could now purchase and play mass-produced music (via the vinyl format) for enjoyment within the comfort of their own homes. By the close of the 1930s, the technological reproducibility of musical forms would lead to the establishment of major recording labels including EMI (est. 1931), Decca (est. 1934), and Columbia Records (est. 1938).

Paired with the corresponding advent of television, the mainstream music industry would prove a significant contributor to the development and reification of distinct youth cultural forms. Indeed, and as Medovoi (2005) argues, the process through which the mainstream culture industry strove to cater emergent musical forms (such as Jazz, Blues, and Rock N' Roll) to a burgeoning market of young consumers contributed to the reification of the Western notion that the "teenager" constituted a unique social group. Above and beyond merely catering to youth cultural tastes, then, Medovoi can be taken to suggest that the mainstream culture industry actually contributed to those processes attuned to correlating distinct musical forms with "adolescence," as well as the demarcation of those practices through which one might reinforce and celebrate their "teenage" identities.

Above and beyond reinforcing the notion that one's distinct personal identity could find constitution through consumption practices, then, the construction of youth culture as a consumer market so too prescribed proper means of broadcasting and validating one's status as a culturally competent adolescent. This process is best exemplified by considering the emergence of Elvis Presley, and the manner in which the performer popularized a range of esthetics and patterns in self-presentation, which would become synonymous with the burgeoning "youth culture" of the 1950s. The culture industry of the 1950s, then, did not merely provide young consumers with a range of cultural goods, but also promoted and reinforced those conventions through which one might "broadcast" their identities as "teenagers" through those proscriptions for practice implicitly contained therein.

CASE STUDIES

Home Taping

> Home taping is killing record industry profits! We left this side blank so you can help.
> (As read on Side Two of the Dead Kennedys' 1981 cassette In God We Trust, Inc.)

The 1979 introduction of the Sony Walkman portable cassette player serves as a particularly salient example of the process whereby cultural and corporate forces popularized the emergent practice of reinforcing notions of selfhood through the consumption of music, particularly through the consumption of specific music technologies. Noting that the Walkman was specifically designed to appeal to young consumers, du Gay, Hall, Janes, Mackay, and Negus (1997) correlate the development of the Walkman with the Sony corporation's tendency of "[keeping] closely in touch with contemporary cultural trends" and designing electronics "in a way which enables the company to make products which both create and respond to consumer 'needs' " (p. 62).

While the original Sony Walkman (the TPS-L2) featured a standard esthetic design and actually allowed two listeners to use the device simultaneously, Sony's discovery that the device had curried favor with a broad range of consumer groups who predominantly used the technology as a personal listening device instigated two significant, and somewhat contradictory, modifications in design and marketing: the walkman was repurposed as a distinctly personal listening device which, nevertheless, was made available in a range of styles through which consumers could "signify" something about themselves. While this consideration serves as a pertinent example of the process through which cultural practices become commonplace through inspiration from the interactions of cultural producers and cultural consumers alike, it so too speaks to the process through which music consumption technologies came to serve as indicators of "lifestyle" and "status" in and of themselves.

As Chen (1998) notes, these intentions are perhaps nowhere better demonstrated than in considering the mid-1990s Sony Walkman advertising slogan "It is not only what you play, it is what you play it on," a tagline that means to suggest "that forms of communication technologies may have consequences for the nature of human experiences [and that] different media may provide different experiences when the content remains constant" (Chen, 1998, pp. 255–256). The Sony Walkman effectively revolutionized music by empowering consumers to enjoy their music anywhere, anytime regardless of surroundings, and to do so fashionably.

This unprecedented accessibility entrenched popular music as an essential element of the teenage identity habitus. Furthermore, the individualistic and private nature of this new technology (vis-à-vis listening through headphones) insinuated that every consumer needed to have their own personal copy of the recording (Resnick, 2001). Sensing the profitability here, recording industry producers commenced wide-scale distribution of digital cassette tapes containing popular music as an alternative medium to long play vinyl records. In addition, industry-wide policies were instituted that ensured music sellers would migrate away from LPs toward newer technologies. By the mid-1980s cassette tape popular sales had eclipsed LPs, and reached an all-time peak of 442 million units sold worldwide in 1990 (Daniel, Mee, & Clark, 1999).

In exercising their control of the industry to direct music consumption habits, music producers had used steering media to colonize the lifeworld with a new consensus on how music was to be consumed. Furthermore, as the controlling interest for the delivery of popular music, the recording industry had effectively established itself as the natural "owner" of these cultural artifacts through the circular logic of institutional rationalism. Simply put, the recording industry had become the controller of music because they were the distributors; and they were the distributors because they controlled the production of music. The significance of this period is that the convergence of technology, habitus, and steering media provided the foundation for a socio-legal framework that specifically targeted RW culture in a contradictory manner.

The cassette tape boom was something of a double-edged sword for the music industry: While users were consuming music individually, they had not given up on sharing it. Home taping, the act of copying music from one tape to another (aka dubbing), had become common practice alongside the popularization of music tapes (Plumleigh, 1990). By the mid-1980s the technology to either dub tapes or record from radio and other mass media had become financially accessible for most users, as had blank tapes. Although the Sony Corporation embraced the unanticipated manner in which consumers used their Walkman, the wider recording industry took great issue with this cultural practice. While no adequate assessment of the impact of home taping or cassette dubbing practices was feasible (Fein, 1983), the perceived financial losses from nonlegitimate use of technology and the betrayal of the recording industry's ownership of popular music led the RIAA to popularize a discourse pertaining to the notion that home taping was effectively "killing the recording industry" (Plumleigh, 1990).

The recording industry has long advocated for a substantive means of legal recourse against music reproducing consumers. The recording industry and those companies responsible for providing the technology rendering home taping possible effectively achieved a compromise with the passage of the Audio Home Recording Act (Sulyok, 1987). Curiously, while the intentions of consumers and the availability of music copying technologies united to institgate the cultural practice of tape dubbing, only the consumer would be rendered legally culpable for the ostensible losses suffered by the wider music industry.

This distrust of the consumer is present in the framework of the 1992 Audio Home Recording Act (AHRA). Implemented at the height of dubbing culture, lawmakers enacted a series of definitions and remedies that targeted music-sharing actions. The act amended the Copyright Act with a 10th chapter specifically targeting "Digital Audio Recording Devices and Media," and implemented a prohibition of copyright infringement actions which it defined as serial copying:

The term "serial copying" means the duplication in a digital format of a copyrighted musical work or sound recording from a digital reproduction of a digital musical recording. The term "digital reproduction of a digital musical recording" does not include a digital musical recording as distributed, by authority of the copyright owner, for ultimate sale to consumers.

Further, the act provided recourse for "interested copyright parties" to receive compensation in the form of royalties from blank media and recording device sales (AHRA, 1992).While the intent of this inclusion may have been to curb the manufacture and/or sale of devices capable of duplicating music, the costs were ultimately handed down to the consumer regardless of their intentions with the device. The act also set the groundwork for a litigious approach to remedy any financial injuries encountered by interested copyright holders against any individual whom they felt owed royalties or who had otherwise impacted their business through copyright circumvention.

Lawmakers had attempted to end the "two-decade-old debate over whether private home taping of copyrighted sound recordings is either fair use or infringement" (McKuin, 1994); however, as McKuin points out, preexisting agreements between the recording industry and audio equipment manufacturers (occasionally entities of the same corporation) were simply codified into law rather than addressing rights to music ownership or use. Instead, the vague definitions within the act and specific remedies for wrongful actions cast a new layer of deviance on music sharing and associated a tangible loss to unpredictable consumer behaviors: $25 per song, regardless of whether the consumer would have ever purchased the music otherwise (AHRA, 1992).

Online Music

Much like the introduction of the Walkman in 1979, the first portable compressed music file players (colloquially called MP3 players) marked a convergent point in technological development that once again engaged consumers to enter new realms of music appreciation and collecting. These small, wallet-sized devices were extremely popular and expensive, and instantly provided social capital to the user. Indeed, the iPod and other portable music devices had many of the same ramifications of the Walkman in terms of mobilizing music and associating it with the development of habitus. However, while use of unique marketing ploys such as white earbuds added another layer of conspicuous consumption, the outward mechanics of the devices did little to differentiate them from other technologies of the time, like CD or minidisc players.

Where MP3 players really stood out was in their capacity to store music: The original iPod, with a now modest 1 GB of storage space, was able to advertise that the consumer could carry the equivalent of 50 compact discs with them on a device that had a footprint smaller than a pack of cigarettes (Apple Inc., 2013). As device functions became somewhat standardized to reflect consumer's patterns of use, manufacturers had to develop new means to attract new/upgrading customers. This was largely accomplished through a space race of sorts: within 5 years of its introduction to the marketplace, the iPod classic's storage capacity had grown exponentially from 5 GB to 160 GB, allowing the user to now hold more than 1,600 full-length albums in their pocket (Apple Inc., 2013).

While these astronomical figures fulfilled the consumer's ability to advertise their cultural identity and communicate their tastes, it also provided them with space to further explore and engage in cultural consumption. Throughout the 1990s the music industry had enjoyed unprecedented record sales and many of the producers had invested in aggressive marketing campaigns to maintain this momentum (Knopper, 2009). Along with a protracted peak in sales, the music industry's application of steering media impacted consumers in a way so as to further entrench popular music tastes as a central element in identity creation. New sub-genres of music and a revitalization of classics through digitization, remastering, and re-release encouraged listeners to expand their music collections, and the extreme capacities of the portable music players afforded listeners the space to do this. However, pricing remained a barrier (Knopper, 2009).

To this end, the popularity of portable music devices and the height of the music industry's expansion coincided with a new approach to the collective nature of music: Napster. In principal, Shawn Fanning developed his music-sharing client to streamline his and his friends' exploration of popular music. In practice Napster became a stepping off point for a new wave of Internet-based music sharing. Recent recording industry-funded studies have estimated that the industry loses $12.5 billion annually due to music downloading, and that as many as 70% of downloaded songs are nonlegitimate downloads that directly replace legitimate purchases of music (Siwek, 2007). While the true financial impact of this phenomenon remains hotly debated (Oberholzer-Gee & Strumpf, 2004), scholarly consensus seems to have gelled on the fact that engagement in downloading is commonplace, particularly among young people (i.e., Gunter, Higgins, & Gealt, 2010).

Despite the popularity of the MP3 and the ubiquity of the MP3 player, conceptual ownership of music reproduction rights has remained solely in the hands of popular music producers. Throughout the late 1990s and the first decades of the 21st century, resistance the MP3 trade has been the target of educational and promotional campaigns by recording industry stakeholders (Knopper, 2009). Moreover, the RIAA, acting on behalf of most of the major record producers in North America, took advantage of its significant share of cultural capital to reinforce the existing institutional rationalism for the record producers' control over music distribution through litigious campaigns. A series of significant lawsuits against music consumers reaffirmed that the right to ownership was determined by the producers, not the end-users. The espousal of this stance by industry celebrities (see Metallica v. Napster, 2000) further manipulated these steering mechanisms.

This process of the lifeworld colonization herein is best described through an examination of one of the earliest decisions against online music sharing (A&M Records v. Napster, Inc., 2001). Whereas the AHRA's stance on copyright infringement placed a significant portion of responsibility in the hands of electronics producers, post-Napster interpretations of the law saw fit to place blame squarely on the shoulders of consumers (Knopper, 2009). A prescient example of this stance is within the discourse of the ruling on A&M Records v. Napster, Inc. (2001). The preamble alone establishes music sharing as an individual action, and as an illegitimate one. For instance, in describing MP3 usage, the findings state that:

> Consumers typically acquire MP3 files in two ways. First, users may download audio recordings that have already been converted into MP3 format by using an Internet service such as Napster. See Lisi Dec. (Tygar Rep.) at 11. Second, "ripping" software makes it possible to copy an audio compact disc ("CD") directly onto a computer hard-drive; ripping software compresses the millions of bytes of information on a typical CD into a smaller MP3 file that requires a fraction of the storage space.

Furthermore, statements present within the decision suggested that most if not all downloaders were acting in a deviant manner, despite a lack of guiding legislation at the time:

> The evidence shows that virtually all Napster users download or upload copyrighted files and that the vast majority of the music available on Napster is copyrighted.

While the case named Napster as the primary defendant, in effect it sought to field a blow against music consumers as a whole. This stance is present in the discourse of several clauses that seek to neutralize common arguments for the use of compressed music files, such as space-shifting (reducing the footprint of music collections by converting them to MP3), promoting new and unsigned artists, and music sampling (downloading new music before purchasing).

CONCLUSION AND THE LEGITIMACY CRISES

In effect, ongoing efforts by the recording industry to mitigate the impact of technology on behaviours of consumption have opened new dialogues about the collective nature of music enjoyment and the true reality of its control. Further, recent attempts to direct consumption habits have worked contrary to their intent, seating the recording industry into a state of fragility that threatens its ability to manipulate legal frameworks. Central to this argument is the relationship between new technologies and popular music tastes: where control over reproduction technologies and the ability to dictate music tastes once rationalized the industry's direction of policy, new realms of technology have opened up the doors for greater diffusion of musical interests and self-directed control over consumption. Fans have realised that they can enjoy music on their own terms, and that the interests of controlling bodies do not necessarily align with their own.

Inasmuch as the unfettered growth of online music trade has been relatively unharmed by prohibitive action, these outcomes seem to suggest a legitimation crisis within traditional control over social steering mechanisms within the realm of legal frameworks dictating music consumption. For instance, Burkart (2010) explained that, initially

> The intrusion of technocratic controls into the activities of collecting and enjoying music with friends and family reflects a colonization of the life-world. Copyright law has helped to "uncouple" the music lifeworld from other social subsystems to the point that the law is no longer called upon to justify itself with reference to its interventions into the music lifeworld. Rather, the law, together with power, money, and communication networks, works as a "steering medium": it works independently of the lifeworld, colonizes it, and converts its cultural communications into formal, instrumentalist, market-based transactions. (p. 15)

However, "the Napster precedent altered legal norms but not other social norms, such that something similar to a legitimation crisis of the music industry has taken place" (Burkart, 2010, p. 91) a situation where tensions over the nature of property rights in cyberspace have led to widespread rejection of normative governing structures. Such wholesale denial of authority has challenged the legitimacy of music producers' rights to control reproduction and distribution of popular music, and further, it challenges the traditional steering mechanisms utilized by these entities (i.e., influencing policy through political and legal processes).

Indeed, this crisis is present in the rich dialogue that has emerged about the legality of music downloading post-Napster where a number of authors have argued against the legitimacy of copyright enforcement on moralistic grounds. For instance Neri (2004) writes that despite advertising campaigns, litigious action, and actions by lawmakers, these efforts "... will fail to convince the general public that downloading constitutes reprehensible conduct equivalent to theft and fail to deter downloading" (p. 735). The author concludes that millions of young people have "thoroughly embraced downloading," (Neri, 2004, p. 757) and that bullying music fans will only strengthen their resolve against what they perceive as unjust laws. Knopper (2009) presented much the same argument, illustrating an entire industry that had alienated itself from throngs of consumers through its attempts to maintain the status quo of music consumption. Knopper (2009) has traced the music industry's growth – and decline – since the late 1970s and has expressed the importance of adaptation to changing perspectives; in what he labels as "Big Music's Big Mistakes, Part 7" (p. 183), Knopper (2009) describes how the RIAA's attempts at suing music downloaders punished a few but led many more to say "what's the big deal?"

Theorists have also challenged the legal foundations upon which the deviant label is affixed to music downloaders. These concerns often accompany state-sponsored attempts to supress downloading, such as the World Trade Organization supported Anti-Counterfeiting Trade Agreement (ACTA) (Ayoob, 2010). Canadian legal scholar Michael Geist has provided a constant voice of reason against criminalizing online behaviors, pointing out that such attempts are misguided. Geist (2005) has insisted that private copying levies created by the governments more than adequately address the revenue losses to music downloading reported by the music industry. He has also demonstrated how international agreement on any form of legal mechanisms will be unlikely to succeed, and even if does, enforcement would be impossible (Geist, 2008). Adding an interesting twist to the debate, Altschuller and Benbunan-Fich (2009) have described the criminalization of downloading copyrighted materials as akin to alcohol prohibitions during the 1920s in the United States:

> From a socially optimistic perspective we would expect that our laws reflect the moral perceptions of society and in turn are obeyed by the majority of morally inclined citizens. However, current events indicate a disconnect somewhere along this path of logical expectation in the case of digital music downloading. As has happened in the past (e.g., widespread disobedience of the prohibition of alcohol in America of the 1920s) society seems to be repelling its own behavioural guidelines. (2009, p. 49)

Others have attempted to provide clarity to the moral and legal ambiguity surrounding file sharing. For example, Lessig (2004) has addressed the need for adaptation, stating that "Copyright law regulates culture in America. Copyright law must be changed. *Changed*, not abolished" (p. 254, emphasis original). According to Lessig, the matter of file-sharing legality can be solved through a simple cost–benefit application. He states that criminalization of file sharing will in fact criminalize countless youth while also burdening legal systems with the associated caseload. In an earlier project, Lessig (2004) noted that attempts by Hollywood to rally support for copyright protection made sense; however, he concluded that their calls for extreme protections were like spraying DDT to kill a gnat (p. 130).

Over the past half century the music industry has efficiently seeded its interests within the habitus of consumers, designing a relatively homogenized spectrum of popular music to be an integral part of personal identity. The steering media that emerged from these efforts also enabled a lifeworld colonization of socio-legal paradigms that rationalized music producer's monopolistic control over the distribution of cultural artifacts. However, as the technologies of music consumption and sharing continue to evolve it seems unlikely that the music industry or legislators will be able rebuff forms of distribution that circumvent traditional controlling mechanisms. Rather than adapting to new paradigms of governance, consumers have simply abandoned these frameworks, choosing collective approaches to music rather than the reification of post-Napster industry ambitions.

REFERENCES

Avdeeff, M. (2012). Technological engagement and musical eclecticism: An examination of contemporary listening practices. *Participations: Journal of Audience and Reception Studies*, *9*(2), 265–285.

A&M Records, Inc. v. Napster. Inc., 239 F.3d 1004, 1011 (9th Cir. 2001).

Altschuller, S., & Benbunan-Fich, R. (2009). Is music downloading the new prohibition? What students reveal through an ethical dilemma. *Ethics and Information Technology*, *1*(11), 49–56.

Apple Inc. (2013). *iPod+iTunes Timeline*. Retrieved from http://www.apple.com/ca/pr/products/ipodhistory/

Audio Home Recording Act (AHRA). § 17 U.S.C. § 1001-1010 (1992).

Ayoob, E. (2010). Recent development: The anti-counterfeiting trade agreement. *Cardozo Arts & Entertainment Law Journal*, *28*, 175–193.

Bandura, A., Ross, D., & Ross, S. A. (1963). Vicarious reinforcement and imitative learning. *Journal of Abnormal Pyschology*, *67*(December), 601–607.

Benjamin, W. (2008). *The work of art in the age of its technological reproducibility and other writings on media*. Cambridge: Harvard University Press.

Borland, J. (2000, July 11). *Musicians launch national anti-Napster campaign*. Retrieved from http://news.cnet.com/Musicians-launch-national-anti-Napster-campaign/2100-1023_3-243021.html

Bourdieu, P. (1990). *The logic of practice*. Cambridge: Polity Press.

Bourdieu, P. (2010). *Distinction: A social critique of the judgment of taste*. Oxon, UK: Routledge Classics.

Burkart, P. (2010). *Music and cyberliberties*. Middletown, CT: Wesleyan University Press.

Chen, S. L. (1998). Electronic narcissism: College students' experiences of Walkman listening, *Qualitative Sociology*, *21*(3), 255–76.

Cooper, T. B. (2009). Appropriating visual form: The iPod "silhouette" campaign as representative form. *Visual Communication Quarterly*, *16*(2), 90–107.

Daniel, E. D., Mee, C. D., & Clark, M. H. (1999). Magnetic recording: The first 100 years. Piscataway, NJ: IEEE Press.

du Gay, P., Hall, S., Janes, L., Mackay, H., & Negus, K. (1997). *Doing cultural studies: The story of the Sony Walkman*. London: Sage.

Fein, J. (1983). Home taping of sound recordings: Infringement or fair use? *Southern California Law Review*, *56*(2), 647–668.

Finlayson, J. G. (2005). *Habermas: A very short introduction*. London: Oxford University Press.

Geist, M. (2005). Piercing the peer-to-peer myths: An examination of the Canadian experience. *First Monday*, *10*(4). Retrieved from http://firstmonday.org/ojs/index.php/fm/article/view/1217

Geist, M. (2008). Copyright reform needs careful consideration. *The Vancouver Sun*, February 19, p. D1.

Gunter, W., Higgins, G., & Gealt, R. (2010). Pirating youth: Examining the correlates of digital music piracy among adolescents. *International Journal of Cyber Criminology*, *4*(1–2), 657–671.

Habermas, J. (1996). *Between facts and norms: Contributions to a discourse theory of law and democracy*. Cambridge, MA: MIT Press.

Hesmondhalgh, D. (1999). Indie: The institutional politics and aesthetics of a popular music genre. *Cultural Studies*, *13*(1), 34–61.

James, K. (2009). Structural change in the music industry: A Marxist critique of public statements made by members of Metallica during the lawsuit against Napster. *International Journal of Critical Accounting*, *1*(1/2), 144–176.

Knopper, S. (2009). *Appetite for self-destruction: The spectacular crash of the record industry in the digital age*. New York, NY: Free Press.

Larréché, J. C. (2008). Momentum strategies for efficient growth: When the sumo meets the surfer. *International Commerce Review*, *8*(1), 22–33.

Lessig, L. (2004). *Free culture: How big media uses technology and the law to lock down culture and control creativity*. New York, NY: The Penguin Group.

Lessig, L. (2008). *Remix: Making art and commerce thrive in the hybrid economy*. London: Bloomsbury Academic.

McKuin, J. (1994). Home audio taping of copyrighted works and the audio home recording act of 1992: A critical analysis. *Hastings Communications and Entertainment Law Journal*, *16*(1993–1994), 311–348.

Medovoi, L. (2005). *Rebels: Youth and the Cold War Origins of Identity*. Durham: Duke University Press.

Metallica v. Napster Inc. CA No. 2:00–3914 (CD California 2000).

Neri, G. (2004). Sticky fingers or sticky norms? Unauthorized music downloading and unsettled social norms. *Georgetown Law Journal*, *93*, 733–758.

Oberholzer-Gee, F., & Strumpf, K. (2004). *The effect of file sharing on record sales: An empirical analysis*. Cambridge, MA: Harvard Business School.

Plumleigh, M. (1990). Digital audio tape: New fuel stokes the smouldering home taping fire. *UCLA Law Review*, *37*(4), 733–84.

Quigley, R. (2010, January 29). *Flashback: How was the iPod received in 2001? (Not well)*. Retrieved from http://www.geekosystem.com/ipod-2001-ipad-bad-reviews/

Reppel, A. E., Szmigin, I., & Gruber, T. (2006). The iPod phenomenon: Identifying a market leader's secrets through qualitative marketing research. *Journal of Product & Brand Management*, *15*(4), 239–249.

Resnick, P. (2001). Beyond bowling together: SocioTechnical capital. In J. Carroll (Ed.), *Human-computer interaction in the new millennium* (pp. 247–272). Boston, MA: Addison-Wesley.

Siwek, S. (2007, August). *The true cost of sound recording piracy to the U.S. economy*. Policy Report no. 188. The Institute for Policy Innovation, Dallas, TX.

Sulyok, T. (1987). The Home Audio Recording Act: An inappropriate response to the home taping question. *Fordham Urban Law Journal*, *15*(2), 436–79.

Veblen, T. (1934). *The theory of the leisure class: An economic study of institutions*. New York, NY: Modern Library.

THE BAND: ARTISTIC, LEGAL, AND FINANCIAL STRUCTURES WHICH SHAPE MODERN MUSIC

Jon M. Garon

ABSTRACT

Purpose – *This chapter focuses on the creative and artistic consequences triggered by legal and business decisions related to the form, structure, and operation of the band as a creative entity, as distinct from its members. The chapter highlights the choices often made by professional musical groups in popular music and the consequences of those choices.*

Design/methodology of approach – *The chapter follows the legal consequences of organizational formation and how those choices impact a band's relationship with its record label, publisher, and audience as well as the relationship dynamics within the organization itself.*

Findings – *Lack of planning often results in tensions that undermine bands, particularly in those bands that form incrementally over time. Standard record label agreements and publishing agreements tend to*

Music and Law
Sociology of Crime, Law and Deviance, Volume 18, 79–99

ISSN: 1521-6136/doi:10.1108/S1521-6136(2013)0000018007

heighten the tension among band members, creating competing economic incentives for various band members.

Originality – *The implications to organizational dynamics for musical groups are rarely analyzed in terms of the band's legal and economic structure either as an academic review or as a professional planning methodology. This analysis and the approach provided herein should provide musicians and their counsel an effective method for planning and anticipating the inevitable tensions that will arise in the various stages of the band's development.*

Keywords: Band name; controlled composition; cross-collateralization; distribution agreement; leaving artist; mechanical fees

INTRODUCTION

The modern musical enterprise known as a "band" in popular music differs from the bands formed in the days before pre-recorded music. A band can be comprised of only instruments, only vocalists, or a combination of both (Shepherd, 2003, p. 6).[1] In the days before pre-recorded music, the musicians who joined a band were paid for their participation – if they were paid at all. Then as now, some musicians are simply employees of the ensemble, hired to perform their parts in live concerts and on recordings (Cirone, 2011; Flanagan, 2008). For pop, rock, country, and other more commercial music forms, however, musicians typically come together, form their musical group, and operate as a band.

The modern band is typically comprised of members who all share a portion of the risk and revenue of the enterprise. Revenue is earned from live performances, music sales, licensed merchandise royalties, and payments for the exploitation of the copyright in the band's music (Schultz, 2009, p. 697). The rights for a musician to earn income for the compositions written and tracks recorded depend not only on the terms of the production and distribution agreements with the record company, but also on the terms of the operating agreements for the band itself. The differing economic and professional risks within the band enterprise can lead to unanticipated problems and ongoing tensions.

LEGAL ENTITIES – DISTRIBUTION OF RISK AND CONTROL

The decision of musicians to play together professionally rather than work as employed musicians will determine many of the legal and economic relationships they face. In the absence of planning, state laws provide legal structures for the artists that may not necessarily be the optimal choices for any of the participants.

General Partnerships

Perhaps to the surprise of many band members, the very act of joining a band is a legal decision to form an entity. When two or more persons engage as co-owners in a business for profit, state laws treat that combination as a general partnership (Revised Uniform Partnership Act §202(a) (1997)).[2] While being paid to perform in a band does not automatically result in each band member becoming a partner in the partnership, the law creates a presumption that may be difficult to overcome. The obligations of a partnership are not limited to the partnership itself or to the contributions of the partners. Instead, partners are jointly and severally liable for all obligations of the partnership, meaning that each partner might be responsible for all debts if the other partners are unable to pay (Duruigbo, 2010, pp. 1047–1048; Freer & Moll, 2013). Most businesses form corporations or limited liability companies (LLCs) to avoid this unlimited liability.

Partnerships are typically defined by the twin attributes of "profit sharing and joint control" (Okorocha, 2011, pp. 5–7). In most bands, both attributes are readily present. Musicians are paid from the revenue derived from each performance as well as some revenue sharing for record sales. Joint control may be less explicit, but evidence of joint control does not require equal say. Choosing where and when to perform, having a voice in which numbers to perform, and deciding whether or not to sign with a publisher or record label all demonstrate some level of control.

Partners owe the partnership and each other a high degree of loyalty. State laws differ on the extent of this loyalty, but all require "partners to account for profits and benefits in all transactions." (Revised Uniform Partnership Act §404 cmt. 2 (1997)). Partners may lawfully seek to benefit themselves as well as the partnership, but they cannot divert partnership opportunities for themselves or compete with the partnership. In practice this means that any conflict between a musician's solo career and the band partnership should legally be decided in favor of the partnership, unless the partners agree otherwise.

To mitigate these rules, state law treats many partnership provisions as default rules, enabling a partnership to tailor its internal relationship. Changes to the default rules should be detailed in a written, signed partnership agreement. As such, a band could choose to identify certain members as the business partners and then hire the remaining performers as employees or independent contractors. The partnership agreement could specify what solo artist activities are considered not to compete with the partnership, to grant permission for partners to also play and record with other bands, or set rules specifying decision-making authority.

In the absence of a contrary agreement, all the partners share equally in the costs of the business and in the profits of the partnership. Because each partner has joint control, each partner can bind the partnership to a contract and any tort liabilities created by one partner (such as through an accident while on tour) would be the responsibility of the partnership and therefore each individual partner (Freer & Moll, 2013). This also results in equal returns even if the band members are not equal in their participation or significance to the group. The failure of the band members to formally agree to distribution interests and ownership establishes a rule of even distribution, so the band members actually make a distribution decision by their inaction (Borden, 2011, p. 1093).[3]

In addition, for a band partnership to have nonpartner members, the partnership should memorialize the arrangement in a written and signed partnership agreement as well as written agreements between the partnership and each of the nonpartner performers. Even then, this may not be enough. Under the doctrine of apparent authority, if a partnership makes it appear a nonpartner band member has authority and a third party reasonably believes this to be the case, then that band member will be treated as if he/she has authority to act on behalf of the partnership. If both partners and nonpartners are all treated as members publicly, then the public may be able to rely on that equal treatment and assume each member is a partner for contracting purposes (Hillman, 2005, pp. 816–819).

Both the unlimited liability and the poor fit of the default rules for partnerships strongly indicate that bands should form limited liability business entities in the form of corporations or LLCs as soon as they choose to operate. As between LLCs and corporations, there are only small differences between the two structures. Both corporations and LLCs serve the band far better than general partnerships (Molitor, 2009, pp. 500–504). In no case should a band rely on the legal default rules without a careful examination of how those rules affect the management of the band.

Corporations and Limited Liability Companies

Both corporations and LLCs come into existence only after the band files the appropriate documents with a state agency. In the case of corporations, the document to be filed is the articles of incorporation; for the LLC, the document is generally called the articles of organization. Because LLCs are more recent legal developments, there is greater variation in nomenclature from state to state.

The prime benefit of corporate or LLC form is limited liability, meaning that the entity is responsible for the contractual and tort liabilities rather than the owners (Molitor, 2009, pp. 500–501). This eliminates guarantee to third parties that each band member will pay for all expenses if the band itself is unable to meet its obligations (Garon, 2007, pp. 133–140). These entities formally distinguish between the owners of the enterprise and those that manage and work for the enterprise.

Tax treatment is an important consideration for the management of the band, but the strategies for minimizing tax liability will vary over time depending on the nature of the income and the ownership. Since owners of LLCs and owners of a species of closely held corporations identified as Subchapter-S corporations can choose to be treated as partnerships for tax purposes, the nature of taxation need not dictate the choice of organizational form.

The creation of a closely held corporation or LLC provides a discrete separate entity that can own the band's assets, enter into employment, production, and other agreements, and help to better distinguish between the band and its members. As such, the formal creation of the band as a corporation or LLC is essential to good band management.

When choosing between the closely held corporation and the LLC, modest differences affect the choice. While both legal forms rely primarily on default provisions that can be modified by internal agreement, the LLC typically has fewer predetermined rules and allows for greater flexibility. Delaware LLC laws, for example, provide "[i]t is the policy of this chapter to give the maximum effect to the principle of freedom of contract and to the enforceability of limited liability company agreements." (Del. Code Ann. tit. 6, § 18-1101(b) (2005)).

Moreover, corporations are required to operate in a more formal basis, with annual shareholders meeting and other formalities unnecessary for the LLC. As such, the LLC is likely the better of the two choices. At the same time, however, the band must utilize a well-drafted LLC operating agreement to specify the rights and duties of the members. In the absence of a comprehensive operating agreement, the default provisions of corporate law may provide a better approximation of the participant's needs than the default provisions of state LLC law. Despite this, the LLC has become the preferred choice of entity.

OPERATING AGREEMENTS

The band's LLC operating agreement must be binding on all of the owners for the agreement to have full effect. LLC owners are referred to as "members" by statute. This membership refers to equity ownership in the business, not participation as a performer in the band. A band can choose to sell equity ownership to nonperformers (subject to state and federal securities laws). Similarly, it can choose to hire performers who are not LLC members. In fact, as discussed below, many of the less prominent members of the band may benefit from this nonequity partner status. Like all other businesses, the operating agreement should provide the identity of the parties, business name and address, business purpose, accounting rules, and other general information. The key issues for bands regarding their internal operating agreements emphasize issues of management and control of the band's operations and the band's assets.

Management and Control of Operations

As a collaborative enterprise, bands operate with all the members serving as managers. This is not required, however, and as the enterprise grows, the band LLC could choose to have professional management that is supervised by the members in their capacity as owners of the LLC. The operating agreement should specify the preferred choice of the band members.

The operating agreement can be used to confirm the dynamic relationships, which serve as the heart of the band. At a minimum, these terms can establish the relative percentages of ownership; percentages of voting control (which might vary from ownership); hiring of new artists, agents, and managers; admission of new members to the LLC; termination and withdrawal; and contributions of funds to the LLC (Passman, 2000, pp. 322–325).[4] Other important protections for members might focus on the payment or withholding of dividends or other nonsalary payments, self-dealing transactions between the LLC and some members, competition between the LLC and individual members, and identification of assets owned by the LLC instead of individual band members (Molitor, 2009, pp. 512–515).

These decisions are often the most important and potentially the most contentious that the LLC will face. As such, the operating agreement may provide that a super-majority vote is required. The super-majority can be set anywhere from a two-thirds majority to a unanimous vote, depending on the goals of the members and minority member's concerns about being mistreated by the majority. The alignment of factions within a band may change considerably after a few years of operations. So the voting rules adopted at the formation of the band should take into account the potential for these changed circumstances.

The particular off-stage duties of band members can also be specified in the operating agreement. Bands can have various individuals or subcommittees designated to manage bookings, recording agreements, merchandise, or investments. By assigning these duties in advance, the band can achieve greater predictability and efficiency. Even if the band contracts with a manager and attorney to recommend and manage many of these decisions, those parties are only consultants. Such consultants sometimes have interests adverse to the band members. The band must review the consultant's recommendations before adopting them and be responsible for its own business choices. The allocation of responsibility within the band helps empower band members and manage that tension. Within the membership or a subcommittee of the members, decisions would normally be specified to be made by majority vote.

Particular to band LLCs, the operating agreement can specify that in the absence of a decision to the contrary, a specified percentage of all recorded songs will feature a particular member as lead singer; describe which instruments each member is expected to play; and set out the opportunities and obligations for authorship of the band's recorded music. Such specificity might not be needed, but it does protect individuals from majority oppression if a controlling group within the band begins to try to oust or undermine a minority group.

More importantly, former band members may still be entitled to revenue from the band. One simple method of managing tension between former and current band members is to provide that management of the band stays with the active performers, while allowing the former members to retain their ownership status. This enables the band to avoid needing to pay the exiting band member the full value of his/her share immediately upon a split.

The responsibilities are particularly important for the most significant decisions, such as the choice of recording company (or the decision to direct-distribute) and the ability to approve members' participation in solo activities or with other projects. These decisions can be assigned to all members while day-to-day decisions are left to the designated managers within the band.

The operating agreement should be very explicit regarding the expectations for its members. If a member's duties are exclusive to the band, then approval would be needed to perform solo, act in a film, or appear in a recurring television role. If the band obligations are not exclusive, then the operating agreement must provide what is expected of each band member.

Band Assets and Band Names

The assets of a band are typically simple. The most valuable is often the name of the band and related trademarks, along with any copyrights retained by the band in compositions and sound recordings (Passman, 2000, p. 320). The other assets typically include the musical equipment, leases on vehicles and other transportation equipment, rentals on lighting and touring equipment, and the intellectual property of the band.

Vesting ownership of the band name in the LLC helps clarify who owns the name and how it can be used. Because of the importance of this asset, the recording agreement will often specify how the name will be used on albums. Band names should always be available to sell the songs recorded under that name. The band name should be registered as a federal service mark, which will help the band assure that other performers are not using the same mark in a confusingly similar manner (Shanker, Guinn, & Orenstein, 2012, § 3.2.1 at p. 3-3).[5]

For touring and merchandise licensing, identifying the rights to the name is critical. Using an LLC, the LLC would own the name rather than any member. Even if all the members changed over time, the entity could still perform using the name and no one who left the band could use the name (Bigger, 2001, pp. 14–15).[6] This practice, however, might not reflect the true understanding among the band members or the expectations of the audience, so some bands make other arrangements. For example, the operating agreement might provide that if the lead singer/composer of the band left, the LLC would transfer the rights in the name to him/her (Passman, 2000, p. 322). The operating agreement might also specify that the name could no longer be used if a majority of band members were not founding members.

In comparison, if a dissolving band were organized as a general partnership operating without an operating agreement, then no individual would have the exclusive right to the band name. Each party might be eligible to use the name as a tenant in common. This nonexclusive use would destroy its value as a source identifier and obviate its federal trademark registration (*see* Bigger, 2001; Shanker, 2012, § 3.3 at pp. 3-10–3-11). The audience would likely be confused as to the identity of the real band and its members. As a result, the public would be harmed and none of the band members would be better off than had a legal entity been created and a trademark in the band name registered.

For both trademark purposes and to maximize value, the rights to the trademark should reflect the public's expectation of the name. A band using the surname of a founding member, for example, might create consumer confusion were it to continue performing after that band member had left the band to play as a solo artist. Such a result could potentially be deceptive to the public. Because the variations are infinite and depend on who was involved in the band's formation, clarifying the ownership of the name is essential to avoid protracted conflict.

Copyrighted Compositions

The songs created by band members might be the other asset of high value owned by the band. But predicting whether the songs are owned by the LLC will be based on many factors. The copyright ownership of the songs will depend on the rules of copyright law, the operating agreement, and the composer's contracts with its publisher. The lyrics, composition, and arrangement are protected by copyright. Under copyright law, a work of authorship initially vests in the author of that work (17 U.S.C. §201(a)). If a person is employed and creates a copyrighted work "within the scope of his or her employment," then the employer is the author of the work rather than the employee (17 U.S.C. §201(b)). An agreement between the employer and employee can alter the law's presumption that copyright vests with the employer, however, meaning the LLC can specify whether the songs written as part of the member's duties to the LLC belong to the band or to the member.

General partners, unlike LLC members, would not be employees, and therefore the work for hire status of the compositions would not arise. A closely held corporation or LLC may or may not treat the band members as employees, depending on how it has been organized. If the composers are not actually employees, then the work for hire rule would not apply. If the work for hire rules do not apply and the band members wish the songs to be owned by the band, then the composers could assign the copyrights in the songs to the band, whether it were an LLC, corporation, or general partnership. If the songs are to stay with the composers, then that decision should also be made clear in the operating agreement. While the copyright owner could be either the LLC or the individual composer, custom remains that the copyright is retained by the composer rather than being transferred to the band (Stim, 2013).[7]

Publishing Contracts

Much of a band's commercial success will come from the exploitation of songs through publishing agreements. The publisher will seek to promote the song for uses in films, television, commercials, recordings by other artists, and publications – much of which is distinct from the band's activities in performing the music and selling copies (Brabec & Brabec, 2013, pp. 13–15). Composers of music and lyrics typically benefit from the commercialization provided by song publishers.

Since the composers benefit from publication, this represents the most explicit conflict of interest within the band. Those members who write the band's songs will benefit from the exploitation of the song's copyrights if the copyrights are owned individually, but the LLC will benefit if the LLC treats the compositions as a work made for hire or the copyrights are assigned to the LLC.

The copyright owner will typically enter into an agreement with a publisher, either for individual songs or on an exclusive basis for a period of time (Johnson, 2001, pp. 132–133). Either the individuals or the LLC would be the writer, depending on the determination as to the work for hire status of the band member.

Since the individual band member or members who created the song will receive the publishing royalties, the LLC may face a situation where the economic interests of some members will diverge dramatically from other members. In a five-person group, for example, if three of those members operated as a successful writing team, then those team members could receive publishing income in addition to the dividends provided by the LLC. Their publishing revenue would increase with each public performance by the band, by use of the songs by cover bands, use in publications, exploitation on television, and in other areas that generated no revenue for the band (Johnson, 2001, p. 130).[8]

If the three writing members of the band had a majority for voting control, they could use their votes in the LLC or influence over the band to increase the band's operating costs. The wealthier majority could insist on fancier hotels, more expensive recording sessions, and other extravagances that nonwriting minority could ill afford.

The nonwriting LLC members, earning money only from the LLC's profits, could be left impoverished by the increased expenses and lack of publishing revenue. Though not a form of corporate lock-out or minority ownership oppression, the conflict of interest triggered by having writing and nonwriting members of the band can lead to dramatic economic conflict within the group.

Alternatively, to assign the copyrights or the publishing revenue to the band contemplates a similar conflict of interest. The composers will receive a proportionate share of that income back in the form of dividends or profits from the LLC, but they may have given up considerable revenue. If the disparities are severe, it could encourage the composers within the band to seek withdrawal as a strategy to retain the publishing income being distributed to the other band members.

The conflict can be anticipated at the time the LLC is formed, so the operating agreement should provide full disclosure of the problem and offer some resolution, if practical. Not all conflicts can be eliminated, but a process for addressing the conflict can be provided.

RECORDING AGREEMENT'S INFLUENCE ON BAND ORGANIZATION

The typical provisions of the recording agreement provide additional pressures on the band organization and should be anticipated as part of the band's operating structure. In particular, the manner in which the publishing rights are addressed by the recording agreement and the treatment of the individual band members by the record deal both affect key operating agreement provisions and should be anticipated in a properly organized band LLC.

Ownership of Publishing Rights and the Controlled Composition Clause

To make a record, the record company (or record label) licenses the mechanical rights to incorporate the composition into a master sound recording. The record label's employee is the producer of the song or album. By recording the song, the record label then obtains the copyright in the master (Brabec & Brabec, 2013, pp. 148–149).[9] The record label must pay a mechanical fee for each copy of the song produced, whether on a CD, digital copy, or other physical embodiment (17 U.S.C. § 115).[10] The mechanical fee is collected by the publisher, which distributes the composer's portion of the revenue back to the artist.

The record label does not wish to pay the publisher for use of the compositions owned or controlled by the band. In the recording agreement between the record label and the band, a controlled composition clause will typically reduce the mechanical fee for each controlled song (or for all songs), often to 75% of the minimum statutory rate (Krasilovsky & Shemel, 2003, p. 21).

The controlled composition clause will similarly limit the number of songs for which the record label will pay the mechanical fees. The excess mechanical fees will be deducted from the band's earned royalties on the album sales. As a result, the band will pay the publishers and composers 25% of the mechanical fees for the first 9–11 songs on the album plus 100% of the mechanical fees for any additional songs on the album.

If the band is recording songs written by artists who are not members of the band, then this is a cost of doing business. If the songs are written and owned by band members, then the LLC is actually paying some of its members for the songs, reducing the profits of the LLC. For example, if an album has three excess songs at a cost of $0.091 per song/per copy and ten other songs at a cost of $0.0182 per album/per copy, then the band would owe the publisher $145,600 for a gold album, meaning distribution of 500,000 albums. Depending on the other contractual terms, this could represent a substantial portion of the band's income on the album (*see* Blake & Stuart, 2001, pp. 371–372).

To alleviate this rather extreme aspect of the conflict of interest between composer and noncomposer band members, one solution would have the composers grant a license to the LLC for those songs exploited by the

LLC itself. In this way, revenues for songs exploited outside of the band are retained by the composer but the band and its LLC never have to pay for rights to its own band members. The publishing income from the controlled compositions would then be returned to the LLC and the conflict of interest would be mitigated.

The Personal Obligations of Each Band Member to the Record Label

The other area in which the recording contract undermines the LLC structure of the band is the manner in which the band is signed. Under the terms of the recording agreement, the record label advances the costs of production for the album and pays for its marketing. In exchange it requires exclusive rights to the services of the band members with respect to recording musical compositions and the rights to use the band name and associated trademarks for the marketing of those recordings (Schulenberg, 2005, p. 188).

Despite the creation of an LLC to serve as contracting party with the band's record label, under common industry practice, the record label will require each member of the band to be bound on a personal basis to the record label in addition to the person's obligations as a member of the band and LLC. Because the value in the band may derive from its makeup, in some agreements, the decision by a member to withdraw from the group will trigger the record label's right to terminate the record deal (Blake & Stuart, 2001, pp. 492–495). In all agreements, the record label will retain the right to approve the new member to the band and require that each member becomes a party to the recording agreement.

The record label cannot insist that a band refrain from breaking up while under contract, though it might exert pressure to discourage (or encourage) group reorganization. At the same time, the record label does not want to risk having the rights to the LLC's musical output but not the contractual rights to the LLC's key members. As a result, the standard recording contract includes language binding each member of the group to the recording contract as individuals in addition to whatever language binds the group to the contract. A sample of such language is provided by the *Musician's Business and Legal Guide*:

> The obligations, liabilities, prohibitions and restrictions imposed upon you hereunder shall be deemed to apply individually and collectively to each of the members of Artist [(e.g., the band)], whether performing alone, with others, or as a member of the Artist, regardless of the name by which the Artist or any of its members may then be identified. … (Blake & Stuart, 2001, p. 400)[11]

The recording contract also protects the record label from losing a valuable member of the band. The record label will include in the band's recording agreement provisions that give the recording company the option to sign any leaving member of the band as a solo artist or any subset of the band members as a new group (Brabec & Brabec, 2013, pp. 146–147). Typically, the contract will require the band and the leaving member notify the record label in writing after which the record label will have a specified period (30–90 days) to exercise its option to sign the former band member to a new recording agreement with the record label (Krasilovsky & Shemel, 2003, pp. 14–15).

The record label can exercise its option to sign the leaving band member on terms identical to those of the band, but negotiations will typically ensue to adjust the relationship. If the leaving artist is likely to be a solo success, the record label will have incentives to make the offer attractive. Otherwise, the leaving artist has little leverage and may find the newly offered terms even more disadvantageous than those of the band's recording agreement. The option to sign the leaving band member will be exercised at the election of the label, not the artist, so an artist cannot avoid contractual liabilities with its label by disbanding, reforming, or seeing its members go solo.

The consequence for the disgruntled band member can be career ending. If the record label elects to exercise its option to sign the leaving band member, that artist is bound to the contract. Although the artist cannot be forced to perform, he/she can be prohibited from performing on behalf of any other label, potentially for as long as the minimum term under the existing contract (Scamman, 2008, pp. 279–280).[12]

In addition, the leaving band member will remain obligated to earn royalties to offset the advances made by the record label for the recording of the album. Album production costs, some video costs, and tour support may be advanced by the record label to the band, but those payments are advances against future royalties. As an advance, it obligates the band to earn back enough royalty income to recoup the advance before the band earns any additional money or receives any cash payments. Moreover, each advance is cross-collateralized with all other advances, so the record label recoups the debt of each project against all royalties earned (Passman, 2000, pp. 223–225).

A leaving band member typically has a proportionate share of this debt assigned to his account with the record label. That cross-collateralized debt will be included in the leaving member's obligations to the record label as a solo artist. Leaving the band provides no relief from unrecouped advances that diminish the actual earnings of the artist. (Krasilovsky & Shemel, 2003, pp. 21–22).

The personal obligation of the recording agreement is directly at odds with the strategy to create an LLC as the signatory for contractual liability. The recording agreement anticipates the use of an LLC to provide personal protections. Instead, the agreement strips individual band members of their ability to operate autonomously.

ORGANIZATIONAL RESPONSES TO COPYRIGHT, PUBLISHING AGREEMENTS, AND RECORDING CONTRACTS

While the structure of the LLC does little to affect the provisions of the standard recording agreement, it can assist the band members to navigate the competing demands of publishers, record companies, and the band's collective interests. First, the LLC allows participants in the band to make choices whether or not to join as equity members. Second, the LLC can be used to set limits on the power of particular members. And third, the LLC can afford some protection to minority factions within the band and minimize disagreements from disabling the band.

Performers Who Should Avoid Joining the LLC

Not all performers may be equally well served by equity membership in the LLC. While every band member may desire the riches, fame, and adoration that come with chart-topping success, most bands are businesses of modest income and significant business risk. Unlike the general partnership, where all members are equal, the LLC allows for different levels of ownership and nonowner participants. This allows each member to determine his comfort level by balancing the risk and the opportunity.

For artists who neither compose the music nor lead the band, the benefits of equal ownership might be outweighed by the obligations to recoup the advances made by the record label and the risks incumbent when financial management is controlled by others in the band with more influence.

For example, if a five-person band led by a charismatic lead singer/songwriter releases an expensive, unsuccessful album, the band will need to recoup the losses against future albums. Further assume that the lead singer quits the band in frustration at the album's failure. The remaining four band members will be responsible for 80% of the unrecouped advances while the lead singer will be responsible for 20%. Since the lead singer is the draw for the band's audience, he/she will be much more likely to recoup on a solo album than through another group album. The remaining band members have little chance of recouping without the lead singer and the debt to the record label may jeopardize renewals with the label or the ability to sign a new recording contract.

If instead, the lead singer/songwriter was a solo artist and the band members were salaried employees, perhaps with modest profit sharing, then the band members could be treated as sidemen under the exclusive artist recording agreement (*see* Krasilovsky & Shemel, 2003, pp. 14–15). While the use of the back-up band as regular sidemen is a bit unorthodox, it will protect both the lead artist and the other band members from an unfortunate financial relationship.

The members of the LLC have control over the band and its name but they also have the financial obligations that come with ownership. For replacement performers thinking to join an existing band, artists who will not be featured by the band, or those with successful solo careers, joining the LLC may not be as favorable as playing alongside.

Limiting Authority with the LLC

The second key benefit of the LLC is the ability of the members to specify proportions of ownership, control, and authority. During formation, band members determine who owns what percentage of the membership interests. Each could own equal shares, but they need not.

If the membership interests are not equal but the band wants each participant to have an equal vote, then the operating agreement can provide that each member is a manager and decisions are made by majority vote of the managers. This creates a one-person-one-vote structure. If the band prefers the voting be reflected by the ownership interests, then the operating agreement can provide that the LLC is member-managed, based on the majority of membership interests entitled to vote. Membership interests are particularly useful in four-person bands. Assuming each person does not have the same membership interest, the difference in membership interests helps avoid deadlock.

Super-majority provisions can force a faction to obtain two-thirds or three-quarters of the votes to authorize a specified list of decisions.

In addition to the common business topics for super-majority provisions such as dissolution, merger, sale of substantially all assets, addition of new LLC members, voluntary bankruptcy, and other fundamental choices, a band may wish to treat the publishing agreement, the exclusive artist recording agreement, any name changes, and the addition of any members as performers as extraordinary items that require the super-majority vote. Any of these decisions could affect the future of the band and should be deliberated carefully. For some bands, the recording budget for each album and the commitment to a national tour would rise to this level. The choice to require a super-majority in more circumstances rests entirely within the band.

At the same time, a super-majority provision can be viewed as a minority veto. If a single person's membership interest is enough to vote down a proposal, the super-majority rules suddenly give tremendous influence over the decision making.

Conflict Resolution and Minority Protection

The ability to craft internal rules provides a critical opportunity to protect the band and its members from deadlock and dissension. Super-majority votes provide one such mechanism because they assume that a greater percentage of the group wants the particular outcome. These votes, however, can serve to further alienate and disenfranchise the minority.

Provisions that invoke third party private mediation for internal disputes may assist bands and avoid public disruption and distraction. Mediation does not guarantee successful resolution of disputes but it provides a very useful method for addressing problems before they spiral into expensive, band-ending litigation (Scamman, 2008, pp. 293–294).

If the parties or the neutral agree that mediation has failed, another possible strategy for maintaining the band is to vest short-term decision-making power in a neutral third party. This party can be an attorney or manager who has not represented the band or any of its members in the past. The operating agreement should specify that the person's powers are limited, but the third party can help the band continue to operate and provide professional stability, which can help avoid a crisis or transition into a healthier arrangement.

If neither of these procedures resolves the conflict, then the band can use binding arbitration to simplify the resolution of disputes that cannot be resolved by the parties themselves without resorting to a series of public lawsuits. In addition, the arbitrator can be selected for both his/her legal knowledge and his/her knowledge of the music industry so that the resolutions crafted fit the business expectations of the parties (*see* Ormsbee, 2011, pp. 239–240).

Finally, special attention should be paid to the provisions on member withdrawal and LLC dissolution. A well-designed operating agreement should cross-reference the obligations under the recording agreement with the terms of a member's withdrawals. For example, the band could provide in its operating agreement that monies owed to the withdrawing member by the LLC are first applied against unrecouped royalties. This would protect the band from simultaneously owing a withdrawing member significant money while not earning any revenue because of the advances previously received from the record label. At a minimum, the advances owed to the record label should be treated as liabilities for purposes of calculating the funds due to a leaving member.

A second aspect of the withdrawing member provision should address the continued revenue for previously recorded albums. The withdrawing artist should be entitled to money flowing from the royalties on albums produced while the person was with the band since the money was earned for performance on the recording. The operating agreement could, however, provide that a formula can be used to set a present value on those royalties and make a one-time lump payment. The choice of a lump-sum payment could be optional and the option granted to either the LLC or the withdrawing member. Whatever the rule, however, the operating agreement should require that any such formulation be applied uniformly to avoid any preferences or oppression.

The need for management of continuing royalties suggests a third special provision for band LLCs. Although the band may no longer tour, there may be sound economic reasons to modify the purpose of the LLC rather than dissolve it, if the band breaks up. The LLC can still promote the previously released albums, encourage sales of branded products and former band merchandise, and promote the music along with the publisher. The band may no longer exist but the business of the band may carry on. This approach is particularly appropriate if a key performer dies. The band might determine it is not appropriate to record new albums, or the band members may elect not to tour under a name that highlights its deceased member, but the business of the LLC could still continue for many years. Separating out the end of the band from the end of the LLC, thus, becomes very important to incorporate into the operating agreement.

CONCLUSION

Bands are central to the modern music business, but their structure is frequently overlooked. As LLCs, they can benefit from unique provisions that take the exclusive artist recording agreement, the publishing agreement, and industry standards into account. Contractually, the band member is often given little attention under these agreements, but these agreements nonetheless shape the lives of the band's members and affect their ability to make music.

By anticipating challenges raised by the highly standardized agreements used by publishers and record labels, the parties to the operating agreement can anticipate and resolve many of the issues that undermine the success of the band. At a minimum, the LLC avoids general liability and undifferentiated management. More than this, addressing the band as a business with unique demands, members of the band LLC and their counsel can craft a more sophisticated business that better prepares the artist and encourages long-term success.

NOTES

1. John Shepherd writes that "[i]n Europe, bands were in existence from the thirteenth century, when men employed by a city as watchmen also formed instrumental bands to perform at ceremonial events" (2003, p. 6).

2. Uniform Partnership Act § 202(a) (1997) provides "the association of two or more persons to carry on as co-owners of a business for profit forms a partnership, whether or not the persons intend to form a partnership."

3. Bradley Borden writes, "[i]n the event partners do not allocate economic items, state default rules allocate them." (2011, p. 1093).

4. Donald Passman writes, "your most important asset is the group name." (2000, p. 322).

5. Shanker explains "[a] growing number of performers and sports figures … have begun to trademark their names in order to protect their use within the growing celebrity endorsement market." (2012, pp. 3–3).

6. Bigger explains "[t]he question of ownership can be simplified to some degree by having the members of the group form a corporation that will own the name. Then, if a federal [trademark] registration is obtained in the name of the corporation, the departure of one or more members will not affect the title to the registration." (2001, p. 14).

7. Stim suggests "[m]any bands also include non-writing members in the income," but this still implies that distributions to non-writing members or through LLC work for hire remains the minority strategy (2013).

8. Johnson reports "[t]here are four general categories of revenue in the music publishing industry: public performance, mechanical rights, print music and synchronization" (2001, p. 130).

9. Brabec and Brabec identify 10 discrete rights granted to the publisher, including public performance on radio, television, and the Internet assigned through a performing rights organization; rights to arrangements and translations; rights to dramatize the work; rights to synchronize the work for audiovisual works such as film and video games; rights to use the works on copies sold as CDs or mp3s; rights to publish the works in print; and rights to exploit the works in new technologies (2013, p. 15).

10. The current statutory rates for mechanical rights start at 9.1 cents per song or 24 cents per ringtone. Effective March 1, 2009. Retrieved http://www.copyright.gov/carp/m200a.pdf

11. Blake and Stuart provide a sample record label agreement providing typical language to bind members forming a band (2001, p. 400).

12. Scamman states that "recording artists are the only class of personal service workers unable to take advantage of Labor Code 2855(a)" (2008, p. 279).

REFERENCES

Bigger, S. (2001). Entertainment group names: Selection and protection. In M. Halloran (Ed.), *The musician's business and legal guide* (pp. 10–21). Upper Saddle River, NJ: Prentice Hall.

Blake, L., & Stuart, D. (2001). Analysis of a recording contract. In M. Halloran (Ed.), *The musician's business and legal guide* (pp. 316–405). Upper Saddle River, NJ: Prentice Hall.

Borden, B. (2011). The allure and illusion of partners' interests in a partnership. *University of Cincinnati Law Review*, *79*(3), 1077–1138.

Brabec, J., & Brabec, T. (2013). *Music money and success*. New York, NY: Music Sales Corporation.

Cirone, A. (2011). *The great American symphony orchestra: A behind-the-scenes look at its artistry, passion and heartache*. Delray Beach, FL: Meredith Music Publications.

Del. Code Ann. tit. 6, § 18-1101(b) (2005) (Delaware Limited Liability Company Act).

Duruigbo, E. (2010). Avoiding a limited future for the De Facto LLC and LLC by Estoppel. *University of Pennsylvania Journal of Business Law*, *12*(Summer), 1013–1097.

Flanagan, R. (2008, January). *Symphony musicians and symphony orchestras*. Stanford University Graduate School of Business Research Paper No. 1989. Retrieved from http://ssrn.com/abstract=1111772

Freer, R., & Moll, D. (2013). *Principles of business organizations*. St. Paul, MN: West.

Garon, J. (2007). *Own it: The law & business guide to launching a new business through innovation, exclusivity, and relevance*. Durham, NC: Carolina Academic Press.

Hillman, R. (2005). Law, culture, and the lore of partnership: Of entrepreneurs, accountability, and the evolving status of partners. *Wake Forest Law Review*, *40*(4), 793–825.

Johnson, N. (2001). Music publishing. In M. Halloran (Ed.), *The musician's business and legal guide* (pp. 130–138). Upper Saddle River, NJ: Prentice Hall.

Krasilovsky, W., & Shemel, S. (2003). *This business of music*. New York, NY: Billboard Books.

Molitor, M. (2009). Eat your vegetables (or at least understand why you should): Can better warning and education of prospective minority owners reduce oppression in closely held businesses? *Fordham Journal of Corporate & Financial Law*, *14*(3), 491–596.

National Commission on Uniform State Laws. (1997). Uniform Partnership Act. Retrieved from http://www.uniformlaws.org/shared/docs/partnership/upa_final_97.pdf (Revised Uniform Partnership Act).

Okorocha, D. (2011). A full 360: How the 360 deal challenges the historical resistance to establishing a fiduciary duty between artist and label. *UCLA Entertainment Law Review*, *18*(1), 1–31.

Ormsbee, M. (2011). Note: Music to everyone's ears: Binding mediation in music rights disputes. *Cardozo Journal of Conflict Resolution*, *13*(Fall), 225–258.

Passman, D. (2000). *All you need to know about the music business*. New York, NY: Simon & Schuster.

Scamman, K. (2008). Note: ADR in the music industry: Tailoring dispute resolution to the different stages of the artist-label relationship. *Cardozo Journal of Conflict Resolution*, *10* (Fall), 269–304.

Schulenberg, R. (2005). *Legal aspects of the music industry*. New York, NY: Watson-Guptill Publications.

Schultz, M. (2009). Live performance, copyright, and the future of the music business. *University of Richmond Law Review*, *43*(2), 685–764.

Shanker, J., Guinn, D., & Orenstein, H. (2012). *Entertainment law and business*. Huntington, NY: Juris.

Shepherd, J. (2003). *Continuum encyclopedia of popular music of the world* (*Vol. II*), New York, NY: Continuum.

Stim, R. (2013). Ten tips for songwriters: Credits, copyrights, and coauthors. *NOLO Law for All*. Retrieved from http://www.nolo.com/legal-encyclopedia/tips-songwriters-credits-copyrights-coauthors-29833.html

PART II
POLITICS AND CULTURE

THE POLICY OF ELECTRO-AMPLIFIED POPULAR MUSIC IN FRANCE: THE LIBERAL CONTEXT AND THE REGULATION OF REBELLIOUS CULTURES

Jean-Marie Seca

ABSTRACT

Purpose – *The aim of this chapter is to theorize and describe the main characteristics of the social construction of the policy of electro-amplified popular music (EAPM) in the French context.*

Design/methodology/approach – *To explain the significance and the institutionalization of EAPM through the conflict and mediation between two modes of legitimation of the rebellion and recognition of identity: deliberative rationality and verbalization of protest, on the one hand, and "musicalization" of revolt and globalization of the rebellious feeling attitude, on the other hand.*

Findings – *The meaning of the so-called "musicalization of revolt" is defined. This phenomenon emerged, in France, at the end of 1960s, after*

Music and Law
Sociology of Crime, Law and Deviance, Volume 18, 103–127

ISSN: 1521-6136/doi:10.1108/S1521-6136(2013)0000018008

a long and traditional period of "politization" and rationalization of protest. The main sociological and economic dimensions of this new historical process are designated: a special standardization of the emotional expression and a transcultural and global matrix of rebellion. Then, the public policy of EAPM is examined in depth. The paradox of the French voluntarism (the regulation of EAPM practices) is accentuated. What to do with the liberal origin of these styles and the institutional policy that began in 1982? Why and for what reasons has this public policy been still going on? What are the advantages of the public support from musicians' as well as local and national authorities' point of view? What are the topics of EAPM public policy (support for social creation, status of drugs, and ritualization of violence)?

Originality/value of chapter – *This academic text offers some key concepts explaining the normalization of the emerging and anarchistic musical cultures.*

Keywords: Electro-amplified popular music; France; hybridization; musicalization; policy; rebellion

INTRODUCTION

Over the past sixty years, in France, like in many other Western European countries, various social scientists and analysts have been witnessing a continuous, progressive global development of electro-amplified popular music (EAPM), with its moments of *statu nascendi* and innovating explosions. This chapter examines the meaning of the relationship between popular rock/electric musical practices and law in a general sense. The "law area" of musical forms can be defined as an extended set of artistic and cultural practices that are marked, both content- and form-wise, by regulations, laws, occasionally committed analytical views held by social sciences scholars, and the effects of national, regional, or local public policies. These musical practices are considered to have received a judicial marking or a variable analytical and theoretical treatment, depending on different contexts or styles. They have nonetheless undergone a scientific, economic, financial, social, professional, psychological, sociological, and creative minimal public regulation. For more than thirty years, they have been benefiting, depending on the time, from a certain orientation and psychological marker, although they emerged before the development of any specific laws, public actions, or decisions affecting their development or limiting their continuation. Social science specialists adopt, sometimes unawares, sometimes deliberately, this categorization as a susceptible element of treatment by a public policy.

After examining popular music from a socio-anthropological point of view, I will then focus on the context of the emergence and the main characteristics and causes of the public regulation of popular music in France. In order to provide a correct analysis of the dialectic between "popular music" and "public policies," I will employ the notion of "electro-amplified popular music" (EAPM), referring to a large set of musical styles (*rock, metal, rap, reggae, techno, punk*, etc.) as well as to its field of study. My aim is to mark out a number of questions addressing the links between these styles and their administrative regulations. I will thus explore a vast area of activities nonspecifically restricted to judicial texts themselves. The set of musical practices and contents to which I refer in this chapter includes historical and sociological elements of EAPM, some key dates of the emergence of popular music public policies, certain decrees and laws, as well as reactions of the public sphere to the various effects of these extremely effervescent phenomena and their relation with addiction or censorship.

THE INSTITUTIONALIZATION OF EAPM AND THE "MUSICALIZATION" OF REVOLT

Music is obviously the most accessible and the most ancient phenomenon of intercultural sharing. From a certain point of view, music, as a cultural form, is the best anticipation of our present. Jacque Attali rightly proposed to analyze the evolution of music production as an exploration of Utopia and of the new socio-economic modes (Attali, 1977). As such, music is the primitive conception of communication, networking, global thinking, and the divination of the future of society.

EAPM: An Anthropological Definition

The term "popular music" is, in this chapter, associated with the qualifiers "amateur" and "electro-amplified," indicating creative, potentially protesting and entertainment tendencies and, at the same time, an electric, technological labeling[1] (Chapple & Garofalo, 1977; Frith, 1981; Hebdige, 1979;

Middleton, 1990; Shuker, 1998; Street, 1986). This expression (EAPM) is used to highlight the double specificity of these trends in France: they are influenced by both Anglo-American matrices (the term "popular music" is very specifically defined in Cultural Studies: Shuker, *op. cit.*) and technological innovations/artistic creativity in the field of electricity (Touché, 1994, 1998, 2007).

Below are some characteristics of EAPM:

1. Communitarian styles and behaviors characterized by conspicuous symbols of marginality.
2. Ambivalent connections with conventions and with most music standards. This structural ambivalence is frequently transformed into both a need for dissidence and a need for stardom. The latter is accompanied by denial of identification with stars and leaders.
3. A position of refusal (characterized by rage and denial) or, conversely, an attitude of overinvestment toward marketing rationality models.
4. Defense (apologia for) and promotion of the popular character of its modes of diffusion/distribution/consumption.
5. A desire to have an audience at all costs ("need for recognition"), even if the public is limited to some friends or a small group of music producers.
6. An ambiguous will to preserve an expressive authenticity and originality.
7. Emergence and renewal of styles (rock, rap, metal, punk, techno) and modes of creation having their origins in technological inventions both in production instruments and in sound diffusion (from electrical guitars to compact discs, from the miniaturization of the means of production to the complete digitalization of the processes of commercial production/distribution).
8. An esthetic and intellectualized dissent (see the different protest songs as well as the punk attitude all over the world) against the mass cultures that have been reduced to strictly entertainment conformism.
9. Numerical hybridization and integration of world folklore and popular styles into a global pop market configuration (Portuguese electro-fado, Spanish and Gipsy flamenco, Latin-American salsa, Cuban nova trova, Algerian raï, African-urban styles, etc).
10. Anthropological phenomena of differentiation and normalization/integration of minority expression into postmodern societies.
11. Social representations (socio-cognitive and ritual systems that have become art doctrine) of music and arts in the amateur and little-known (or amateur, or garage) bands.

12. Increasing propagation of neo-pagan religions and experiences, which is associated with the emergence of ever more musical trends and bands (Maffesoli, 1988, 2012).

Ever since the end of the Second World War, there has been an increasing global dissemination and standardization of different EAPM trends (from be-bop jazz to rock'n-roll, rap, reggae, soul, and punk). They illustrate the typical process of creating social differentiation, entertainment, and pleasure (Buxton, 1985). This global process is connected with an ideological (social representations) and commercial model of innovation and uniqueness. It generates an esthetic and emotional reflexivity that generally expresses an urban everyday life rejection, anxiety, or criticism as well as an alternative/utopian/ecological social life project. Some of these critical and political representations have been propagated through this effective and global model of business, esthetics, and socialization.

"Musicalization" of Revolt Versus "Politicization-Verbalization" of Dissent

I propose the expression "musicalization of revolt," which is probably connected with an innovative, original artistic protest process, which emerged toward the end of the First World War (Marcus, 1989). This movement is mainly opposed to that of "verbalization/politicization/militarization of dissent." The latter developed, in Europe and in The United States, from the beginning of the 19th century to 1945 and flourished during the 1950s and the 1960s, more particularly with the hybrid style of the protest song. "Verbalization/politicization of revolt" is an ambiguous term because it includes not only "military and war" action in which most Western nations were involved, but also the rise of the study of everyday life as an academic field (Enlightenment philosophy movement, human rights actions, and also the criticism of consumption worlds). This ambiguity corresponds in fact to that of national identity affirmation: from its onset, during the 18th and 19th century, the fight for Enlightenment, modernity and democracy became, nationalistic, practical, and warmongering.

The EAPM styles (rock and roll, rap, techno, metal, world music) appeared during the World and Cold Wars (1910–1960), a time of inversion/transformation of these rationalistic and nationalistic values. They were – and they are – exemplary crystallizations of another expression of crowd behavior. This "musicalization" illustrates the end of a certain type of coordinated protesting organization, also centered on fundamentalist,

Marxist, and communist beliefs. At the same time, it materializes a global entertainment model and a current, dominant love and emotional group-feeling culture (or *ordo amoris* process: see Scheler, 1973):

> Social movements, and subcultures, especially those associated with youth, were seen in a much more positive light, at best as positive stages in social development mapping out non-established routes to adulthood, at worst as the unfortunate extremes of youthful idealism and alienation. (Eyerman, 2002, p. 444)

As it is widely known, the claim for flower power in the 1960s was not solely a poetic attitude. It also symbolized the transformation of both majority norms and minority groups in terms of mobilization. Furthermore, the "musicalization" process has structural, political, and sociological characteristics. The use of an enlightening metaphor of the evolution of the erotic of the masses may illustrate this process. Hardly anyone ever dreams of having a notorious politician as lover or parent. However, this is how a wonder-struck nun, working as a warder in a psychiatric hospital, consoles the young Ida Dalser, Mussolini's tearful ex-lover: "Be happy that you've met this man and made you pregnant." Ida, whose life was turned into a film entitled *Vincere* by Marco Bellocchio, had sold everything to finance Benito Mussolini's propaganda newspaper, *Il Popolo d'Italia*,[2] only to be rejected and ignored by him afterwards. She would fight in an asylum for the rest of her life to claim her role as Mussolini's wife and mother of their son, Benito Albino Mussolini. In the 1930s important political leaders were considered ideal men. Mussolini had hundreds of lovers (Olla, 2011). Adolf Hitler, despite his unattractive appearance, would arouse the boundless admiration of German women (Leutheusser, 2001; Schaake, 2012). Ever since, the star-system has caused political leaders to gradually and inevitably go out of fashion. The Knight of the Sad Figure embodied by Silvio Berlusconi in Italy or Dominique Strauss-Khan's libertine behavior in France can only breed commiseration, contempt, or mockery in today's society. They become totally hermetic due to the reversal of values triggered in the Occident by the worship of heroes who are more evanescent, seducing, and close to the masses (reality-shows). So the need for submission remains. These values are now projected around entertainment, esthetics, and music. However, this does not prevent ultraliberal or insidious totalitarianisms (pernicious programming of cultural contents) from spreading across Europe and beyond. This also explains why the present chapter argues in favor of an anthropological, musical, and esthetic meaning of revolt/conformism (Godelier, 2009). In other words, the "musicalization" of revolt is the blank, projective, and virtual space of various institutional, political, and social needs. In this lengthy and strange movement, that includes a new *ordo amoris*, the "traditional" societies of Africa, South-America, or North-Asia rejoin the dominant and rationalist Western countries.

A Standardization of Feeling Emotions Despite Local Cultural and Stylistic Heterogeneity

In order that the musical message should be "heard", it is necessary that a social knowledge of the environment as well as a manner of feeling emotions should be increasingly of prime importance. It is futile to attempt to analyze the integrality of the stakes of the "standardization of feelings" as it is too lengthy a process and outside the scope of this chapter (for further reference see: Seca, 2005, 2006, 2009). The standardization of feelings and of some corporal attitudes (erotic habits, fashion, and narcissist behavior) is part of this specific global ideology of EAPM. It complements the cultural heterogeneity in the local productions and the consecutive specific internalizations of these styles. The confrontation between the global electro-amplified rhythmic predominance of these styles and the local diversity of their reception explains why there is a continuation and even a stronger propagation of violent and enraged new creations. It is as if the conflicting impact of the standardization of feelings generates various "replications" and partial transformations of the previous reproductions, as in the case of the retrovirus in biology. Consequently, the controversial (standardization/heterogeneity) impact of these different styles seems to be in latent contradiction with their intercultural benefits and financial profit.

But in reality, there is no contradiction between the contribution of these expressive and stylistic modes, which are socio-economically reproduced, and their paradoxical and terse innervation of the social element because the expression of anger is frequently associated with rock, pop, rap, techno, hard-core, and metal. These styles are specifically the formalization of these tensions, contradictions, and various latent conflicts in all societies. In others terms, there is no real inconsistency between these different phenomena (differentiation/"replications"/standardization/communication/global development/conflict generated during the reception of an innovation). They are all elements of the same process: need for social recognition of the personal uniqueness in a collective reference. The expression of rage in musical underground styles and local contexts is naturally connected with the modulation and adjustment of communication, as well as with this need for differentiation and imitation (Seca, 2012). There are numerous examples from various countries where the pattern of this kind of protesting attitude both in esthetics and in EAPM has different consequences in terms of expression of feelings, emotions, anger, and repression (Seca, 2007). Additionally, in various Western countries and globalized spaces, one notices nowadays the emergence and diffusion of six stylistic forms implying a technical deepening and an emotional intensification of esthetic explorations of EAPM experiences (Lebrun, 2009; Seca, 2007). Here are the aforementioned stylistic forms:

- populist and identity rocks, among others;
- free parties (techno) practices;
- hard-rock and metal trends;
- reggae and soul/funk roots and hip hop/rap movements;
- punk revivals and hardcore styles;
- global world and specific folk music revivals.

A number of questions can be addressed at this stage. In spite of the nuances of regional and local appropriation described above, can one talk about the advent of a transcultural matrix of rebellion? Is this matrix ever a source of change and transformation? This seems highly unlikely. If there is a standardization process, founded by these musical forms, is this tendency in relation to an accentuation of individuation (to be singular in small similar groups) and psychopathological regression? Or is it the opposite, that is to say this process encourages, crystallizes, and materializes an ever more important dissemination of minorities' behaviors and patterns of real creativity? This second interpretation seems far more plausible. Furthermore, the "musicalization" of revolt is strongly associated with the influence of a specific model of "internality" (very often studied in social psychology: Beauvois, 1994; Dubois, 1994). The increase in the internalized causal attributions in different cultural and organizational fields (and in musical practices) means that this trend goes hand in hand with:

1. a general psychiatrization/psychologization of social relations;
2. an excessive obsession with individual/standardized/marketing/influenced bodily cultures;
3. an ideology of charismatic, gifted personality;
4. a worship of the body and modified states of consciousness;
5. a narcissistic "instrumentalization" of otherness.

There is a symbolic meta-system (social representations) that organizes the influence of EAPM productions and their latent impact: it is more effective than traditional propaganda because it is centered on the after-effect of minority as private influence (Channouf, 2004; Moscovici, 1977; Moscovici & Mugny, 1987; Nemeth, 1987). This global ideology of minorities and of individuals spreads naturally and emotionally in the reserved daily life of the people and is a mirror of a global dissent. It is no surprise if some philosophies, such as "situationism" or Nietzschean thinking, have become more meaningful and illustrative of the apologia for EAPM trends and "minority attitude" (Debord, 1967; Marcus, *op. cit.*). As mentioned above, there are ever more Dionysian or pagan rituals as well as esthetic emotions (François, 2006; Mombelet, 2009; Walzer, 2007). They consist of acts, symbols, and crystallizations of this matrix. They are structured as a system of socially shared assertions about rebellion, community, body, pleasure, future, and self-conception in the world.

This symbolic and representational matrix of EAPM also includes a puritan and religious refusal/promotion of idolatry (Seca, 1991). It shows a permanent and structural rebellion against institutions and law (Martin, 1979). Simultaneously, there are colossal networks of fans, multinationals, official leadership, stardom, etc. (see the internationalized funeral of Michael Jackson in 2009; for more on fan cultures see: Ferrand, 2010; Le Bart, 2000). This explains why this specific culture, qualified as "utopia" by its organic supporters or intellectuals, or as commercial ideology by its critics, is greatly influential (Adorno, 1989, 2001; Bloom, 1987; Finkielkraut, 1987; Seca, 2010). In the eyes of conservatives and academics, these "cultures" are defined as "an ideology" and a source of "addiction attitudes." Within this academic trend, EAPM is a symptom of the relative decline of the "logos" and Kantian deliberative philosophy (Dufour, 2007; Stiegler, 2008), holding the advantage of an essentialist, narcissist, and communitarian conception (a claiming/protesting democracy value; for more on this view, see: Taylor, 1989).

Conversely, an idealization of "neo-tribalism" is emerging among producers, supporters, poets, and musicians: in a large number of video clips featuring a style or a group, recurrent images of crews, tribes, posses, and gangs are put on the screen. This apologia for the basic and tribal group supporting a musical style has been dealt with at length in English cultural studies or by some French sociologists (Maffesoli, 1988, 2012). This group idealization implies a prevalence of fetishism (accentuation of the image of a specific style) and a "fluidic" representation of musical action, that is, an increasing promotion of the hypnotic efficiency of art and of what Maisonneuve calls the "*corporization*"/"bodyism"[3] (a general body interactive feeling ideology: *cf.* Maisonneuve, 1976; Seca, 2001). Another constructive characteristic of the matrix of EAPM is a specific design of creativity: self-training, technological and instrumental minimalism, and individuation career with functional use of the group, in spite of the formal promotion of collective benefits. This use of DIY (Do It Yourself) pertains to a cultural position that is extremely hybrid, at times incoherent and at best "innovating," supported by a solidarity/brotherhood philosophy and a libertarian–individualistic inspiration. Depending on the point of view, it can be liberal, neo-tribal, resourceful, emergent, adaptable, or, on the contrary, progressive, radical, rebellious, disjunctive, anti-familist, autonomous, loyal, utopist, alternative (Bey, 1997; Deleuze & Guattari, 1972; Guibert, 2006; Hein, 2012).

THE MAIN CHARACTERISTICS OF THE FRENCH PUBLIC POLICY OF EAPM

Ever since the 1980s the French public policies of these electro-amplified styles have constituted, in a way, a rare national experience of long-term (modest, but constant) voluntary funding of production and dissemination of protesting cultures, in Europe and in the world. As a preamble to the explanation that follows, it is important to stress that these musical styles, more than other cultural forms, represent, due to their mode of emergence and dissemination, a minority and liberal culture whose origin can be placed between the cinema, the dream, and the mythical North American territories whose frontiers first reached London. This profound and ancient impact of North American cultures upon Europe and France is not a sensational discovery, but it is essential to point it out. For example, we note a well-known and old tradition of the "French touch" in Jazz music (e.g., Stefan Grappelli, Django Reinhardt, and more recently Michel Pietrucciani). Like in many European countries (e.g., Lonnie Donegan in Great Britain: Price, 2010), rock and jazz music began to be listened to in the very early 1950s, for example, with artists using an English surname in the Latin countries (Touché, *op. cit.*).

One also notices an increasing popularity of rock music protests in France (1979–1988): identification of many young people with the punk model and English new wave, during the stage of my first investigations: 1979–1987 (Seca, 1988). Since 1982–1983, there have been numerous and various appropriations of American hip hop in the French suburbs (Marseille, Lyon, Paris, etc.), giving birth to a mixed and relatively original

French rap. Still in the 1980s, the concept of "world music" began to be diffused in Paris by Nova Radio, for example (an audio broadcast of the underground music periodical *Actuel*). From 1995 onwards, a multiplication of other trends has emerged (mainly techno, straightedge, cyberpunk, and metal). Recently, some revivals of punk and a commercial standardization of French rap could be observed. Like in other Western countries (the United Kingdom, the United States, Scandinavia, Italy, or Germany), all these trends are strongly structured and organized. They have networks, periodicals, websites, and radios. These networks consist of active consumers and small groups of producers and artists, who are present both in cities and in villages, with their own associations, their lobbying activities, and the intention to influence the decisions of the Parliament, the government, or the regional and local authorities.

The "Cause of Musicians" Following the "Cause du Peuple"

After the *Cause du Peuple*,[4] a French Maoist newspaper, forerunner of *Libération*, and sold by Jean-Paul Sartre in the 1960s, "the cause of musicians" has gradually and metaphorically emerged. It has often been used as an "object of strategic transaction" since the 1970s, including by the unions of disc producers (Kaiser, 2012; Zafiropoulos & Pinell, 1982). This tendency toward the instrumentalization of artistic activities greatly exceeds the concerns and specific interests of esthetes and artists themselves, be they "guerrilleros of style or protest," "skilled entrepreneurs of easy-listening songs," or "creators of genius (Scheler, 1933)." A perfect illustration of this would be the ethnography of the "2000 Parking" lot (Seca, 1988, 2001). At the beginning of the 1980s, there was a quarrel over a Parisian underground parking lot, which had been abandoned by motorists and turned by punk, West Indian, reggae, or hard-rock amateurs into a place for rehearsal and musical creation. As a result, a battle of image and "points of view" between the Ministry of Culture (of socialist orientation with Jack Lang at its head) and the City Hall of Paris (governed by Jean Tibéri, a Gaullist conservative close to Jacques Chirac) took place in the press.[5] The amateur groups of this parking lot had tried to take advantage of this rivalry, albeit without success for they were gradually expelled around 1986–1989. This symbolic battle projected around the legitimacy of rock practices taking place in a sordid underground parking lot is indicative of the utter destitution existing in the rehearsal and concert premises of the then EAPM producers. This conflict stereotypically broke out between the two parties either to glorify or to justify the disparaging of marginal experiences as well as a certain type of youth "in the name of security" or "against drug trafficking." This type of "dispute," which received a lot of media coverage, is also indicative of the context in which certain leftist politicians or cultural advisers deliberately chose to support EAPM at the time.

Consequently, the public policy of EAPM began in 1982 in correlation with the access to power of socialist movements (1981–1986; 1988–1992; 1997–2002). A significant moment was the creation of "La Fête de la musique"[6] in 1982 by the Left Party Minister Jack Lang, former founder of the Theatre World Festival in Nancy, an event that has enjoyed tremendous success ever since. After its accession to power, the left-winged government put at the center of its philosophical policy the notion of creation as a general and quasi-anthropological objective of cultural policies (Decree of 10 May 1982), which defined the mission of Jack Lang, the then Minister of Culture, as follows:

> Allow all French people to cultivate their capacity for invention and creation, to express their talents freely and to receive the artistic training of their own choice; to preserve the national, regional, or social heritage to the benefit of the entire community.

One of the aims was to "attain cultural democracy" with EAPM becoming an emblematic practice, continuing the endeavor of the popular history of the Maisons des Jeunes et de la Culture[7] (a network of cultural democratization initiated during the Front Populaire in the 1930s and after the Second World War, in 1944) and the spirit project of the preceding governments round the idea of "cultural development" (André Malraux). July 22, 1982 marked the founding of the Youth Inter-ministerial Committee. Starting 1982, ministerial notes aimed at "encouraging youth cultural practices (focus on neighborhoods, promotion of cultural activities in educational settings, spare time, and vacations)" (Teillet, 2003, p. 160).

More broadly, various experts called for the development of a logic concerning the projects to be implemented as well as for the need to multiply a diversity of places of cultural investment by young people. EAPM had a privileged role in this quest to adjust to the needs of the so-called "young groups" (at the instigation of the following ministerial advisers: J.-M. Lucas, J. Hurstel, and B. Lion). As an example, the cultural militant Bruno Lion became in 1989 "project adviser for rock music" for Jack Lang. He would promote a dynamic of voluntary action in the field of EAPM (creation of a network of small and large concert halls, federations of musical actors, devices of professionalization, opening of rehearsal, and creation centers).

As a result, the conservative, liberal, or social governments that followed would continue the general philosophy initiated in 1982 by Jack Lang's nebulous advisers and those for cultural and creative development. The continued existence of funding devices and envelopes would then be ensured (especially to help the foundation of local and regional scenes or to guarantee minimum professionalism in these sectors). An example of the continuation of this policy is a statement that Jean-Jacques Aillagon, minister of culture and communication in the conservative government of Jean-Pierre Raffarin, made in 2002 speaking of EAPM:

> I intend to give them a place in accordance with their pre-eminence in the cultural practices of young generations. The government's commitment to reduce VAT rate on discs is above all a policy for young audiences and musicians, who produce and consume most of these discs. Besides, the Ministry of Culture and Communication will continue to support local collectivities concerning the implementation of *musiques actuelles* halls, rehearsal studios, festivals and will favor the progressive opening of music schools [...]. More than often [...], the towns want to offer young people music venues. I believe that we have to support their projects by also proposing training and vocational programs for the musicians who wish to attend such courses.[8]

The political framework for EAPM was thus set out and has been continued to this day with its low but also strong moments, such as the concerted action supporting the performing arts by the Ministry of Culture of Catherine Trautmann, between 1998 and 2002 (Dutilh & Varrod, 1998).

The Emergence of a Sector of EAPM Social and Solidarity Economy

A priori, it is difficult to understand this type of public policy in favor of EAPM, because, from an American standpoint, it addresses trends that remain singular, emergent, elusive, free, diversified, anomic, deviant, and innovating, thus dependent on a culture permeated by the market or anarchic spirit. It is important to remember that these extremely effervescent and evanescent creative and artistic forms are indicative of a Darwinian vision of minorities who "should become successful through their own commercial outlets and the satisfaction of the public," which is sometimes promoted (rightly or wrongly) in more liberal contexts, such as the United States. All these remarks help to render the political aspect of EAPM funding ever since 1982 in stark contrast to the marketing matrix of promoted practices. This originality and mismatch characterize a real cultural French specificity in this field (Dauncey & Le Guern, 2010; Le Guern, 2007; Le Guern & Dauncey, 2007). It is certainly not a paradox that emerging cultural activities should be regulated. On the contrary, it is a standard feature of numerous cultural policies, particularly the propagandistic ones. Nevertheless, it is rare that protest cultures should be continuously supported publicly and nationally (ever since 1981). What is the genesis of the idea to publicly fund the most of the various projects pertaining to groups whose objectives are often anomic, inconstant, mischievous, marked by free market principles, and symbolizing, at the same time, a spirit of protest as much as the lightest form of entertainment?. Doesn't this kind of policy of public support lead to a new orthopraxis and conventionalism of "chosen" cultures by certain (semi) public actors (associations) and consequently to neo-conformist and "funded EAPM"?

A sociological and philosophical characterization of this type of state intervention accounts for a French specificity: regulation of dissemination, support for production, protection of emergent experiences, dialog with social minorities, and recuperation of atomized rebellions by an open participation on the local scene. The origin of this attitude of public support (at a state, regional, or local–communal level) can be identified in a number of ideological discourses defending counter-cultures (IRMA, FEDUROK, or UFISC: http://www.ufisc.org/presentation-de-l-ufisc/manifeste-statuts.html). These discourses stem from a political and philosophical glorification of the public and corporatist preservation/appropriation of countercultures. They are inspired or influenced, at least in France, by a radical ideology emerging in the 1960s in the United States and Europe, as described in the "The Institutionalization of EAPM and the "Musicalization" of Revolt" of this chapter (situationism, DIY ideology, activism, libertarian leftist ideology, influence of Bourdieu's sociological ideas, and popular education drawing upon a wide range of sources, be they Christian, personalist, communist, or libertarian). This public policy of current musical practices has led to:

a. a reasoned and comprehensive assessment of opposing minds;
b. a will to help to pre-professionalize activity sectors seen as socioeconomically, technically, and esthetically marginal, but potentially useful to cultural production systems (see IRMA: a national EAPM association financed by the minister of culture and communication: http://www.irma.asso.fr/);
c. a desire to culturally counter, transform, and even sublimate the deviances and anomy of deprived urban neighborhoods (Lafargue de Grangeneuve, 2008).

This institutionalization and professionalization process of EAPM leads to the development of the so-called "Third Sector." The term is an excellent example of how the intercultural practice is developing in a specific area, in this case within the French social welfare system. From the point of view of cultural activism and of the French amateur and professional EAPM associations, the term "Third Sector" is connected with the revolutionary and connotative concept of "Tiers État" (Third State) that concentrated, in 1789, all the representatives of the People in the Parliament. Metaphorically speaking, "Third Sector" also reflects an alternative economic and social solidarity of some enterprises and nonprofit associations.[9] What's more, "Third Sector" indicates all kinds of alternatives to industries and services controlled by strictly stock exchange and financial logics. Various national associations (TECHNOPOL, FEDUROK, IRMA, etc.), different kinds of networks of concert halls, several independent productions, numerous conferences and festivals of musicians and producers (FORUMA, Transmusicales of Rennes, Festival of Bourges, Rock en Seine – in Paris), many professional training courses, as well as technical and commercial help activities, confirm the existence of a strong institutionalization of amateur and EAPM policy.

Ever since the 1980s, there have been innovative trends in the public regulation of popular music in terms of social and solidarity economy. This blurry but politically and discursively active sector of activity is developing alongside the market economy of music production (associations, groups, musicians' federations, professionalization structures, multiplicity of festivals supported, to a great extent, by public funding). The state or regional/local support for the production/dissemination of popular music (rap, techno, world music, rock, metal, jazz, etc.) has been also part of an irrigation strategy of fluid and renewed networks of artists and groups. This also led to investments in a wide network of concert halls covering the entire French territory through the policy promoting halls of *musiques actuelles*: the SMAC operation[10] represents about half of the national subsidies granted to EAPM. The possibility of performing in these locally and nationally funded concert halls comes to be a new criterion for the recognition of emergent groups. This was completed by the implementation of a radio quota of francophone songs (in 2000) and a data protection law combating digital piracy (Law HADOPI 2009–669 of 12 June 2009 promoting online diffusion and protection of musical creation).

One observes, in this public policy of EAPM, a functionalist and utilitarian relation with the law and the state and administrative institution, whether it concerns the management of digital copyright (the combat of the conservative government of François Fillon between 2007 and 2012) or the support for production/diffusion venues. In such a judicial and administrative context, French counter-cultural musical styles are strangely free, conformist, at once savage and domesticated, autonomous and dependent on subsidies obtained through a complex system of associations funded indirectly by local or national authorities. At the same time, we have been witnessing, ever since the 1990s, a stylistic diversification of trends related to rock, pop, and rap, as if the strongest dissemination of "authentic cultures" were accompanied by a stronger sophistication of auditor musical expertise and subsequently by an exacting and informed segmentation of taste. Previously dissident styles, such as rock, end up acquiring an "academic status" and to a certain degree a canonical status; additionally, other cultures come into being through counter-differentiation (Coulangeon, 2010; Lescop, 2012).

A concerted, administrative process between actors aiming at enforcing the professionalism of these musical practices was superimposed on the public regulation and segmentation of cultural taste. Disc industries, organizers of festivals, tours, and concerts agreed to create a commercial, administrative, and vaguely socializing appellation (in French "musiques actuelles") so as to neutralize the stylistic, reductionist, and political connotations related to rock and rap. The term "musiques actuelles" has become a strategy to better communicate with the Legislator and public decision makers as well as to classify a wide range of styles.

> The term "musiques actuelles" has been preferred, from the beginning of the 1980s, following its usage by the actors themselves. Indeed, it seems that M. Lidou, who participated in the creation of Transmusicales of Rennes and the Center for Information and Resources of Musiques actuelles, used it when addressing political leaders so as not to refer to the political and sound dimensions that other designations suggested, even though the actors in question seem to have preferred the terms of "rock" and "pop." Musiques actuelles still means to the (French) political leaders all non-elitist musical forms, from jazz to rock, including *chansons, variétés*, rap and techno styles, but also "traditional" music, which is even more problematic. Hence the existence of the National Center for chanson, variétés, and jazz (CNV), regional centers for musiques actuelles. (Kaiser, 2012, pp. 191–192)

The collective and bureaucratic creation of this special expression ("musiques actuelles" in French) to designate this kind of music indicates how the specialization of the State Administration in this field of music policy is developing. It is another indicator of the official handling of EAPM. Studies on music and amateur practices have abounded from 1973 onwards, especially after 1982 (DEP of the French Ministry of Culture[11]: http://www.culture.gouv.fr/dep/). At the same time, one can observe a continuous nonevaluation and noncontrol of cultural expenditures by many local authorities, with consequences such as a prevalence of favoritism/

nepotism or ideological choices in financing decisions (Le Guern & Dauncey, 2007). This situation is a potential source of conflict. One can also spot an increasingly institutionalization and a certain disorder in some locally activated public policies. Obviously, it is not easy to control the satisfaction of the proliferating Dionysian need in rock practices and other types of electro-amplified music. The main demand of rock and rap bands, ever since the origins of these movements (especially in American "garage bands", for example), has been to be treated equally ("we can do it too"). The characteristics of this public policy in local urban spaces are in direct contradiction with the aim of punk or rock revolt. As mentioned above, EAPM was born in anomic and deregulated contexts. French policy is inspired by a regulatory (rationalistic? humanistic?) philosophy of culture and social control. This paradox explains and justifies the diffusion of an often plaintive and "underground/rebellious" mini-technocracy claiming subsidies and requiring even more attention. This can lead to unequal support of some styles, at the expense of others. In other words, the French regulation model of music bands will potentially help to legitimate certain artists rather than others, more or less wild or conformist. This contradiction does not hinder a parallel maintenance of a hierarchical representation of cultural values (between elitist and classical music and EAPM, for example). One observes a typical and stereotypical direction of the public resources when it comes to culture: a small amount of the money goes to amateur EAPM bands, whereas ever more financial support is provided for jazz, opera, avant-garde, experimental, or classical music.[12]

Last but not least, this kind of policy ("Third Sector," local and national subsidies, maintained hierarchies of arts, and a continued preference for some kinds of EAPM bands or trends) and that of the market (small companies linked with great labels and desire for success) lead to a chaotic but also tonic development of these musical trends in France.

About Other Interference Between Legislation and EAPM

It is impossible to review here all of the phenomena lying at the intersection between EAPM and its politico-judicial regulation. As already mentioned, certain consecutive sociological effects of this integration/regulation (e.g., a sort of vulgarization/dissemination/segmentation of rock, rap, techno, and metal experience), whether judicial or administrative, can be explained by the virulence of a pro-active and pro-youth EAPM philosophy continuing since 1982. It has led to a normalization/integration/recognition of esthetics of contestation and to the attribution of an academic status to this rebellious/commercial/emergent music. The consequence was a sort of "underground orthopraxis" opposed to the nonprogrammed draft modes of creation and production reigning in these circles. This underlying and inexorable "legitimation of a traveling entertainer" and this enchanted valorization of youth cultures often take place so as to recognize, on the one hand, the most diversified aptitudes of the new generations, and on the other hand, cultural innovation. The change that this large process of institutionalization of rebellious cultures has inscribed in the semantics of these musical styles is the result of years of concerted public action. It implies immeasurable psycho-sociological and political consequences on the management of social rage and its esthetic dissemination. One of these effects is the annexation of revolt and intellectual opposition to the field of *admissible cultural programming*.

The question of the status of addiction and drugs in general also marks legislative and pro-active interventions, for example, in the field of techno-festive events ("free parties"). The application in France of the 2002 Mariani decree on the obligation to declare to the Police Commissioner any festive events bringing together more than 250 people has decreased the number of free parties and altered their form ever since the first seizures of equipment made by law enforcement agents. A large number of "non-scheduled" techno events have been closely monitored for various reasons (whether from an ethnological or administrative point of view or police related: Epstein & Fontaine, 2005; Pourtau, 2005, 2006). One notes in particular that, after the Mariani decree on controlling drug trafficking in techno musical events, illegal sales have been transferred to other venues, less marked by psychedelia. The strategy employed by offenders has been to roam the nightclubs and other festive venues marked by other stylistic trends. The relation with substance abuse is regularly evoked as a pretext for the control of a lot of festive events and their risks. In France, these types of behavior are not a private affair.

The reasoning may be the same for everything related to sectarian practices, closely monitored by the Central Bureau of Worship (BCC) of the Minister of the Interior and by the MIVILUDE (the Inter-ministerial Mission of Vigilance and Fight against Sectarian Abuses), dependent on the prime minister. This latter institution is based on an individualistic, rationalistic, and universalistic philosophy of the French republic where any occult group or movement, or having a mysterious influence on individuality, is regarded as potentially dangerous. The individual is defined in the French Constitution as the only legal entity of republican conceptualization of citizenship, in the name of the principle of secularism separating religion and political life. In this context, a sect or any collective entity may be, if its hold becomes too strong, declared harmful to the individual's mental equilibrium. According to the MILIVUDE, a sect leads to:

> the perversion of the freedom of thought, of opinion, or of religion violating public order, laws and regulations, fundamental rights, security, and individual integrity. It is characterized by the implementation by an organized group or an isolated individual, irrespective of its nature or activity, of pressure or techniques with a view to create, maintain, or exploit the individual's state of psychological or physical subjection, partially depriving him/her of his/her free will, with damaging consequences on that individual, his/her circle, or society at large. (see: http://www.miviludes.gouv.fr/)

As an example, this inter-ministerial group examined at length the satanical activities of metal bands in France and their harmful effects on youth (MIVILUDES, Report 2007, April 3, 2008). Shortly after the publication of this report, militant sociologists protested, rightly[13] arguing that a large number of these amateur metal musicians did not take themselves seriously by worshipping Satan in their concerts (Bobineau, Bisson, Mombelet, & Walzer, 2008) or adolescent pranks, despite 92 cases of satanical profanations identified by the authors of the report of the MIVILUDES between January 2007 and November 2007.

Then, there is a whole range of battles of unemployed artists and regulating interventions in the employment of artistic workers that include musical practices and pertain to the relationship between law and music. Job management is thus a subject classically associated with "culture" as an economic driving force by left-winged parties. This type of discourse is regularly heard and read in audiovisual and written media. The French sociologist Pierre-Michel Menger (of the EHESS-Paris) studied the entertainment industry in great detail, noting the artists' capacity for survival by managing on their own and using more favorable unemployment benefits (Menger, 2002, 2011). With regard to EAPM, half of the musicians studied in the doctoral research of Gérôme Guibert were professionalized by using the unemployment benefits for artists and entertainment workers (Guibert, *op. cit.*).

Finally, the relation with the law is significantly present in France (as well as in the United States) in the judicial monitoring of certain lyrics and clips of musicians trying to either defend their royalties or promote a radical cause through provocation or transgression by being sexually vulgar or by chiefly attacking the police or the French nation. In the United States there were parental protests against "explicit lyrics" and certain trends considered very provoking (Benetollo, 1999). The French Ministry of the Interior prosecuted mainly rap bands (including various and more or less popular and financially successful groups such as Ministère Amer, Suprême NTM, Abdul X, Morsay and his gangsters, Sniper, etc.). In France, as in the United States, the attitudes of certain musicians in battles of the bands border on gangsterism. One notable event is an exchange of videoclips posted on Youtube between La Fouine (a rapper from Yvelines department, close to Paris) and Bouba (from the department of Hauts-de-Seine, still in the Paris area). These two artists challenged each other for the most unpredictable reasons through insults and provoking rap. The latest episode culminated in a pistol shot fired at La Fouine's car close to his home. Publicity stunt? Real violence? Overstatement? The judicial inquiry will answer these questions. The chronicle of anathema against the French state or police authorities is too long to be listed. It implies dreaded issues related to law but also counter-counter-cultural reactions (e.g., the Gabber movement, which claims an antirap and ultranationalistic position).

CONCLUSION

As a conclusion, this chapter examined EAPM as an appropriated and interiorized socio-cultural phenomenon in the French economic and political sphere while addressing a number of topics related to legislation and public regulation. There are many other examples. We did not tackle the complex legislation[14] with regard to the French language radio quota. These laws have nowadays some influence on the esthetic and linguistic strategy of many French EAPM emergent bands, such as the language (English or French) used in their shows. The implementation of cultural policies is not a strictly French prerogative to act. It is nonetheless rare to read the history of a country so accurately when it comes to cultural public policies. It is well known that songs are indicators of current events and form a useful system of indicators for the study of the mentalities of a culture. As such, the image of EAPM in France reflects at once the influence of cultural globalization strongly influenced by musical movements of Anglo-American origin – but also African and West Indian – as well as a long political history of revolts and dissidences typical of this country. The impact of 1968 and everything related to it in terms of emotions and memories (anger, rage, transformations of sensitivities, ideological after-effect of American cultural radicalism, fashion movement, feminism, passage from combative leftism to rock and other musical forms of activism, and emergence of an alternative punk scene toward the end of the 1970s) also play a primordial role in France, enabling us to understand why so many people wanted to bring to the forefront sounds and words, creative and representational aptitudes, which were attributed to cultural minorities and despised by the elites and dominant groups of the 1970s and 1980s. This instrumental and romantic combat fitted perfectly within a long revolutionary history, which is excellently illustrated in the novels of Victor Hugo and Emile Zola and which is part of the emotional fiber of a large part of popular categories whether they are politically oriented or not. However, it is important to note that even the French far right tried to favor an "identity rock," following the example of the English National Front, which attempted to instrumentalize the skinheads of the 1980s (Lescop, 2007). Philosophical and intellectual battles aiming to define the nature of emergent cultural situations are as such neither innocent nor neutral when it comes to the consequences of their sociological, judicial, administrative, and political categorization, whether in the medium or long term.

NOTES

1. See International Association for the Study of Popular Music (http://www.iaspm.net/).
2. Like some groups that sacrificed themselves for an idolized music band.
3. In French the neologism is "Corporéisme."
4. In English: "The Cause of the People."
5. The Minister of Culture descended to the fourth basement of this parking lot, in 1985, for strategic and political motivations: "Jack Lang fait une descente dans le 4e sous-sol du rock," *Libération*, 25 avril 1985.
6. Translation: "The Music Day."
7. Trad.: Cultural and Youths Centers.
8. *In Trax. Magazine des musiques électroniques*, no. 56, October 2002, p.62.
9. This entrepreneurial, social, and social science research movement led to the creation in 2012, under the French socialist government, of the position of minister of social and solidarity economy and consumption.
10. SMAC: Scène de Musiques Actuelles (operation officially initiated by a Ministerial Circular of August 18, 1998 after about ten years of "café-musique," "festivals," and "Zenith network" support). The SMAC mission promotes the diffusion of both Jazz and EAPM, accompanying practices including rehearsal, training, creation, and cultural action. The SMAC network consisted of 150 locations in 2011, out of which about 70 were nationally subsidized (about 9 million euros was

granted by the French Ministry of Culture). Supplementary SMAC subsidies come from local authorities (more than 55% of its public support).

11. Despite this increasing institutionalization, the academic recognition of the social scientists specialized in the study of musical studies is not at the same level and legitimacy as what they are in British and American universities (see Dauncey & Le Guern, 2010).

12. Other and larger subsidies are invested for more legitimized musical activities in "National Scene" (50 million euros), "National Centre of Musical Creation" (3 million euros), "Opera Houses" (more than 26 million euros), and "Classical and operatic Orchestra" (more than 22 million euros).

13. Raphaël Liogier, "Révolution culturelle dans la lutte antisectes," *Le Monde*, March 3, 2008.

14. These laws of 1986 and 1994 were modified on August 1, 2000.

REFERENCES

Adorno, T. (1989). *Théorie esthétique, trad. fr.* (1st ed.). Paris: Klincksieck (in German language: 1970).

Adorno, T. (2001). *Le Caractère fétiche dans la musique et la régression de l'écoute, trad. fr.* (1st ed.). Paris: Allia (in German language: 1973).

Attali, J. (1977). *Bruits: Essai sur l'économie politique de la musique*. Paris: PUF.

Beauvois, J.-L. (1994). *Traité de servitude libérale. Analyse de la soumission*. Paris: Dunod.

Benetollo, A. (1999). *Rock et politique. Censure, opposition, integration*. Paris: L'Harmattan.

Bey, A. (1997). *The temporary autonomous zone. Ontological anarchy, poetic terrorism: Anarchy and conspiracy*. London: Forgotten Books.

Bloom, A. (1987). *The closing of American mind*. New York, NY: Simon & Schuster.

Bobineau, O., Bisson, D., Mombelet, A., & Walzer, N. (2008). *Le Satanisme. Quel danger pour la société?* Paris: Pygmalion.

Buxton, D. (1985). *Le rock, star système et société de consommation*. Grenoble: La Pensée Sauvage.

Channouf, A. (2004). *Les Influences inconscientes. De l'effet des émotions et des croyances sur le jugement*. Paris: Armand Colin.

Chapple, S., & Garofalo, R. (1977). *Rock'n'roll is here to pay: the history and politics of the music industry*. Chicago, IL: Nelson Hall.

Coulangeon, P. (2010). *Sociologie des pratiques culturelles*. Paris: La Découverte.

Dauncey, H., & Le Guern, P. (2010). *Stereo: Comparative perspectives on the sociological study of popular music in France and Britain*. Farnham: Ashgate Publishing Limited.

Debord, G. (1967). *La société du spectacle*. Paris: Gallimard.

Deleuze, G., & Guattari, F. (1972). *L'Anti-Œdipe. Capitalisme et schizophrénie*. Paris: Minuit.

Dubois, N. (1994). *La Norme d'internalité et le libéralisme*. Grenoble: PUG.

Dufour, D.-R. (2007). *Le Divin Marché. La révolution culturelle libérale*. Paris: Denoël.

Dutilh, A., & Varrod, D. (Ed.) (1998). *Rapport de la Commission nationale de musiques actuelles à Catherine Trautman, Ministre de la Culture et de la Communication*. Paris: Ministère de la Culture et de la Communication.

Epstein, R., & Fontaine, A. (2005). De l'utilité des raves: consommation de psychotropes. *Mouvements*, *42*, 12–21.

Eyerman, R. (2002). Music in movement: Cultural politics and old and new social movements. *Qualitative Sociology*, *25*(3), 443–458.

Ferrand, L. (2010). *La Vie en rock. Une approche compréhensive de la culture rock par ses acteurs : les amateurs*. Ph.D., under the direction of Prof. M. Maffesoli, CEAQ/University of Paris-V, Paris.

Finkielkraut, A. (1987). *La Défaite de la pensée*. Paris: Gallimard.

François, S. (2006). *La Musique europaïenne: ethnographie d'une subculture de droite*. Paris: L'Harmattan.

Frith, S. (1981). *Sound Effects. Youth, Leisure and the Politics of Rock'n roll*. New York, NY: Pantheon Book.

Godelier, M. (2009). *Communautés, sociétés, cultures: trois clés pour comprendre les sociétés en conflit*. Paris: CNRS.

Guibert, G. (2006). *La production de la culture. Le cas des musiques amplifiées en France. Genèse, structurations, industries, alternatives*. Paris: Irma/Mélanie Séteun.

Hebdige, D. (1979). *Subculture: The meaning of style*. New York, NY: Terence Hawkes.

Hein, F. (2012). *Do it yourself! Autodétermination et culture punk*. Congé-sur-Orne: Le Passager Clandestin.

Kaiser, M. (2012). *Les politiques publiques liées aux musiques populaires en France: la dimension culturelle en question*. Ph.D. under the direction of E. Prof. Maigret, University of Paris-III, Paris.

Lafargue de Grangeneuve, L. (2008). *Politique du hip-hop: Action publique et cultures urbaines*. Toulouse: Presses Univ. du Mirail.

Le Bart, C. (2000). *Les Fans des Beatles. Sociologie d'une passion*. Rennes: PUR.

Lebrun, B. (2009). *Protest Music in France. Production, Identity and Audiences*. Farnham: Ashgate Publisher.

Le Guern, P. (2007). En arrière la musique! Sociologies des musiques populaires en France. La genèse d'un champ. *Réseaux*, *141*, 15–45.

Le Guern, P., & Dauncey, H. (2007). De la difficulté d'émerger sur les scènes de "musiques actuelles": les exemples de la France et de l'Angleterre. In J.-M. Seca (Ed.), *Musiques populaires underground et représentations du politique* (pp. 84–112). Cortil-Wodon: InterCommunications.

Lescop, G. (2007). De la fascination musicale: stratégies et représentations de l'extrême droite. In J.-M. Seca (Ed.), *Musiques populaires underground et représentations du politique* (pp. 244–271). Cortil-Wodon: InterCommunications.

Lescop, G. (2012). Skinheads: du reggae au Rock Against Communism, d'une contre-culture à une "contre-contre-culture" sous influence musicale. *Volume! Contre-Cultures, Théories & Scènes*, *9*(1), 129–149.

Leutheusser, U. (Ed.). (2001). Hitler und die Frauen. München: W.H. Verlag.

Maffesoli, M. (1988). *Le Temps des tribus. Le déclin de l'individualisme dans les sociétés de masse*. Paris: Klincksieck.

Maffesoli, M. (2012). *Homo eroticus. Des communions émotionnelles*. Paris: CNRS.

Maisonneuve, J. (1976). Le corps et le corporéisme aujourd'hui. *Revue française de sociologie*, *17*(4), 551–571.

Marcus, G. (1989). *Lipstick traces: A secret history of the twentieth century*. Cambridge: Harvard University Press.

Martin, B. (1979). The sacralization of disorder: Symbolism in rock music. *Sociological Analysis*, *40*(2), 87–124.
Menger, P.-M. (2002). *Portrait de l'artiste en travailleur, Métamorphoses du capitalisme*. Paris: La République des Idées.
Menger, P.-M. (2011). *Les intermittents du spectacle. Sociologie du travail flexible*. Paris: EHESS ed.
Middleton, R. (1990). *Studying popular music*. Milton Keynes: Open University Press.
Mombelet, A. (2009). *Le Metal. Un projet mythologique articulé au jeu et au don*. Ph. D. under the direction of Prof. M. Maffesoli, CEAQ/University of Paris-V, Paris.
Moscovici, S. (1977). *Social influence and social change*. London: Academic Press.
Moscovici, S., & Mugny, G. (Eds.) (1987). *Psychologie de la Conversion. Études sur l'influence inconsciente*. Fribourg: Delval.
Nemeth, C. J. (1987). Au-delà de la conversion: formes de pensée et prises de décision. In S. Moscovici & G. Mugny (Eds.), *Psychologie de la conversion. Études sur l'influence inconsciente* (pp. 239–250). Fribourg: Delval.
Olla, R. (2011). *Il Duce and His Women: Mussolini's Rise to Power*. London: Alma Books Ltd.
Pourtau, L. (2005). Les interactions entre raves et législations censées les contrôler. *Déviance et Société*, *29*(2), 127–139.
Pourtau, L. (2006). Consommation de substances psychoactives et transe fonctionnelle dans les fêtes techno. *Psychotropes*, *12*(3–4), 163–181.
Price, J. (2010). Lonnie Donegan, Rock Island Line, et la corne d'abondance. *Volume*, *7*(2), 115–140.
Schaake, E. (2012). *Les Femmes et Hitler. Leur rôle dans l'ascension du Führer*. Paris: R. Laffont. (1st German edition: 2000).
Scheler, M. (1933). Vorbilder und Führe. In *Schriften aus dem Nachlass*, Berlin (*in Gesammelte Werke*), Trad. In French: 1958, *Le Saint, le Génie et le Héros*, Lyon, Vitte Ed.
Scheler, M. (1973). *Selected philosophical essays*. Evanston: Northwestern University Press.
Seca, J.-M. (1991). Les purificateurs du rock. *Les Cahiers internationaux de Sociologie*, *90*, 121–130.
Seca, J.-M. (1988). *Vocations rock. L'état acide et l'esprit des minorités rock*. Paris: Méridiens-Klincksieck.
Seca, J.-M. (2001). *Les Musiciens underground*. Paris: PUF.
Seca, J.-M. (2005). Formatage du ressentir et représentations underground. *Sociétés*, *90*(4), 57–69.
Seca, J.-M. (2006). Représentations et ritualisations de la violence : quelle position scientifique peut-on avoir face aux musiques "extrême"? *Les Cahiers de psychologie politique, 8*. Retrieved from http://lodel.irevues.inist.fr/cahierspsychologiepolitique/index.php?id=1068
Seca, J.- M. (Ed.). (2007). *Musiques populaires underground et représentations du politique*. Cortil-Wodon: InterCommunications.
Seca, J.- M. (2009). Musiques extrêmes, déviance et violence: normalisations et conversions: entretien avec Julie Cerizay. *Les Cahiers de psychologie politique, 15*. Retrieved from http://lodel.irevues.inist.fr/cahierspsychologiepolitique/index.php?id=832
Seca, J.-M. (2010). *Conduites minoritaires et représentations sociales*. Saarbrücken: Éditions universitaires européennes.
Seca, J.-M. (2012). Colères et ordo amoris dans les styles rock. *Sociétés*, *117*(3), 15–33.
Shuker, R. (1998). *Key concepts in popular music*. London: Routledge.
Stiegler, B. (2008). *Prendre soin de la jeunesse et des générations*. Paris: Flammarion.

Street, J. (1986). *Rebel rock – the politics of popular music*. New York, NY: Basil Blackwell.

Taylor, C. (1989). *Source of the self: The making of the modern identity*. Cambridge: Harvard University Press.

Teillet, P. (2003). Publics et politiques des musiques actuelles. In O. Donnat & P. Tolila (Eds.), *Le(s) public(s) de la culture* (pp. 155–180). Paris: Presses de Sciences Po.

Touché, M. (1994). *Connaissance de l'environnement sonore urbain. L'exemple des lieux de répétition*. Vaucresson: Rapport de recherche CRIV-CNRS.

Touché, M. (1998). *Mémoire vive. Premier tome de recherches menées avec l'association Musiques Amplifiées d'Annecy*. Paris: CNRS/Le Brise Glace.

Touché, M. (2007). Muséographier les "musiques électro-amplifiées". Pour une socio-histoire du sonore. *Réseaux*, *141*, 97–141.

Walzer, N. (2007). *Les Imaginaires satanique et païen : le cas de la musique metal extrême : une volonté de puissance schizomorphe*. Ph. D. under the direction of Prof. M. Maffesoli, University of Paris-V, Paris.

Zafiropoulos, M., & Pinell, P. (1982). Drogue, déclassement et stratégies de déqualification. *Actes de la recherche en sciences sociales*, *42*, 61–75.

STRATEGIC AFRO-MODERNISM, DYNAMIC HYBRIDITY, AND BEBOP'S SOCIOPOLITICAL SIGNIFICANCE

Cynthia R. Nielsen

ABSTRACT

Purpose – *I argue that one can articulate a historically attuned and analytically rich model for understanding jazz in its various inflections. That is, on the one hand, such a model permits us to affirm jazz as a historically conditioned, dynamic hybridity. On the other hand, to acknowledge jazz's open and multiple character in no way negates our ability to identify discernible features of various styles and esthetic traditions. Additionally, my model affirms the sociopolitical, legal (Jim Crow and copyright laws), and economic structures that shaped jazz. Consequently, my articulation of bebop as an inflection of Afro-modernism highlights the sociopolitical, and highly racialized context in which this music was created. Without a recognition of the sociopolitical import of bebop, one's understanding of the music is impoverished, as one fails to grasp the strategic uses to which the music and discourses about the music were put.*

Music and Law
Sociology of Crime, Law and Deviance, Volume 18, 129–148

ISSN: 1521-6136/doi:10.1108/S1521-6136(2013)0000018009

Design methodology/approach – *I engage in an interdisciplinary study of jazz via analyses and commentary on selected texts from several scholarly disciplines.*

Findings – *To acknowledge the hybridity and social construction of jazz esthetics in no way nullifies the innovations and leadership of African American jazz musicians whose artistic contributions not only significantly shaped modern jazz in the mid-twentieth century but also whose musical voices continue to sound and set esthetical standards in contemporary expressions of jazz (and beyond).*

Originality and value – *My chapter is highly interdisciplinary, bringing philosophical explanations of race, discourse, and the ontology of music into conversation with numerous sociological and (ethno)musicological insights about jazz.*

Keywords: Afro-modernism; hybridity; jazz esthetics; bebop; race; jazz discourses

INTRODUCTION

In this chapter, I argue that if race is socially constructed (and I believe it is), then jazz esthetics must also be understood and more carefully articulated as socially constructed. Both race and jazz esthetics are conditioned by cultural, political, legal, economic, and myriad other social narratives, discourses, and practices. As social realities, neither race nor African American or European musical styles emerge from an immutable essence or consist in a fixed set of characteristics purporting to define (once and for all) what it is to *be* black or authentically "black" bebop or "white" cool jazz. An analysis of the complex social ontology of jazz esthetics reveals both the hybridity of jazz and provides a model for understanding dynamic identity. Although a historical and thoroughly social reality, jazz (and by extension this applies to European classical and other musical genres, styles, and inflections) communicates something about the social context, history, and the pre-history in which it is created and performed. For example, the bebop of the 1940s–1960s is of course intimately connected to the histories and struggles of African Americans, both of which were played out and developed in relation to whites of various political, religious, national, international, social, and esthetic sensibilities.[1] In short, my claim is that music (and bebop in particular), like other social realities, is an ever-morphing mulatto.

To claim that categories such as race, blackness, whiteness, black esthetics, and the like are socially constructed is in no way to deny the stark differences in lived experience of various ethnic groups – in particular, the numerous injustices experienced by blacks due to racist practices and residing in a racially structured society that exploited blacks and benefited whites. Nor is it to deny that specific musical characteristics at particular historical moments are often associated with Afro (black) or Euro (white) musical styles and esthetics. Lastly, to argue for the social construction of esthetical categories by no means negates the decisive, formative contributions, innovations, and leadership of musicians such as Dizzy Gillespie, Charlie Parker, Miles Davis, and countless other African American artists whose "musical signatures" both significantly shaped modern jazz in the mid-twentieth century and whose voices continue to sound and re-sound in current expressions of jazz.

Although Afro-modern esthetics and European classical esthetics are not fixed essences but like "race" are dynamic, historical, social realities, they nonetheless exhibit a provisional fixity or fluid identity. This dynamic identity or ontology is shaped and maintained by historically specific sociopolitical structures, as well as particular discourses and practices. Moreover, the affirmation of the historical and constructed character of various musical esthetics in no way negates our ability to identify their (historically shaped and always permeable) characteristics and features. Stated otherwise, musical esthetics are socially conditioned and highly fluid realities; yet such fluidity coexists with a "staying power" or nonpermanent fixity allowing one to identify (via musical theoretical analysis and aural skills of various degrees) a clearly recognized esthetic, style, or genre. Thus, particular esthetics and styles such as blues, Afro-modernism, French Impressionism (as a style within European classical music), tonal serialism, etc., can congeal into something quite recognizable and transferable and yet remain open to alterations and (re)harmonizations creating new (future) styles.

Here it is instructive to draw upon Michel Foucault's notion of historical a prioris. According to Foucault, as the qualifier emphasizes, *historical* a prioris are historically conditioned structures or rules that make possible the emergence of various kinds of knowledge and discourse. In addition, they define by way of fulfillment requirements what counts in a particular historical epoch as valid or legitimate expressions of knowing, being, or doing. However, unlike Kantian a priori conditioning structures, Foucauldian historical a prioris are themselves subject to change over time. In other words, Foucault's structures are mutable and historically particular – or as he might put it, episteme-specific. Yet given their function as conditioning *structures* that make it possible for certain kinds of discourse, knowledge, and practice to appear, they change less frequently and can last for decades and even centuries, thus allowing various styles, traditions, and recognizable esthetical expressions to come into focus, gain momentum and esteem, and, as it were, take on lives of their own.

By employing Foucault's insights regarding historical conditioning structures and the analyses of ethnomusicologists and other scholars of African American music cognizant of race and musical esthetics as socially constructed realities, I argue that one can articulate a historically attuned and analytically rich model for understanding jazz in its various inflections. That is, on the one hand, such a model permits us to affirm jazz as a historically conditioned, ever-open dynamic hybridity. On the other hand, to acknowledge the hybridity and fluidity of jazz in no way negates our ability to identify discernible features commonly recognized as constituting, for example, Afro-modernist jazz inflections such as bebop, as well as multiple other musical styles and esthetics.[2] Of course, music-making as creative human activity takes place in specific historical contexts. Hence, not only multiple musical streams but also sociopolitical, cultural, legal, and economic structures and practices influence and condition all types of music-making.

Given America's long history of racism – and in no way denying that definitive emancipatory gains had been won – unjust racist structures and practices remained entrenched throughout the twentieth century (and many, no doubt, continue today). Such racialized structures, which privileged whites, created significant barriers for African Americans in their pursuit of equal recognition and opportunities to live a life of human flourishing. Although black jazz musicians were often recognized by the dominant society for their extraordinary talents, such recognition existed simultaneously with "Whites Only" signs. In other words, even when black musical talent was publicly affirmed and lauded, discrimination in the world of music was just as prevalent as discrimination in other social and economic spheres, making it difficult for African American musicians to earn a living wage. Moreover, white ownership of clubs, hotels, concert halls, and record companies created a power differential, which when operative within a racialized society, meant that white musicians often received the best performing venues with respect to both monetary and cultural capital. In contrast, blacks were given less prestigious performance sites and regularly received inadequate and incommensurate pay for their artistic creations and musical performances (see, e.g., Monson, 2007, Chapter 2). To bracket this history in the study of jazz is to fail to hear what the music *says* and to fail to recognize the power of music – even instrumental music – both to (re)narrate collective (and personal) identity and to sound a polyphonic, multi-layered sociopolitical critique. As Guthrie P. Ramsey puts it, "the political import of bebop could not be (and was not) ignored. [...] these were signifying texts, indeed" (Ramsey, 2003, p. 108; see also, Thomas, 1995; Kelly, 1997).

I begin by explaining how particular American legal discourses and social practices constructed "blackness" and helped to establish artificial and harmful black–white binaries. I then focus on jazz's mixed heritage. In this section, I especially emphasize the sociopolitical dimensions of jazz. The notion of music as a site of struggle is a natural segue into an exploration of bebop as an instance of Afro-modernism. Having highlighted the hybridity of bebop and its sociopolitical import, I then examine how traditional Western discourses privileging the composer over the jazz improviser worked in conjunction with early copyright laws to disadvantage the latter economically and socio-culturally. Following the discussion of bebop as a strategic inflection of Afro-modernism, I turn to an analysis of Foucault's work on historical a prioris and the acceptability conditions of discourse, as well as Monson's analyses of jazz discourses and her notion of sonic signifyin(g).

LEGAL CONSTRUCTIONS OF RACE: THE ONE-DROP RULE AND THE CONSTRUCTION OF (FALSE) BINARIES

As students and scholars of race and African American history observe, the one-drop rule plays an especially important and rather idiosyncratic role in the legal construction of blackness in the history of the United States. Although the one-drop rule was an "unofficial" social practice during the years of chattel slavery, it was employed regularly as a way to maintain a strict black–white divide. Children who were the offspring of white and black sexual unions – many of which were born as a result of white masters raping their black female slaves – presented a problem for the dominant society. The hybridity of the mulatto child posed, on the one hand, an ontological challenge to the artificiality of the white-constructed color line and a potential threat to the social, political, and economic advantages created by this one-sided system. To deal with this categorization "problem," Southern states created and applied the one-drop rule: anyone possessing "one drop" of so-called black blood or any trace of African ancestry was considered black. Consequently, biracial children of slave women were deemed slaves at birth and thus became the property of their white masters – masters who were also their fathers.

However, the one-drop rule did not disappear after slavery was abolished. In fact, during the Jim Crow era, the one-drop rule became codified as law (see, e.g., Khanna, 2010, esp. 98–101). As expressed in its nineteenth-century manifestation and working hand-in-hand with Jim Crow legislation, the one-drop rule proclaimed that any person with "traceable black ancestry" was considered *legally* black. Tellingly, the percentage or trace of black ancestry legally constituting an individual as black varied over time and from state to state. For example, until 1910 in Virginia, a person was classified under law as "colored" if he or she had one-quarter or more African ancestry; however, from 1910 to 1924 Virginia decided to "lower" the requirement for blackness to include those with one-sixteenth black ancestry (Monson, 2007, p. 8). Following this period (post-1924), Virginia declared that in order for a person to be judged legally white, he or she must possess no trace of African ancestry – not even "one-drop" of "black" blood (Monson, 2007, p. 8).

Many who were one-eighth black or less exhibited none of the outward markers associated with African or African American descent. In other words, they could "pass" as white since they were extremely light-skinned; and skin color, given its visibility, tended to be the outward "sign" most heavily scrutinized. Since the requirements of the one-drop rule varied from state to state, those who were legally classified as black in one state might be judged white in another. Thus, the act of crossing a state border could (at least given the "logic" of the theory) change one's racial classification and significantly impact one's life-course. In addition, those who in a former period were not considered "colored" because they were only one-sixteenth black – were they still alive – would be legally deemed black in a later period when the African ancestral percentage-requirements became stricter. These examples highlight the mutability of race as well as the ways in which legal constructs and social practices and discourses combine in order to shape and produce race for political, economic, and other purposes. Moreover, what was in fact a wide color spectrum and a diverse mixed heritage, including not only black and white mixed ancestries but also black and Native American as well as black and Native American and

European and Native-American combinations, was forced into an unnatural black–white binary. What existed in reality as a mixed heritage or hybridity was presented as a rigid, fixed, impenetrable dichotomy. As Monson explains, the purpose of the one-drop rule was to preserve and uphold "white purity and domination by assigning intermixture to the legally subordinate category. [...] The strict binary racial classification of Jim Crow attempted to legislate a clear division in a society that was far more hybrid than segregation laws admitted" (Monson, 2007, pp. 8–9).[3]

Along similar lines, discourses about jazz have arisen that mirror these artificial, binary white–black classifications and thus imply and perpetuate the false notion that a fixed racial essence informs musical esthetics and styles. Utilizing the insights from multiple scholars and disciplines, I reject this overly rigid, ahistorical characterization of musical esthetics. In its place, I present a historically sensitive understanding of jazz – focusing mainly on bebop – that, on the one hand, takes seriously the contributions and innovations of canonical African American musicians such as Dizzy Gillespie and Charlie Parker, yet on the other hand, recognizes the hybridity of music-making and the dynamic ontology of music itself. In addition, my model embraces the notion of music as a site of struggle and a means for collective and personal (re)narrations and sociopolitical censure. In the following section, I discuss (1) the ontology of jazz – its hybridity and dynamic identity – and (2) the sociopolitical dimensions of jazz both musically (i.e., the music itself) and discursively (i.e., the discourses about jazz).

JAZZ'S MIXED HERITAGE: POWER DIFFERENTIALS AND STRATEGIC DISCURSIVE AND SONIC SIGNIFYIN(G)

In a recent short essay, Ronald Radano highlights the power of slave music to exceed the controlling, exploitative grasp of white slave owners (2010, p. 366). How is this possible? How can that which is produced by the master's "property" somehow free itself from the master's chains? Slaves, of course, were not "things," and their ability to create beautiful, profoundly moving music underscores the absurdity, greed, and self-deception upon which chattel slavery was built. Humans, not inanimate objects, create music.[4] In other words, the ability to compose music not only for esthetic but also for strategic sociopolitical purposes – whether bebop, Baroque, avant-garde, or hip hop – is a distinctly human capacity. As complex social, intellectual, affective, and creative acts, music-making and the enjoyments of music are human activities that, among other things, allow our stories to be told and our sufferings and joys to be heard and shared. Moreover, like great works of literature and philosophy, music carries within itself a multiplicity of voices – past and present – creatively harmonized and crafted into an identifiable form and content, yet always open to future (re)harmonizations and (re)interpretations. As a social and cultural artifact, music often arises from sites of struggle. For example, black spirituals and much of the blues and jazz styles created and performed by African Americans was birthed amid intense social and political struggle. Given this racialized and exploitative social context, music-making was not a mere autonomous, art-for-art's-sake activity. As Ramsey explains, "the cultural politics of African American music has developed within powerful ideologies surrounding race. For that reason, the principle of artistic autonomy could not develop within black culture in the same way as it had with regard to the Western art music tradition" (Ramsey, 2003, p. 109). This is neither to disown the modernist impulses and influences on jazz and bebop in particular nor to deny bebop's status as art music; rather, it is to claim that in addition to its esthetic value as a human artistic work, music-making and performance functioned as powerful sociopolitical (nonviolent) "weapons," challenging dominant narratives and providing a way for African Americans to re-narrate a white-scripted history while leaving their esthetic mark on American culture (and beyond).

Just as slaves intentionally engaged in distinctly human creative acts and often for strategic, counter-hegemonic purposes, African American jazz musicians of the 1940s–1960s likewise gifted American culture with landmark musical contributions, many of which carried intentional social and political messages. Even a musician such as Thelonious Monk, who is often labeled as an apolitical jazzman, was well aware of the daily racial injustices blacks experienced. Monk, for example, devoted his time, talent, and money to the African American struggle for civil rights and economic equality through benefit concerts and other venues. In other words, there were many different ways in which a jazz musician might express his or her allegiance to and participation in the civil rights movement. Some musicians such as Max Roach and Abby Lincoln were outspoken figures who composed specific musical compositions with conspicuous political protests (see, e.g., Monson, 2007, Chapter 5).[5] Others believed that by dedicating themselves to the creation of outstanding, ground-breaking music, the excellence of their artistic contributions would help to expose the absurdity and falsity of long-held negative assessments of African Americans' intellectual, moral, and esthetic capabilities. Yet even with this latter approach where the focus is on the music itself, one of the intended and anticipated outcomes is to participate in the communal struggle of dismantling unjust structures and re-writing racialized narratives in order to establish a more just and equal social, economic, and political standing for African Americans.

America's history of unjust and exploitative treatment of African Americans – from the Jim Crow South color-coded laws to the Northern ghettos, urban riots, and the various protests and activities that led to the passage of the Civil Rights Act of 1964 – significantly impacted the lives of African American jazz musicians and their artistic creations. For example, commenting on the jazz modernism of the 1940s, Eric Lott observes, "it is impossible to absorb the [be]bop attack without its social reference" (1988, p. 597). Of course, individual musicians channeled their frustration, anger, disappointment, and countless other emotions differently. Some chose the route of open protest via association with black nationalist or other political groups dedicated to dismantling racial, sociopolitical, and economic inequality. As mentioned earlier, others chose different strategies and expressed their frustrations and protests primarily through their music. For example, scholars have commented on how African American jazz musicians, given their unequal economic and social treatment in the music world, intentionally created complex musical harmonies performed at blinding tempos that allowed them to display their virtuosity while leaving their white counterparts at times baffled and unable to compete (see, e.g., Lott, 1988). This situation, of course, was not the case for all white jazz artists, as some were quite capable of navigating bebop's extended harmonies and lightning tempos. However, the interracial tensions and societal structural inequalities that African Americans jazz artists experienced undoubtedly impacted their creative compositional responses to the music's evolution and oft-associated key characteristics. Commenting on bebop in general as well as Charlie Parker's contributions and *artistic* participation in the broader African American struggle for equality, Lott states: "Bebop was about making disciplined imagination alive and answerable to the social changes of its time. [...] jazz was a struggle which pitted mind against the perversity of circumstance, and that in this struggle, blinding virtuosity was the best weapon" (1988, p. 597). In short, one might say that the racialized social, political, and economic contexts served as at least partial conditions making possible some of the important harmonic and other musical innovations and characteristic features of bebop.

Along similar lines, consider the by-and-large positive experiences of African American jazz musicians such as Dizzy Gillespie and Charlie Parker as they toured and spent time in Europe (see, e.g., Monson, 2007, p. 86). Quite unlike their thoroughly racialized and exploitative socio-economic context in the United States, Europe presented them with a context in which they were not only admired for their artistic abilities – which was the case in America among certain jazz connoisseurs and aficionados – but also, and more importantly, where they were treated as fellow human beings: moral and intellectual equals worthy of respect and dignity. This favorable treatment African American musicians experienced while performing in Europe serves as an important backdrop for understanding the complex relation that black jazz musicians have had with the modernist or "high art" tradition.

Bebop as a Hybrid Inflection of Strategic Afro-Modernism

Although it shares several features and impetuses with so-called classical modernism – for example, formal innovations and reaching new heights of expressivity – Afro-modernism of the mid-twentieth century (roughly 1940–1960) manifests distinctive characteristics arising from and related to the particular sociopolitical and economic struggles of African Americans. Guthrie P. Ramsey highlights one aspect of Afro-modernism as the process of African Americans grappling with their place in the modern industrialized, capitalistic world and working out their thoughts, feelings, and stances artistically and collectively (2003, p. 97). Whether we find Afro-modernist overtones expressed via bebop's structural expansions, exceedingly complex harmonies, extended and virtuosic improvised solos, or hybrid African, African American, and Afro-Cuban musical styles, one must also take into account the tension-ridden, racially conflicted socio-political and economic context from which the music emerged.[6] To illustrate, consider my earlier statement that it is a mistake or at least an incomplete characterization to describe bebop as chiefly concerned with the principle of artistic autonomy. Granting this claim and considering the racialized context in which it operated, bebop artists and advocates strategically employed a modernist narrative of autonomy in order to challenge and subvert stereotypical depictions of black musicians as mere entertainers (for whites). In the process of deconstructing white-imposed narratives of what a black musician is or ought to be, bebop artists self-consciously appropriated modernist tropes and discourses to construct their own personal and collective Afro-modernist stories. Yet as Ramsey explains, not only do the new black-scripted modernist narratives proclaim that bebop was neither "dance music" nor "conceived for mass consumption," it also asserted that bebop was "not designed for traditional 'high brow' concert audiences" (Ramsey, 2003, p. 106).

Although it drew upon past sources – from both the Afro and Euro traditions – and was thus clearly hybrid in nature, bebop as an *Afro*-modernist art form was something new. Having broken down the traditional rigid barriers and antagonisms between so-called "high" art music and "folk" music, as well as discourses claiming that art music has no political import, bebop opened up a new musical horizon whose artistic excellence carried sociopolitical substance. As Henry Louis Gates Jr. might put it, bebop musicians' (re)harmonizations and transformations of musical "texts," traditions, and discourses were signifin(g) acts. That is, not only the discourses about bebop but also the musical pieces themselves are instances of "black double-voicedness" and repetition with a "signal difference" intentionally and strategically enacted to speak to social, political, and economic issues (1988, p. 51; see also, Chapter 2). In short, bebop's harmonic, rhythmic, and structural complexity coupled with its blinding, virtuosic improvised solos and distinctive grooves combine to create an expression of *black* art music or strategic Afro-modern jazz, whose innovations and contributions, given the racialized context in which they emerge, carry with them multi-layered sociopolitical significations. To imagine that African American bebop musicians were simply performing and creating works for art's sake in line with the Western art music tradition's discourses on artistic autonomy is to ignore the harsh, racialized reality and lived experience of African Americans in the U.S. history and to conceive of music as an ahistorical artifact untouched by its particular sociopolitical and cultural contexts.

Although, as mentioned earlier, bebop artists were, on the one hand, decidedly not creating music for mass consumption or for traditional "high brow" audience. Moreover, like other highly skilled professionals, they desired and rightfully expected a living wage. However, the complex of American racism and modern capitalism created a particularly constricting and slanted framework – a framework whose laws, discourses, and practices privileged (white) copyright owners while diminishing music-makers, especially black improvising music-makers. Before concluding this section, let me illustrate how bebop as an inflection of strategic Afro-modernism worked within and against these slanted structures and discourses in order to resist and transform the commodifying practices of capitalism – and of course simultaneously struggled against racist (il)logic.[7] From a music-theoretical perspective one could make a strong argument that composition and improvisation are emphases on a single continuum and thus differences between the two are more matters of degree; however, in the socio-economic sphere the difference between the socially prestigious label, "composer," and the socially stereotyped label, "improviser," is stark.[8] The traditional Western notion privileging the composer over the jazz improviser or the "mere" performer per se views the composer as the sole or primary originator and author of the musical piece. This understanding of what a composer is and does is intimately tied to the development of musical notation. A musical score takes the live, dynamic performed music and reduces it to signs on a page. From one perspective, such technologies are completely understandable, legitimate, and even helpful to the process of preserving and transmitting music to subsequent generations. From another perspective, these fixed (silent) signs make it easy to ascribe ownership and thus creative primacy and economic privileges to specific individuals. Within the framework of modern capitalism and its drive to commodify, ownership and copyright laws go hand in hand. Since the improviser is viewed as a mere performer, a conduit or tool, his or her significant contribution – or better co-creation – that transforms the silent signs on a page into (actual) music is diminished. Moreover, this diminishment is made manifest in the economic realm.[9] As Scott DeVeaux observes, even as the artistic talent of a jazz legend such as Charlie Parker is publicly recognized by musicians, critics, and jazz fans across the ethnic spectrum, nonetheless "in a music industry designed to funnel profits to the owners of copyrights, improvisers have found themselves in an anomalous and frustrating position. The history of jazz can be read, in part, as an attempt by determined musicians to close the gap between artistic ambition and economic reward" (DeVeaux, 1997, p. 9).

In fact, as many scholars have pointed out, the original Copyright Act of 1909 itself presupposes that only musical expressions that correlate to a written composition or score qualify as copyrightable material; thus the composer, rather than the performer, is given artistic preference, which, in a capitalistic system, translates into economic privilege. Prior to the 1970s' amendments to copyright laws, recorded versions or improvised performances based on but exceeding and often transforming written scores were not granted a legal copyright-protection status.[10] Consequently, songwriters (composers) and publishers received the bulk of royalty payments, whereas performers (improvisers) were typically paid a one-time fee and their share of the royalties was significantly less (Monson, 2007, p. 336).

Monson provides an excellent example of how such laws favored the composer/songwriter economically and continued to reinforce the idea that the composer/songwriter is the sole musical creator, whereas the improviser/performer is simply a conduit giving expression to the composer's musical intentions. Take, for instance, Miles Davis' 1956 recording of "My Funny Valentine" by Rogers and Hart. Here we have an improvised performance that includes significant harmonic and rhythmic additions, as well as masterful improvised solos creating a new form that many deem superior to the original version. However, as Monson notes, "Davis's unique version of the tune was not copyrightable." Moreover, not only did the songwriters and publisher receive the mechanical royalties, but when Davis's version was heard on radio or TV, additional broadcast royalties were earned by the songwriters and publisher and collected by the American Society of Composers, Authors, and Publishers (ASCAP) (Monson, 2007, p. 30). Such a system clearly exhibits an unfair economic benefit for (mainly white) composers, publishers, and those controlling the radio and television broadcasting industry.

Having discussed bebop's hybrid character, its strategic deployments as an expression of Afro-modernism, and the problematic aspects of the early twentieth-century copyright laws, I turn now to a more technical discussion about discourses. Specifically, I shall bring Foucault's analyses of conditioning structures, discourses, and acceptability conditions into conversation with Monson's work on jazz discourses and sonic signifyin(g).

Foucault on the Social Layers and Acceptability Conditions of Discourses

As Foucault has taught us, what surfaces as the prevailing discourses of a particular period in no way exhausts the reality or complexity of phenomena. In his work, *The Archaeology of Knowledge*, Foucault concerns himself not merely with traditional philosophy of language inquiries such as what counts as a true or false statement. For Foucault, an equally important question is: what are the conditions that make possible a statement or a discourse showing up so that it actually counts at a particular moment in history as a statement or discourse "worthy" of being judged as true or false? In other words, Foucault's analyses focus upon the circumscriptive background "space" that allows various discourses and statements to emerge in the first place. This circumscriptive space, or to use Foucault's terminology, the historical *a prioris* of various epochs, consists of sets of rules or standards that determine not which statements are veridical (*dire vrai*) but which statements are in the true (*dans le vrai*) (see also, Thompson, 2008, esp. p. 12).

Stated from a slightly different angle, to be in the true is inextricably linked with what Foucault calls the "acceptability" of truth and the "acceptability of a system" such as the carceral system or the healthcare system (see, e.g., Foucault, 2007, p. 61). Acceptability conditions speak of the conditions that allow a statement to show up as a recognizable statement while bracketing questions of the statement's truth-value. Thus, for Foucault, a proposition that has already been received by a particular discipline such as music, physics, biology, and so forth is a proposition *dans le vrai*; however, its status as *dans le vrai* does not equate with its truth; it may in fact be received as true yet proven false at a later date. Once we recognize Foucault's focus on the acceptability conditions of propositions and discourse – rather than on the truth-value of statements – we can better understand his claim: "[a] discipline is not the sum total of all the truths that may be uttered concerning something; it is not even the total of all the truths that may be accepted, by virtue of some principle of coherence and systematization" (Foucault, 1972, p. 223). Take, for example, the former (pseudo-)scientific discourse concerning race as a bio-behavioral essence determinative of one's intellectual and moral value. Although such claims were considered true in several academic and other discourses (and thus achieved the status of *dans le vrai*), they were in fact false (and thus did not have the actual status of *dire vrai*). As noted earlier, this past notion of race is no longer the consensus view among social scientists, anthropologists, and scholars of race and ethnicity; yet the discourse regarding race as essentialized and fixed in biology, even though false, had a widespread and injurious impact upon American society. Lastly, a statement qualifying as *dire vrai*, can, paradoxically, be both true (*dire vrai*) and not true (*dans le vrai*).[11] For example, the present widely accepted discourse regarding race as a social construction – a discourse that is today accepted as *dire vrai* – would not have "shown up" as a potential candidate to consider. In other words, the acceptability conditions for such a discourse to be heard were not present as they are in contemporary academic discourses. In short, historically specific structuring (acceptability) conditions that function as historical *a prioris* have the ability, as it were, to silence true (*dire vrai*) propositions and discourses; that is, they can prevent true discourses from appearing at all. Thus, these muted or unarticulated discourses can and often have emerged in a subsequent historical period whose acceptability conditions allow new discourses not only to sound but also to be heard – a hearing that then allows for the possibility of judging their truth or falsity.

Monson on Racialized Jazz Discourses and Saying Something Sonically

Drawing upon Foucault's notion of discourse as, generally speaking, linguistically articulated ideas used to establish one's argument and to justify one's position, and which "possess the authority and prestige to order how we think about the world," Monson describes the multiple musical, cultural, and sociopolitical discourses and strategic practices operative in the world of jazz in America in the mid-twentieth century (2007, p. 24). In addition, Monson's Foucauldian-influenced account helps us to understand better why certain discourses about jazz emerged and why others did not (and could not) until a later period.

As Monson explains, jazz discourses of the 1940s–1960s had become overly binary and highly racialized. On the one hand, we find a liberal, universalist, colorblind discourse depicting jazz as neither black nor white but rather as "a colorblind art music open to all who master its repertory, improvisational mode of musical creation, and demand for individuality and originality" (Monson, 2007, p. 70). On the other hand, we find black and white musicians, scholars, critics, and supporters who reject the colorblind discourse and emphasize the African American origins of jazz; however, their arguments often presupposed and deployed an unhelpful, essentialized notion of blackness to articulate the constitutive esthetic elements of jazz. For many in the latter group, to insist on a colorblind discourse was just another variation on a long history of white confiscation of (and profiting from) black cultural contributions and innovations. Given the long history of racism, the exploitation of African American musicians, and the continuation (although in different forms) of entrenched racialized structures and unjust economic practices, one can understand why the discursive framework shaping jazz discourses had become so polarized well into the 1960s. Rather than an either/or – that is, jazz as either universal, colorblind, and untouched by history, or as ethnically particular and *essentially* black, Monson articulates a third way beyond this impasse. That is, she highlights the porousness and hybridity of jazz esthetics and demonstrates how the very construction of a jazz Afro-modernism not only represents an innovative and significant artistic contribution but also says something or signifies (in Gates's sense) in the sociopolitical realm. This signification occurs not only via the discourses surrounding jazz but also in the music itself, which communicates irony, humor, and sounds a critique of the unjust social, political, and economic system (see also, Floyd, 1995, Chapter 4; Monson, 1994).

For example, take John Coltrane's transformation of the popular Broadway tune, "My Favorite Things." Coltrane's "signification" upon the tune is a multiple-layered example of structural, harmonic, melodic, and rhythmic modifications. The modifications so alter the original tune that jazz esthetes – both black and white – acknowledge Coltrane's version as superior. As Monson explains, Coltrane's creation, "makes the interludes, not the verse, the subject of the performance; it transforms waltz time into a polyrhythmically textured six-feel; and it transforms a sentimental, optimistic lyric into a vehicle for a more brooding improvisational exploration" (1996, p. 116). Moreover, the Coltrane version carries within it and communicates (to those with ears to hear) ironic overtones. The new polyrhythmic groove and the protracted improvised solos re-write the lyrical images of "girls in white dresses," "snowflakes on eyelashes," and other "white things" and communicate a weighty, contemplative, and at times menacing feel. Given that Coltrane's version of the tune emerged during the years of the Civil Rights Movement, it is certainly possibile that Coltrane intended his musical interpretation to make an ironic and socially critical statement. Even if this was not the case, one need not limit the possible range of meanings of a musical work to the intentions of the composer(s). Just as the dynamic ontology of texts allows for multiple interpretations over time by different interpretative communities and traditions, the same is true with musical pieces. In addition to these examples of sonic irony, Monson highlights how Coltrane's transformation of "My Favorite Things" strategically employs European American musical standards for its own purposes. That is, by traditional standards of Western classical music, the original tune and arrangement would be judged as exceedingly basic and unoriginal. However, Coltrane's version with its sophisticated harmonic and rhythmic textures not only surpassed the original when judged by jazz esthetical standards but also illustrated how jazz musicians can "invoke selectively some of the hegemonic standards of Western classical music in their favor" (Monson, 1996, p. 120). Lastly, these strategic moves occur simultaneously with the creation of something new – an African American jazz esthetic that becomes an evaluative standard by which non-African American music and musicians are judged.

In order to demonstrate the hybridity of bebop, Monson highlights the multiple esthetic streams constituting jazz. These streams include: blues, gospel, R&B, American popular songs (e.g., Tin Pan Alley), modern classical music, African and Afro-Cuban esthetics, and Indian, as well as other non-Western, esthetics (Monson, 2007, p. 71). What emerges from this creative and strategic harmonization is, as we have already noted via Ramsey, a new Afro-modernist esthetic – a new black modernist esthetic that was, on the one hand, "more populist than its European art music counterpart, and on the other, committed to articulating its elite position relative to the more commercial genres of R&B and rock and roll" (Monson, 2007, p. 71). Thus, the creative artistry and sociopolitical astuteness of bebop musicians like Gillespie, Parker, and a host of others actively defined the "aesthetic center of this canonic period in jazz," transforming and bringing into existence an Afro-esthetic – a "blackening of modern aesthetics, which would ultimately serve as a standard against which any player of jazz would be evaluated" (Monson, 2007, p. 71).

On this model, African American jazz musicians such as Gillespie, Parker, Davis, Coltrane, and others are acknowledged as the creative innovators whose standard-setting contributions and leadership made bebop and continues to exert significant influence on contemporary jazz musicians. However, this model starts with and employs a view of race and esthetics as socially constructed rather than "natural" and fixed.[12] Although structures and discourses can become entrenched and can impute meanings to physical characteristics (in the case of "race," phenotypic markers) and musical features (in the case of jazz, syncopated rhythms), such meanings are open to change over time as practices "on the ground" work to change the discourses and structures. Thus, by rejecting an essentialist-informed and hence fixed notion of bebop's Afro-modernist esthetic, one can acknowledge its hybridity and avoid overly rigid and often stereotypical definitions of "authentic" black music – stereotypes that all too often fail to acknowledge the extensive esthetic range of African American musicians. Yet this model also allows one to draw attention to the differences in lived experience between white and black jazz musicians given the institutional and structurally racist system. For example, due to structural white privilege, white jazz musicians, many of whom were talented and acknowledged as so by their black counterparts, received the highest paying gigs and widespread and sustained press coverage in jazz and other publications, and were granted disproportionate radio and television performance opportunities in comparison to black musicians. Likewise, many black jazz players whose talents surpassed their white counterparts were not only denied prestigious performance opportunities but also regularly subject to unjust, disdainful, and even violent treatment both onstage and offstage and especially when touring in southern states. Here Monson emphasizes an important distinction between an "individual's self-conscious identity (whether ethnic or political) and that person's treatment as a citizen within the larger sociology of race relations in the United States" (2007, p. 73). A white, liberal progressive may possess a heightened ethnic consciousness and have no intentional desire to benefit from white privilege; nonetheless, he or she does in fact benefit daily from racially skewed sociopolitical and economic structures. Similarly, whether white or black, a musician can choose and develop skills allowing him or her to participate in multiple musical esthetics, styles, and traditions; however, exercising one's "aesthetic agency" and achieving recognizable musical skills does not *by itself* change the larger sociopolitical and economic structures. Policies, legislation, cultural, and other discourses must also change. This is not to negate an individual's esthetic choices; it is, however, to acknowledge the complexity of the structural strata constituting society and the fact that structures change at a much slower rate than practices and require transformations from multiple spheres.

CONCLUSION

In this chapter, I have argued that jazz esthetics and inflections of jazz such as bebop are socially conditioned, dynamic, and hybrid in character. To affirm the fluid and hybrid character of jazz, bebop, and Afro-modernist esthetics neither renders impossible our ability to identify discernible features of particular styles and esthetic traditions nor requires that we accept a colorblind discourse about jazz. Rather, my model, following Monson and a host of others, affirms that sociopolitical, cultural, legal, and economic structures and practices influence and condition all types of music-making. Bebop as an inflection of Afro-modernism is of course no exception. In fact, I have emphasized that in order to have a historically rich and comprehensive understanding of bebop, one must consider the social, political, and highly racialized context in which this music (and its discourses) emerged. To neglect the sociopolitical import of bebop is to display one's ignorance of the African American signifyin(g) tradition. Moreover, it is, as Lott puts it, to fail to see that the "self-conscious advances of bebop" are part of "a moment, the early forties, in which unpaid historical bills were falling due" (Lott, 1988, p. 587).

NOTES

1. Admittedly, I have already set up an artificial binary with my discourse of white and black. Other ethnicities, groups, and esthetical traditions likewise contributed to the sociopolitical struggles of the period and to the ongoing creation of various jazz styles (e.g., Afro-Cuban and West Indian influences).

2. Of course, these "discernible features" are themselves hybrid in nature having arisen from multiple musical genealogies, practices, and appropriations.

3. Monson further explains how these binary impositions "collapsed ethnic and cultural distinctions within populations of African descent" (e.g., Caribbean populations and Creoles populations in Louisiana) and likewise flattened and masked the ethnic diversity among European immigrant groups (2007, p. 9).

4. One could argue that other animals such as birds also create music. To an extent, I certainly agree. However, I would argue that the level of harmonic, melodic, and rhythmic complexity, the double-voicedness, and the strategic and political intentional purposes of both the instrumental and vocal music I examine in the present study are distinctively human cultural products.

5. Monson provides a helpful analysis of the political context and message of Max Roach's work, *Freedom Now Suite*, and the sociopolitical ideals and philosophies that inspired both Roach and Abby Lincoln (Monson, 2007, see esp. pp. 171–181).

6. Ramsey discusses several mid-twentieth century "processes and their contradictions and paradoxes" including: mass migration, the (mis)use of black bodies, an emerging black defiance that helped to fuel effective political strategies and collective actions, and lastly, the multiple and "conflicting discourses on art's role in social change" (2003, p. 98, see also, Chapter 5, "We Called Ourselves Modern," esp. pp. 98–105).

7. For a discussion of the resistance elements of bebop within the marketplace, see DeVeaux (1997, esp. pp. 20–27).

8. For a theoretical analysis deconstructing the assumed rigid dichotomy between composition and improvisation, see Nielsen (2009).

9. DeVeaux sums up this process nicely: "Notation imposes upon music the idea of a permanent text to which authorship can safely be ascribed and ownership securely established. Such fixity is a necessary precursor to commodification" (1997, p. 10).

10. The federal copyright laws were amended in the 1970s to cover recordings. See, Monson (2007, p. 336, no. 2). See also, DeVeaux (1997, esp. pp. 11–12). As DeVeaux explains, the growing ascendancy of recordings over sheet music did not change the economic privileges and power structures. "[E]conomic power remained stubbornly in the grip of music publishers, who insisted (with the help of copyright law) that all financial benefits to creativity must flow to officially recognized composers. Since royalties for performance per se were relatively rare (contracts typically dictated a modest one-time fee), 'mere' performers saw very little of this money, unless they somehow managed to claim the role of composer" (p. 12).

11. It is also the case that a statement can be false and yet true (*dans le vrai*); such was the case with the aforementioned dominant view of race as a

bio-behavioral racialized essence in the nineteenth century. It passed the "acceptability test," yet it was clearly false.

12. Monson's model and mine share many similarities such as our affirmation of the hybridity and dynamism of jazz esthetics as well as its socially conditioned character. Likewise, we both emphasize the innovative and standard-setting contributions of African American musicians in creating and developing jazz and bebop in particular.

REFERENCES

DeVeaux, S. (1997). *The birth of bebop. A social and musical history*. Berkeley, CA: University of California Press.

Floyd, Jr., S. A. (1995). *The power of black music: Interpreting its history from Africa to the United States*. New York, NY: Oxford University Press.

Foucault, M. (1972). *The archaeology of knowledge and the discourse on language* (A. M. Sheridan Smith, Trans.). New York, NY: Pantheon.

Foucault, M. (2007). What is critique? In S. Lotringer (Ed.), *The politics of truth* (pp. 41–81). Los Angeles, CA: Semiotext(e).

Gates, Jr., H. L. (1988). *The signifying monkey. A theory of African American Literary Criticism*. Oxford: Oxford University Press.

Kelly, R. D. G. (1997). Dig they freedom: Meditations on history and the black avant-garde. *Lenox Avenue: A Journal of Interarts Inquiry*, *3*, 13–27.

Khanna, N. (2010). If you're half black, you're just black: reflected appraisals and the persistence of the one-drop rule. *The Sociological Quarterly*, *51*, 96–121, esp. pp. 98–101.

Lott, E. (1988). Double V, double-time: Bebop's politics of style. *Callaloo*, *36*, 597–605.

Monson, I. (1994). Doubleness and Jazz Improvisation: Irony, Parody, and Ethnomusicology. *Critical Inquiry*, *20*, 283–313.

Monson, I. (1996). *Saying something. Jazz improvisation and interaction*. Chicago, IL: University of Chicago Press.

Monson, I. (2007). *Freedom sounds. Civil rights call out to jazz and Africa*. Oxford: Oxford University Press.

Nielsen, C. (2009). What has Coltrane to do with Mozart: The dynamism and built-in flexibility of music. *Expositions*, *3*, 57–71.

Radano, R. (2010). On ownership and value. *Black Music Research Journal*, *30*, 363–369.

Ramsey, G. (2003). *Race music: Black cultures from bebop to hip-hop*. Berkeley, CA: University of California Press.

Thomas, L. (1995). Ascension: Music and the black arts movement. In K. Gabbard (Ed.), *Jazz among the discourses* (pp. 256–274). Durham: Duke University Press.

Thompson, K. (2008). Historicity and transcendentality: Foucault, Cavailles, and the phenomenology of the concept. *History and Theory*, *47*, 1–18.

CULTURAL NORMS OF JAPANESE FOLK AND TRADITIONAL MUSIC

Masaya Takahashi

ABSTRACT

Purpose – *The main purpose of this chapter is to discuss cultural norms in the process of handing down traditional folk music. In doing so, I focus on learning what successors of the tradition think about the orthodoxy of their music and what they think is the ideal way to pass down cultural heritage. In addition, considering that cultural norms are socially constructed in the moment, it should be also examined what leads people to have such notions.*

Design/methodology/approach – *To achieve these purposes, I look at practices of handing down traditional folk music in Japan, developing five case studies of various* ohayashi. *I also analyze* yosakoi, *which is modernly arranged local folk music that is widely spread across the country in the form of community festivals.*

Findings – *The successors of traditions tend to consider tracing the roots of their music as an obligation. On the other hand, in the case of music with no exact origin, its successors seek to find their identities by learning lessons from local anonymous ancestors. Meanwhile, there*

Music and Law
Sociology of Crime, Law and Deviance, Volume 18, 149–165

ISSN: 1521-6136/doi:10.1108/S1521-6136(2013)0000018010

are people who consider its economic value as a raison d'être for traditional music.

Originality/value – *What gives originality to this chapter is that I adopt an approach, employing regional and urban sociology methods, of comparing the characteristics of the regions in which local folk music is based. Along with perspectives on macro social changes and the principle of music group formation, I also discuss the transformation of expertise in folk culture associated with the rise of institutional reflexivity.*

Keywords: Cultural norm; tradition; heritage tourism; local history; reflexivity

INTRODUCTION

In this chapter, I seek to discuss the cultural norms of traditional music. When we try to gain an understanding of music as a tradition, it is important to consider the trends in tourism practices that affect people's cultural identity. Culler (1981) describes mass tourism as follows: "All over the world the unsung armies of semioticians, the tourists, are fanning out in search of the signs of Frenchness, typical Italian behavior, exemplary Oriental scenes, typical American thruways, traditional English pubs" (p. 127). In modern society, to meet such expectations of tourists is a critical issue for successors of traditional music as a tourism resource, and particular norms have urged them to satisfy the tourists.[1]

Mass tourism has been criticized for undermining the vernacular values of "place." However, this criticism also faces the objection that it is not wealthy people but the middle class who see mass tourism as a problem, because they cannot ensure their own untouched places the way the rich can (Beckerman, 1974, pp. 50–52). In any case, to merely criticize either tourism development or the egotism of the middle class contributes nothing to the understanding of traditions. One way of bridging the positions is to focus on the proactive practices of cultural successors and the processes by which they come face to face with the history that is closely connected to their identities. Handing down a tradition surely provides its successor with a foundation for identity. Using that meaning, the cultural norm that a tradition should be valued, which firmly establishes people's raison d'etre and orthodoxy, is readily formed.

In modern society, as the homogenization of time and space progressed, people instead began to cast an esthetic look at places that had unique histories and traditions. By knowing the differences, they have understood themselves and their social worlds (Schivelbusch, 1986). In essence, tourism is a reflexive practice of forming identity by utilizing information technology and high mobility (Beck, Giddens, & Lash, 1994). Because reflexive people constantly refer to their self-descriptive knowledge, successors of tradition are also sensitive to the evaluation of their music by experts, and they are concerned about how other music is handed down and regarded. It is now quite easy to go and see different festivals, and videos are available on YouTube. That is, the performers keep their audiences in view. Therefore, the successors believe their music must be more sophisticated so that it will hold up under keen observation.

To make the local folk music sophisticated, every successor makes an effort, and many hope their music will become an intangible cultural asset for the nation. As Anderson (1983) argues, traditional culture is a requirement of nation-states that contributes to a sense of belonging. Recently, a set of campaigns for World Heritage registration was actively developed because cultural successors wanted for their own national culture and traditions to be held in high regard and meet global standards.

On the other hand, the process of globalization, in which nation-states are more like revolving doors than defined borders and various "flows" cross each other, is ongoing (Appadurai, 1990). In this process, the framework of the nation-state becomes fuzzy in terms of cultural practices, and opportunities for domestic cultures to interact with foreign local cultures are increased. Today, the various media undermine a sense of history tied to particular places, and all local traditions need not be representative of national cultures (Meyrowitz, 1985). New norms are occurring under which every cultural practice should adapt to the dual situation of both globalization and its backlash.

In recent years, alternative tourism that emphasizes the value of unique experiences and the narrativity of place has become a booming market replacing mass tourism. This type of tourism does not offer the same old attractions to tourists as semioticians but urges tourists to establish inherent relationships with the places and relate to the experiences in their own ways. Reflecting this trend in tourism, successors of local folk music began to think that they should make their traditions into attractive "texts" that would be worth reading and talking about so that the traditions would take on many interpretations by tourists. However, this participative approach to tourism also requires local music successors to determine how far they allow tourists and the acceptable range of interpretation.

As Bauman (2000) argued, using an excellent metaphor, even traditional cultures cannot stay solid in the liquid modern world. The traditions that are handed down and those that are to be discarded are not stable. In a sense, music is now something people can choose but that they do not require, and so they are free to choose their favorites. In this situation, building a disjunctive network can be critical in bringing together those who selectively hand down the traditions or choose not to. Thus, the existing methods of organizational management for the solid modern world are not enough to sustainably pass down local folk music.

As shown, the reality of surrounding folk and traditional music is changing from moment to moment. To establish the current state of affairs, I look at the practices of handing down traditional folk music in Japan, developing five case studies of various *ohayashi*. *Ohayashi* is traditional music generally performed with dance in dedication to the Shinto god of a shrine or the Buddha of a temple on festival days. For example, I analyze *yosakoi*, modernly arranged local folk music that is widespread throughout the country as a form of community festival. I also look at a folk song that was restored as part of a project relating to civil engineering heritage.

These unique cases will demonstrate the new phase of tradition and cultural heritage. Truly "the age of preservation" is upon us in which reflexive people who have museological desires attempt to preserve every human deed for later reference (Ogino, 2002). However, paradoxically, these traditionalists tend to have conflicts over what is worth preserving and handing down and why. The contemporary norms and value consciousness about the traditions, the main focus of this chapter, are reflected concretely in such conflicts and so we must examine them carefully.

EXPLORING THE ROOTS OF TRADITIONS

It is a historical practice to pass down folk and traditional music. Almost every successor of folk performing art calls him- or herself an orthodox flame keeper; their art forms part of their cultural identity, and their practices are based on historical thinking. Here, historical thinking means exploring the roots of their heritage. All traditions certainly have particular roots, and the successors emphasize the continuity of these roots.

The successors tend to pride themselves on being involved in authentic music that is central to the national culture rather than peripheral. For example, today we see many people exploring the roots of their local folk music in the style of Kyoto or the style beloved by the Heian aristocrats over 800 years ago. This is because Kyoto and its aristocratic culture have been historically considered the proper home of Japanese culture.

However, because the cultural prototypes have been transformed even in Kyoto, it is difficult to recognize it as such. In fact, from the perspective that regional differences in culture reflect the process of culture diffusion, we can possibly find the styles of music that are closer to the prototypes not in the major cities but rather in the local ones.

Folkloric cultural assets, into which traditional music is categorized, are defined under the Law for the Protection of Cultural Properties in Japan as follows: "subject matter essential to an understanding of the transition of people's lives, including manners, folk performing arts, folk technologies and other objects which are related to clothing, food, and housing, regular vocation, religion, and annual events." Although traditional music reflecting the transitions of people's lives is highly regarded, music with no definite roots cannot receive high marks as a cultural asset. Therefore, the successors are eager to explore the roots of traditional music so that their heritage earns high regard.

I will provide a specific example. There is an intangible cultural folklore asset called the Hanawa-Bayashi in Akita Prefecture, an area of heavy snowfall. *Hayashi* is a traditional style of music performed with bamboo flutes, Japanese drums, and gongs for Noh, Kabuki, shrine festivals, and other events. In particular, *Hayashi* performances dedicated to shrines with the purpose of amusing the gods are very lively and energetic, and performers riding on floats play their instruments and get people dancing. The Hanawa-Bayashi has been dedicated to the guardian god of Hanawa for over 800 years, since the shrine was founded. The Hanawa-Bayashi is considered one of the three major *Hayashi* of Japan along with the *Gion-Bayashi* in Kyoto and the *Kanda-Bayashi* in Tokyo.

There are various views on the origin of the Hanawa-Bayashi. Among these, it is widely believed that a nobleman from Kyoto introduced the Hanawa people to a way of playing the bamboo flute with Kyoto flavor at the end of the Heian Period. Later, people began to perform the music with Japanese drums, gongs, and *samisens* (similar to a banjo). A tune called "Gion," one of the 12 tunes handed down to date, closely resembles the *Gion-Bayashi* in Kyoto, and thus people consider Kyoto the origin of Hanawa-Bayashi. In addition, because of their self-contempt, people have thought there was no way for their culture to survive without the influence of Kyoto.

Recently, there have been several debates on the history of the Hanawa-Bayashi between the young and old locals and the experts. The debates focus on the reasons the Hanawa-Bayashi lost its popularity for more than 40 years after the Sino-Japanese War and why the *samisen* was added to the composition of instruments. According to one expert, because the Hanawa-Bayashi had developed as entertainment by *geishas* rather than as festival music dedicated to shrines, *samisens* were played with the other instruments. However, as the country entered a period during which pastimes such as *geisha* parties came to be disliked, the Hanawa-Bayashi fell out of favor. During that time, blind strolling musicians had handed down the tradition, and 40 years later, farmers in nearby villages, who had learned the Hanawa-Bayashi from the blind musicians, set the stage for the revival of the tradition.

It is true that there was a period when the Hanawa-Bayashi had become more entertainment than tradition and had been maintained not by locals but by outsiders. This fact is difficult to accept for those who believe that the nobility and authenticity of the Hanawa-Bayashi were derived from its origins in Kyoto.[2] Not a few people hold the view that both locals and experts should not actively spread the fact because the Hanawa-Bayashi has been performed abroad, for example, in San Francisco, Nice, and Shanghai, and is known as representing Japanese traditional music. Thus, those involved claim that they should seek the continued success of this heritage industry.

One expert reported being harshly told by local elders not to damage the images of the Hanawa-Bayashi and its orthodoxy when he was serializing articles on the roots of the Hanawa-Bayashi in a newspaper. However, he continued the series and insisted that people should not rely on orthodox images of Kyoto as their cultural center but should try to identify the true roots and history of their heritage. Actually, it took a great deal of courage for him to express this opinion. He was originally an owner of a kimono shop on the Hanawa shopping street and he was also friendly with local elders and other owners who were successors of the Hanawa-Bayashi. As it turned out, because of his earnestness he gained more of their understanding, and some people cheered him for writing about the critical role played by the blind strolling musicians in passing on the traditions.

From this case study, we can see that there are two cultural norms among successors in terms of exploring the roots of traditional music. One is the norm, or ruling idea, that local traditional music, if it is truly valuable, should be historically rooted in a cultural center and continuously handed down by locals. The second is the norm that successors should try to identify the roots of their music in an objective way. These two norms are occasionally at odds with each other because they do not always meet their desired objectives. Therefore, what is important is to patiently address the dilemma between the two norms without choosing sides.

THE HYBRIDITY OF TRADITIONAL MUSIC

The styles of traditional music cannot be divorced from the local industry. When an industry changes, the workers in the area are partly replaced by others, and their lifestyles also change. Such industrial change results in transformations of who hands down the local folk music and what people are looking for in music. The local industry is also deeply connected to the regional image, and the local music is utilized as a tool for forming favorable images of the region. Thus, if you wish to sustain the regional image of industrial prosperity, you should preserve and hand down the familiar music of the workers who had worked there.

This local folk music is not always designated an intangible cultural asset. However, there is a kind of local music that truly represents the regional image and history, despite the lack of defined roots worthy of being designated a cultural asset. The traceability of tradition, a basis for the evaluation of cultural assets, is greatly dependent on the simplicity of historical lineage. Here, it must be properly noted that the multilineal development of traditions and cultural diversity are conditions for being highly regarded. In this sense, the hybridity of local folk music should not be considered as disorder or frayed cultural continuity.

A traditional event called the Kosaka-Tanabata has been held every year in Kosaka, Akita Prefecture. The Tanabata stems from Chinese customs based on the folk legend that a couple separated by the Milky Way meet once a year on August 7. It was introduced to Japan as an event of the noble courts in the Nara Period and spread, together with Japan's indigenous religion and ancestor worship, to farmers and townspeople in the Edo Period. Therefore, the Tanabata is now considered the ritual for prayers of agricultural fertility, good health, and so on; the forms of the festival differ according to area.

Kosaka is a region composed of the rural part where farmers live and the town area where mine workers live. Thus, the Kosaka-Tanabata is held to pray for the god of agriculture and the victims of the mining industry. The Kosaka-Tanabata began in roughly 1900 and has a history of more than 100 years. At that time, there were many itinerant miners who belonged to the Tomoko Union, which served to promote a fictional kinship. They would wander from mine to mine all over Japan with the approval of the Tomoko Union. Because they brought festival cultures from around the country to Kosaka, the Kosaka-Tanabata gradually changed to be a hybrid of these cultures. One year they made a festival float, and the float style was transmitted to the neighborhood areas.

The Kosaka-Bayashi is played with bamboo flute, Japanese drums, gongs, and harmonica. To be precise, the locals use short-cut rails from the mine carts by which miners transported heavy ore. In addition, playing *ohayashi* on the harmonica, which was imported to Japan right at the time Kosaka-Tanabata started, is remarkably unique. Elementary school children learn how to play harmonica in music class and begin to participate in the festival from an early age. Although the Kosaka-Bayashi using the "rail gong" and the harmonica is not rooted in the traditional music of the Middle or early Modern Age, this local folk music properly reflects the vigorousness of the old industrial city.

Although the *ohayashi* of the Kosaka-Tanabata has a different rendition in every colony, no one can explain each origin adequately. Additionally, because there is no practice of tracing the roots and restoring the old songs, this *ohayashi* is not designated as an intangible folk cultural asset. However, no resident thinks the *ohayashi* is empty of value because the *ohayashi* of the Kosaka-Tanabata has played an important role in forming the local image of Kosaka as a mining town.[3]

Since the Kosaka Mine closed 20 years ago, a new key industry has been started that takes of the refinement technology of the mining station, but the population in Kosaka has decreased severely. Thus, discussions of mergers with other local governments near Kosaka have been held once or twice. In this tough situation, the local image of the mining town that once had the highest output in Japan is the precious property of Kosaka. The playhouse, which was built as the welfare facilities for a mine 100 years ago, was renewed and now draws record audiences, and Kosaka town has built the practical use of the modernization heritage into the core of city planning.

Now, tourism involving viewing a play and enjoying the Kosaka-Tanabata has won popularity, and sightseeing of the industrial culture in the mining town is prosperous. The presentation of the Kosaka-Tanabata in which miners have brought their festival culture shows the past panache and openness of a mining town. Moreover, the locals have passed on methods of cultural exchange and multisystem development as traditions of Kosaka, such as traveling to neighboring regions to study float building.

This case illustrates that there is traditional music with the value of historical records, which is more important for knowing how people worked in Kosaka and what they lived for than is tracing the roots of the music. Moreover, even if such traditional music has not been designated a cultural asset, the people there consider that *ohayashi* should be handed down to the next generation. As proof of this, although former miners received large amounts of retirement allowance, they did not leave Kosaka and they maintained the traditions of *ohayashi* and the float. Thus, the *Kosaka-Bayashi* in Tanabata, which had been accepted as an event of ancestor worship in Japan, is now performed for successive miners as the fictional ancestors of the locals.

SINGING THE HOPE OF BACKWATER

Music that reflects past dreams and hopes may encourage people who are in a pessimistic situation. When we know that the locals who once lived there sang positive songs, in contrast to the modern people, we should be encouraged still more.

There is an area called Nobiru in Miyagi Prefecture that suffered serious damage from the Great East Japan Earthquake. Nobiru was once a site of large-scale national land development planning in the Meiji Period. The first modern port construction in Japan as a governmental direct control enterprise was planned in order to build a base of northeast development under the "promotion-of-industry" policy of the Meiji government. The Dutch engineer who received the appointment of the Japanese government performed appropriate site selection, and Nobiru was selected as the first proposed site.

The contents of the first-term construction were a river inner harbor and the port entrance from the inner harbor to the sea, excavation of a canal, and improvement of the newly developed urban area. Although the Nobiru Harbor opened completely in 1882, most piers were passed by the large-scale typhoon that came only two years afterward. The port construction fell through because the leading mode of transportation traffic shifted to the railroad. Because there was no reconstruction, Nobiru has become a "phantom harbor." Only a canal and a lock remain now.

Although the history lovers and native historians had individually studied the history of Nobiru Harbor for so long, there was no collective action by local residents such as handing down the history of harbor construction from generation to generation. The first turning point was a commemoration project by the Japan Society of Civil Engineers. The members of this academic society – researchers, private constructors, and consultants – are conscious of their responsibility to participate in the provision of social overhead capital as engineers. As part of bridging civil engineering technology and society, the northeast branch of the Japan

Society of Civil Engineers began tracing the history of Nobiru Harbor, regarding the Nobiru Harbor construction as their modern civil engineering heritage. A native of Nobiru was also in the Japan Society of Civil Engineers, and the "Nobiru Harbor Fan Club" was also formed to take advantage of the individual network.

However, although the Nobiru Harbor Fan Club posted five points – "protection and preservation of heritage," "activation of the town," "information gathering," "further research," and "the succession of the local culture," as the purpose of their activities, the actual practice was mainly elders gathering to tell each other the same old stories of Nobiru. Whether the engineers had special discussions or amateurs told the old stories, it was not an effective practice of clarifying the historical value and the concrete image of Nobiru Harbor as a heritage site. Then, the "excavation" of traditional music became the second turning point. This succeeded in reproducing the folk song of Nobiru Harbor, recording it and taking notes.

Although the existence of this folk song had been spoken of for some time, the memories of many people were ambiguous. However, a certain resident remembered clearly and was able to sing while striking the drum. The lyrics of this folk song show the past prosperity of Nobiru Shinmachi, which was the town newly developed in the Meiji Period along with the harbor construction. According to the lyrics, "In this town, we don't need a broom, for the skirts of the women who go back and forth will sweep the floor." This cheerful folk song had been dedicated in the float festival of the Shirohige shrine near the seashore, but it stopped in 1950 or so.

With the discovery of this folk music, the members of the Nobiru fan club could have concrete images of past prosperity in Nobiru. Because singing this song was simply enjoyable, it drove their motivation for handing down the history of Nobiru Harbor. Moreover, because the civil engineering technology involved in Nobiru Harbor was good for the environment, preserving the heritage was also meaningful in a modern context. The music and technology of Nobiru Harbor give the cultural successors' practices the legitimacy of preserving a cultural heritage "without form."

On the historical side, Nobiru is an unfortunate place because the harbor's development suffered a setback; railroad development was also advanced in the early Modern Age, and cars passed by Nobiru along bypass roads at the beginning of the automotive age. Moreover, because much sediment flowed from a river and the shallow seashore, the Nobiru Harbor was bypassed by the typhoon and also suffered tsunami damage from the Great East Japan Earthquake. Thus, the folk song is curing and encouraging people who have faced a severe situation and they believe folk music ought to exist.[4] There is now also a cultural norm of believing that folk music has the power to change people positively.

COMMERCIALIZING THE TRADITION AND CREATIVITY

There is a festival called the Yosakoi-Soran that developed nationally from Sapporo-city, Hokkaido, and is now about the style of production of community events rather than the music itself. The Yosakoi-Soran festival literally unites the Soran in Hokkaido with the Yosakoi of Kochi Prefecture. A young man came up with this curious fusion of the traditional music 20 years ago. When Mr. Takeshi Hasegawa (now an upper house member), who was a student of Hokkaido University, visited an elder brother in Kochi, he was moved by seeing the activity of Yosakoi and came to think that he would like to create such a lively festival at his university.

The Yosakoi is originally a folk song of the early Modern Period in Kochi Prefecture, and the Yosakoi festival is a relatively new festival that was established to compete with the Awa dance of Tokushima Prefecture in the 1950s. In the early Yosakoi festivals, Mr. Eisaku Takemasa, a composer, hit upon the idea of performing with a *naruko* (Japanese castanet) and dancing along with the Yosakoi, and the festival became popular. However, the dance was like the Bon festival dance and was somewhat modest at that time. Because the composer allowed people to arrange his song in contemporary ways with the condition that his original melody should be saved, junior composers began to use their creativity to present the song in rock, flamenco, and samba styles. With this change, the number of spectators increased drastically, to nearly 1.8 million.

When Mr. Hasegawa saw the Yosakoi, he planned to borrow its style of incorporating a *naruko* and dancing along with the local folk music, and created a new festival, the Yosakoi-Soran.[5] Although Soran itself had been a historic folk music style since the early Modern Age, there had been no popular Soran festival. Because the festival in which people could dance to Soran was new, it was especially supported by the young and vibrant people.

The Yosakoi-Soran has been getting better each time, "Yosakoi-Soran" was registered as a trademark, and its governing organization became an incorporated company. Additionally, the Yosakoi-Soran became a huge business; for instance, a vocational school that taught Soran musicians was established, and designers who made the clothes for the dancers also gathered in Sapporo. In a word, this festival produced industry and employment.

A Yosakoi-Soran-style festival is a quick method for local governments to renew prosperity in a central city area. Each sector of the region always tries to reactivate its towns, so various measures are taken, but if people do not come to the town, they cannot see these devices. At this point, the Yosakoi-Soran is a suitable event that attracts people to the town and catches their attention with music and dance. This kind of festival is called a "festival without god," and the dance and the *ohayashi* are not dedicated to any particular shrine. However, because there is no religious nature to this festival, anyone can participate regardless of faith and the local government can support the festival financially. So to speak, in the festivals of the Yosakoi-Soran style, regional vitalization is the noble aim, and the people who are eager to achieve the goal live blessed existences.

However, such commercialization of the festival has also received much criticism. There are also those who feel the traditions have been disturbed by changing Yosakoi into a noisy rock. Since Mr. Hasegawa became a politician, there are also those who criticize his desire for improvement using Yosakoi-Soran, meaning that he is using traditional music for business. On the other hand, there are negative views in terms of cultural diversity. By widely spreading the single format of one festival, instead of highlighting the differences among the various folk music styles, putting on the Yosakoi-Soran with much the same arrangement every time is said to cause a lack of local endemism.

It surely seems that this festival has attracted homogeneous people with similar personalities and motives.[6] Moreover, those who are excited by such a festival and those who lose interest or feel alienation are clearly divided, and the latter do not generally go to see the Yosakoi-Soran.

However, it may be evaluated that local musicians collectively, rather than by their star potential, cultivated a new field of performance and even raised it to an industry by taking advantage of traditional music. Furthermore, musicians' being active not only in a studio or live venues but also in communities, and addressing not only their fans but also the local residents, are affirmative changes for local music. The same is true of designers. Thus, certain cultural norms are formed that both the creativity and the marketability of music that has been commercialized should always be called in question.

In this context, the present situation that each Yosakoi festival is almost the same must be taken more seriously from a viewpoint of creativity. Due to this point, the audience of the Yosakoi festival has started to decrease. Either way, the ironical paradox that featuring local folk music causes a lack of local endemism should be solved in the process of ongoing cultural industry.

ENHANCING THE SYMBOLIC POWER

Even though a style of traditional music is commercialized and widely expanded, the music, which is not only for the players themselves but also for symbolic icons, will be special. This holds true especially when the symbolic icon is something of a father figure for locals.

For example, there has been passed down the *ohayashi* of the sparrow dance in Sendai, Miyagi Prefecture. The Sendai sparrow dance is an improvisational free dance with its origin in a masonry party stunt introduced to the feudal lord, Masamune Date, at the completion ceremony of Sendai Castle in 1603. To be exact, it was a dance for encouraging masonry when pulling a heavy stone with a rope. The dancing figure is like a sparrow walking, and because the family crest of the lord Date was called "a sparrow in a bamboo forest," the dance was named the sparrow dance.

The *ohayashi* of the sparrow dance as a traditional music form is performed in three urban festivals every year, that of the Setaya Fudouson (temple), Osaki Hachimangu (shrine), and the Sendai Aoba. Many groups of dancers and their *ohayashi* as traditional music are organized, so this cultural heritage has been passed down with a very broad base.

The Setaya Fudouson was constructed in 1672 and was located in the area of the masonry community. These stonemasons were brought from Osaka by the feudal lord, Masamune Date, for building a castle and had lived in a castle town. They constructed Setaya Fudouson to pray for their safety at work. Even now, several stone dealers live in the area, and they conduct the festival of Setaya Fudouson. The Sendai sparrow dance has been dedicated to this festival for a long time.

Next, Osaki Hachimangu, the shrine of the national treasure, was founded for the worship of a guardian god in 1607. Its festival is very popular, with a parade of carrying a miniature shrine and archery on horseback as a ritual. This shrine is near the masonry settlement, so the Sendai sparrow dance was dedicated in the festival of Hachimangu, and a group for the preservation of the orthodox sparrow dance has also been organized with the support of shrine parishioners.

In addition to Osaki Hachimangu, there is Sendai Toshogu, where Ieyasu Tokugawa, the founder of the Edo Shogunate, is enshrined; this shrine is designated as a nationally important cultural asset, and it had been popular to have floats at the festival of Toshogu. However, because of urbanization, it became more difficult to parade floats and so the float event was lost for decades. In addition, there is the Aoba Shrine, where Masamune Date, the feudal lord of Sendai, is enshrined; its festival is also popular, with a parade of miniature shrine. Combining these festival customs, the sparrow dance with *ohayashi*, the parade of miniature shrines, and that of floats, the Sendai Aoba festival began in 1985. The festival as a hybrid of festival cultures in Sendai is held every year, mobilizing roughly 800,000 spectators.

The sparrow dance and its *ohayashi* that are performed at the Sendai Aoba festival are not orthodox but are arranged in a contemporary style that is relatively easy for a broad range of people to dance along with or to play. The governing organization of the Sendai Aoba festival conducts a promotion group of the sparrow dance and *ohayashi* and holds citizen-oriented lessons periodically.

In this case, the *ohayashi* of the sparrow dance is the ordinary kind with the general composition of bamboo flutes, drums, and gongs; there is neither the *samisen* nor the harmonica, and it is not designated as a cultural asset. However, it is interesting that the process in which the dance of masonry was expanded to a civic dance and the formative process of the historical image of Sendai city intensifying the power of Masamune Date as a symbolic figure progressed in a parallel way.

Today, the sparrow dancers and their *ohayashi* players in both Sendai and Osaka, where masons lived, teach their ways to each other. Traditional music is handed down as successors retrace the footsteps of masonry. Sendai is the so-called branch economy of Tokyo, and there are also many people who put down roots in Sendai after job transfers. It could be said that handing down the dance of masonry that was invited to Sendai all the way from Osaka has a special meaning for people who have experienced job transfers.[7]

Sendai residents have great respect for Masamune Date, and his symbolic power is greater than anything. It is repeatedly emphasized in the festival that dancing and playing the music of the masonry sparrow dance that served Masamune Date is veneration to him. There may be cultural norms through which traditional music should determine to whom it is dedicated and should be used to heighten the symbolic power of that entity.

CONCLUSION

The main purpose of this chapter is to examine the cultural norms involving the practice of handing down folk and traditional music. I will briefly organize the findings from the five case studies into a conclusion.

First, from the case of Hanawa-Bayashi, it was considered to be a successor's mission to retrace its roots, with the specific desire for the traditional music to have its roots in Kyoto, the center of historical culture or aristocratic culture. However, the searches for such roots have not always produced desirable results. As a result, local folk music successors came to learn the fact that succession had once stopped but was revitalized by geisha girls, strolling blind musicians, and farmers other than local residents. At the same time, trying to learn the "truth" by the objective criticism of historical materials is also considered part of the sincere nature of succession. Thus there is the cultural norm that traditional music should be equal to academic verification while providing people with the historical pleasure of having traced their roots.

Next, from the case of Kosaka-Tanabata, it seems that people are proud of their cultural hybridity, which was brought by the itinerant miners, rather than trying to trace the origin of their music with no exact roots. In other words, it is an essential practice of reinforcing identity to search for a fictional ancestor in local history. Using the short-cut rail of the truck and the harmonica imported during the golden age of the mine is an aspect of the musical style that is specified by the reproduction of the local image of a mining town. There, we can find the cultural norm that the traditional music has to represent diversity, hybridity, and a progressive nature.

Third, from the case of the Nobiru Harbor construction, it could be said that people today sometime "discover" local folk music under "institutional reflexivity" (Beck et al., 1994), which is the nature of utilizing history to build history. The folk song with no name, which sang of the past prosperity of Nobiru Harbor, was almost forgotten. However, in Nobiru, where people had been left behind by the marine business, the railroads, cars, and the "history of mobility," singing the folk song to learn the history of harbor construction is finally considered what they need. After the Great East Japan Earthquake, the meaning of this folk song has increased more. There, we can see the cultural norm that local folk music has to sing of the history of people who are not in the mainstream.

Fourth, from the case of the Yosakoi-Soran, we explore the process by which traditional music diffuses at once. By the fusion of Yosakoi and Soran, a style of music was produced that was easier to dance along to in the street. Moreover, the local music is arranged in a modern style, and it is also easy to teach young people because of the simple principle of using the melody of origin and dancing with a *naruko*. The style of the Yosakoi-Soran, as a participatory event from which the effect of regional vitalization is expected, rapidly expanded all over the place. In recent years, "Yosakoi-Soran" was registered as a trademark and the festival became a business. The company that makes the Yosakoi-Soran's music and clothes was established, and a vocational school that develops talented people to perform the Yosakoi-Soran was also established. There, traditional music has the cultural norm that it is more desirable to induce an economic effect while functioning as a stage of new creation.

Last, from the case of the Sendai sparrow dance, through the process by which the music of masons was transformed to that of ordinary citizens, traditional music has played the role of amplifying the power of a symbol. The Sendai sparrow dance is performed with *ohayashi* from the masons who were invited from Osaka to construct a castle for Masamune Date, the feudal lord of the Edo Period. This *ohayashi* was originally played by masons to cheer themselves up while carrying stones, and it has been dedicated to the temple where they prayed for their safety at work. Masamune Date, the feudal lord, has national popularity even now, and the *ohayashi* of the sparrow dance is strengthening the power of this symbol. Dance and *ohayashi* lessons for ordinary citizens are now offered periodically, and the successors increase in number every year. Here, we can see the cultural norm that traditional music should be a symbol of unity and increase sympathy for it.

In these ways, various cultural norms have been formed at the scenes of handing down folk and traditional music, and those who can conform to such norms with ownership became successors. The future of folk and traditional music is up to such reflexive people and their historical imagination. In the meantime, the music should be flexible so that people can interpret the music in many ways. The diversity and flexibility of music are deeply connected to the characteristics of the region where the music is rooted.

NOTES

1. As Walter (1982) argues, there is a distinction between the physical carrying capacity and the perceptual capacity of a tourist site. Thus, even if a tourist site has sufficient physical carrying capacity, sometimes it does not have enough capacity to satisfy the perceptual desires of tourists.

2. Lowenthal (1985) defines the concept of nostalgia as "memory with the pain taken out" (p. 8). In handing down cultural heritages, the accompanying memories should be sorted out.

3. "Their own memories of a way of life in which economic hardship and exploited labour were offset by a sense of community, neighbourliness and mutuality" are essential for the integration of local residents (Mellor, 1991, p. 100).

4. Global stages have emerged to preserve the cultural heritages of "little platoons" and the memories of the people who were bombarded by the state (Urry, 2000, p. 157). The discarded industrial heritages have become preserved, for example, railway engines, canals, and derelict coal mines (Corner & Harvey, 1991; Dicks, 1997). On the surface, these things appear to represent the strength of the modern nation. However, in fact, these are not "the national past" but memory devices for the little platoons that survived in serious condition.

5. As hooks (1991) notes, "home is no longer one place. It is locations" (p. 148).

6. For the people who belong to mobile communities and take on variable identities depending on the context, it is quite easy to share contingent relationships with others (Plant, 1997).

7. Berman (1983) characterizes the nature of urban capital as a "maelstrom of perpetual disintegration and renewal" and states that through this process, we always plan strategies "to make oneself somehow at home" (pp. 15, 345).

REFERENCES

Anderson, B. (1983). *Imagined community*. London: Verso.

Appadurai, A. (1990). Disjuncture and difference in the global cultural economy. *Theory, Culture, and Society*, *7*, 295–310.

Bauman, Z. (2000). *Liquid modernity*. Cambridge: Polity.

Beck, U., Giddens, A., & Lash, S. (1994). *Reflexive modernization: Politics, tradition and aesthetics in the modern social order*. Cambridge: Polity.

Beckerman, W. (1974). *In defense of economic growth*. London: Jonathan Cape.

Berman, M. (1983). *All that is solid melts into air: The experience of modernity*. London: Verso.

Corner, J., & Harvey, S. (Eds.) (1991). *Enterprise and heritage*. London: Routledge.

Culler, J. (1981). Semiotics of tourism. *American Journal of Semiotics*, *1*, 127–40.

Dicks, B. (1997). The life and times of community. *Time and Society*, *6*, 196–212.

hooks, B. (1991). *Yearning: Race, gender and cultural politics*. London: Turnaround.

Lowenthal, D. (1985). *The past is a foreign country*. Cambridge: Cambridge University Press.

Mellor, A. (1991). Enterprise and heritage in the dock. In J. Corner & S. Harvey (Eds.), *Enterprise and heritage* (pp. 93–115). London: Routledge.

Meyrowitz, J. (1985). *No sense of place*. Oxford: Oxford University Press.

Ogino, M. (2002). *La sociologie des patrimoines: Du Louvre au dome de Hiroshima*. Tokyo: Shinyosha.

Plant, S. (1997). *Zeros and ones*. London: Forth Estate.

Schivelbusch, W. (1986). *The railway journey: Trains and travel in the nineteenth century*. Oxford: Blackwell.

Urry, J. (2000). *Sociology beyond society: Mobilities for the twenty- first century*. London: Routledge.

Walter, J. (1982). Social limits to tourism. *Leisure Studies*, *1*, 295–304.

SCRAPING THE BARREL OF ANALOGUE AMNESIA: THE SOFT RESCUE OF MAGNETIC OBSCURITY OVER THE FINAL EMBERS OF 'EXPANDED' POP STARDOM

Heitor Alvelos

ABSTRACT

Purpose – *This chapter observes the dynamics between various aspects of current pop music production, particularly in respect to digital culture, and the preservation and access challenges faced by a wealth of analogue sound artefacts. I argue for the need to consider the activity of 'fringe piracy' – that is online music distribution that specialises in out-of-print analogue editions and bootleg trading – as worthy of civic merit: as participatory heritage recovery, preservation and dissemination.*

Methodology – *I narrate and interpret a series of contexts pertaining to deep changes in popular music production and consumption in the last decade. I will do so primarily by focusing on online activity, while*

Music and Law
Sociology of Crime, Law and Deviance, Volume 18, 167–178

ISSN: 1521-6136/doi:10.1108/S1521-6136(2013)0000018011

unravelling its relationships with traditional modes of music production, dissemination and consumption (i.e. the music industry as defined by vinyl records, cassettes and CDs throughout the second half of the Twentieth Century). I further contrast the mechanics of 'grey areas' of online music access against mainstream web platforms such as iTunes. The author has performed extensive participant observation throughout various online platforms in the last decade, particularly the ones mentioned along the chapter. Additional content has been developed as a consequence of both online and offline discussions, as well as conference panels and symposia (Codebits, 2010; South By South West, 2011; Syracuse University London, 2011).

Findings – *I argue that the current, wide field of possibilities for music production and dissemination stands in radical contrast with an ongoing and strengthened orthodoxy on the part of media labels and distributors. I further argue that, in contrast with this orthodoxy that stems from consumer culture, an exponential availability of recording and editing tools is encouraging a discreet civic mission of digital transcription, and subsequent historical preservation, of analogue artefacts that would otherwise face the prospect of fading into obscurity and possible definitive loss. This, however, seems to be occurring in gradual oblivion of contextual placement, but rather in line with a culture of interchangeable sampling of a purely sensorial and/or affective nature.*

Originality – *Most debates on the subject of music piracy tend to focus on a polarisation of the underlying issues, while mainly addressing its legal and political aspects. There is a need to unravel the cultural, aesthetic and civic parameters that emerge from a phenomenon that is, ultimately, anything but polarised: instead, one finds it is paved with complexity and ambivalence.*

Keywords: Analogue preservation; music piracy; cultural heritage; Sharity

INTRODUCTION

The year is 2013, and it is becoming increasingly difficult to remember how life felt before the Internet. Similarly, online access in the early days of Internet dissemination seems a distant, clumsy experiment devoid of flow, albeit bursting with intensity of experience: dial-up access was slow and intermittent, but when it worked it opened the gates to late-night discussions in newsgroups, the intuition of post-geography and the wonderment of shared information and knowledge. The odd picture or sound file would surface, painfully slow in revealing itself, yet already hinting at the prospect of audiovisual abundance as data transfer speeds themselves promised to increase.

Yet perhaps what was unexpected was not so much the current abundance of audiovisual content, but rather its ubiquity. Current online content stands in contrast with the above scenario: multiple video connectivity, the demand for edutainment, plug-in-driven, self-regulated audiovisual production, the replacement of unmediated perception by continuous recording of daily existence – all is now, literally, at the pressing of a seamless gadget. Yet this all seems to betray a default expectation of constant immersion, a sense of connectivity as a given, an absence of effort. And with this absence of effort a lack of engagement seems to surface.

"You've never been so easily entertained", touts the slogan on the iTunes website as of 2 May 2013. The expectation that music content is, first and foremost, about providing easy entertainment creates and consolidates a mode of listening that seems fairly devoid of investment. Recommendations based on prior purchases, low-bitrate sound files, impeccably groomed youth, neatly identified genres, random audio playback: it all seems to foster a lack of adventure, and this lack of adventure (Jean Baudrillard would no doubt call it the *simulation* of adventure) seems to be the default mode of music access and consumption for the large majority of citizens with continuous, multi-platform online access.

DISCRETION AS KEY TO ENGAGEMENT

A parallel model of music access and engagement has flourished in relative obscurity for a decade now. While the embers of Napster cooled down as its first incarnation as the founder of peer-to-peer content exchange succumbed to widely covered court cases and subsequent bankruptcy, a discreet paradigm shift went public in the early hours of 1 January 2003.

On that date, a website named 'The 365 Days Project' launched, and its authors, a loose collective of amateur audio archivists, proposed to reward the faithful daily visitor with one 'cool and strange and often obscure audio selection' per day throughout the whole year. One must remember the almost complete absence of online social networks at that point in time, as well as the fact that most users accessed the Internet via dial-up modem:

these were the very early days of the home implementation of broadband or ISDN, a privilege of few: downloading one audio track for everyone else could, *in extremis*, take various hours to accomplish.

The proto-aesthetics present in the 365 Days Project, implicit rather than rendered visible, revealed an inclination towards former editorial experiments in Exotica compilations in the 1990s (as epitomised by the Ultra-Lounge compilation CD series, started by Capitol Records in 1996), thematic re-visitations of forgotten vinyl tracks carefully edited and re-packaged in CD format for post-modern consumption. Yet a series of particular aspects stood apart in the context of the 365 Days Project: the fact that the curatorship was ensured by a collective of regular web users, rather than music label experts; the sheer temporal length of the exercise; and, most importantly, the significant widening of the provenance spectrum of artefacts in order to embrace home recordings, lo-fi audio documents, spoken word, sounds that resist categorisation. The 'Utica Club National Carbonation Beer Drinking Song' gave way to home recordings of radio shows denouncing 'Hidden & Satanic Messages In Rock Music', which in turn gave way to extracts from a full LP of heart sounds to be heard 'Only with Stethescope' [SIC] and a Hindi rendition of ABBA's hit 'Dancing Queen': one literally never knew what to expect next. And most importantly in this context, all were free for immediate downloading.

Free, the ambivalent term whose distinct sorts of impact have been thoroughly dissected by Anderson (2009), was an obvious given in the labour of love that was the 365 Days Project; besides, the sheer oddity of most of its content would most likely discourage potential consumers from paying. In truth, a significant part of the content in this Project was copyrighted, and could technically be considered piracy; yet the collective rightly posited it was possible (and actually easy) to traverse the tightrope of legality, as the overwhelming majority of this copyrighted content was long out of print, and the copyright holders would, if anything, potentially benefit from this exposure, however small. A disclaimer offered to take down any content at the request of the respective copyright holders, and this in fact did occur once (on 21 January 2003). All other content is available to this day in online archive form (it is worth mentioning that a second edition of the 365 Days Project took place throughout 2007, faithfully replicating the purpose and underlying structure of the original project. However, the momentum seemed to be gone, and it didn't quite conquer the same enthusiasm or commitment among fringe music communities).

As broadband access disseminated, and as the standard for home and private Internet access and download speeds increased, the expectation of larger quantities of online content to be accessed rose accordingly. The steady 'diet' of one track per day was therefore soon replaced by a flood of digitised vinyl of obscure provenance: thus the Sharity community was born, and flourished via the dissemination and dynamics of broadband and blogging. If the 365 Days Project was still defined by a 'one-to-many' editorial structure, the then-nascent 'music blogs' were the shattering of this scenario, as they adopted a de-centralised, unstable and networked and mode of cooperation. The underlying logic, however, remained: a substantial segment of what was being shared in these 'music blogs' was copyrighted, yet as long as the content was out of print, there was a tacit understanding that no harm was being done, as there were no actual sales to be sacrificed. The principle of takedown at the copyright holder's request was generally followed as well, as was the principle that stated that, should any of this content be the object of a commercial re-release in digital format, the vinyl transfer would equally be taken down.

SHARITY GOES MEGA

This basic code of ethics would soon be superseded by a flood of actual pirate blogs dedicated to free dissemination of in-print musical content, some blogs going as far as specialising in making pre-releases of the latest pop albums and chart-toppers freely available to anyone with Internet access. The advent and gradual rise in popularity of one-click hosts such as Rapidshare and Megaupload ensured a conundrum that took years to clarify in legal terms: users would upload a confidential, often password-protected file to one or various of the file hosting companies; they would then provide the link(s) via a personal blog, while providing links to a broader network of other music-sharing sites. The catch came soon enough: free downloading was severely limited, whether in terms of number of music files, allocated bandwidth and/or download speed; in order to keep up with the flood of available music and download unlimited files simultaneously, users had to purchase premium accounts with these one-click hosts, who in turn rewarded frequent uploaders, allegedly with a percentage of this profit. Free music became not-so-free, after all: its price tag was simply being diverted elsewhere.

File host companies thus began in effect profiting from users' uploads, and this in effect constituted an early sign of the current trend that shifts away from content production to service provision and interface usability:

away from artists, music labels and promoters, into the hands of unofficial distributors whose main attraction would be an indiscriminate ease of access. Sign up, click once, the whole World opens up. Furthermore, the sheer volume of available musical content began pointing towards a divorce between the ownership of music content (regardless of its legality) and the actual enjoyment of this content: it became possible to download music at much faster rates than it was actually possible to listen to it all.

Meanwhile, a conundrum took shape: host companies denied responsibility over content uploaded by their users, music uploaders took advantage of the confidentiality clauses regarding both content and identity offered by the host companies and blog hosts in turn denied responsibility over the content of their users' blogs. A link is simply a link, it was stated. All this essentially stemmed out of the legal vacuum originated by such exponentially rapid rise of digital capacity and speed of transmission. The media was simply too new and too *radical* to be contained within former legal readings. The exploitation of this ambivalence went further, involving digital payment platforms such as PayPal and the strategic location of mediators in countries where this legal vacuum could be further ensured. Rapidshare even went as far as moving its operations from Germany to Switzerland in 2007, most likely as a consequence of the approval of tighter laws regarding music distribution in Germany (the timing coincided). A court injunction actually took place in January 2007, whereby GEMA, the German Society for Musical Performing and Mechanical Reproduction Rights, attempted to minimise alleged damages for copyright infringement. Since then, Rapidshare has walked a legal tightrope of counter-argumentation and measured implementations to ensure the ongoing viability of its business.

This legal no man's land soon became the centre of the debate, and reached its apex in the Megaupload raid of January 2012, along with the proposed U.S. Stop Online Piracy Act of October 2011. This hardened landscape opened up the gates for a politicisation of cultural artefacts, rapidly obscuring the fact that not all content could be neatly categorised, not all issues of profit could be promptly deciphered. The fact is underneath the unresolved controversies of piracy, a civic service was still somehow being performed.

Shirky (2010) proposes a fundamental distinction between two types of vocation for social networks: communal, when the network concerned their own internal narratives, and civic, when the mission is the betterment of external contexts. Somehow inadvertently, Sharity communities fulfilled the characteristics and expectations of both types: they primarily flourished for the enjoyment of their members' thirst for the outer limits of exotic, quasi-extinct musical heritage, yet simultaneously inaugurated a loose, collective endeavour of digital transcription of otherwise doomed historical audio documents. The problem, it seemed, was that this original ambition was at some point 'bundled' with a wider territory of indiscriminate dissemination of music content, regardless of context or availability. Yet could it be that even the unauthorised sharing of copyrighted content could ultimately benefit the artist?

BORN-AGAIN BOOTLEGGING

Sharing niche content on the fringes of mainstream was obviously not new, and the ambition to preserve otherwise lost musical content through webs of transcription or documentation may be observed in the unauthorised recordings of live concerts, also known as bootlegs. Fan-made audience recordings are as old as popular music itself, and while a loose fan network based on the aim of recording live shows for personal enjoyment and memory amplification soon gave way to a parallel, illegal industry in its own right (detailed by Neylin, 2003), digital environments have meanwhile re-established a balance towards the former. It is also worthy of note that not all musicians maintain a hostile viewpoint towards unofficial recordings made by fans: The Grateful Dead not only authorised the recording if their concerts by audience members, they often reserved the seats with best acoustics in order to accommodate those who wish to do so. As a direct consequence of this authorisation, the Grateful Dead now have an exclusive section dedicated to their live heritage on archive.org, and as such may well be the most well-documented live band in popular music.

It is important to point out that a significant part of this music archiving work actually takes place within closed, discreet communities: namely, peer-to-peer networks that specialise in the dissemination of unreleased music content. While technically dedicating themselves to illegal activity, as they do share recordings that are unauthorised by the authors, these invitation-only communities have flourished discreetly by ensuring a zero tolerance observation of a series of internal rules:

- Absolutely no content that has been released by official channels.
- At the artist's request, his/her work may be stopped from being shared.
- Users must maintain a fair upload/download ratio.

These online 'bootleg' networks themselves cultivate a profound disdain for the act of selling unauthorised recordings, and as such regard themselves as providing a service of cultural preservation of music content, as well as helping ensure others do not profit from an artist's work. A 'hall of mirrors' emerges, whereby musicians have themselves, in specific cases, reclaimed these bootleg recordings and re-released them as historical documents. Robert Fripp stands as a prime example of this re-appropriation: since establishing his own online music distribution platform (DGMlive), Fripp has steadily provided (i.e. sold) various audience recordings of early King Crimson concerts that would most likely not have survived, were it not for the persistence of bootleg trading networks, first via analogue tape, subsequently via peer-to-peer activity.

SKYROCKETING SALES

The debate returns, then: how much of this bootleg activity actually does damage sales? How much of it is about the author being able to control their own output? A further entanglement of this paradox may come via, of all places, the Monty Python YouTube channel. While not an example stemming from the music context, and certainly not an episode involving bootlegging, the expressiveness of its facts makes it worthy of mention. In 2008, in apparent frustration with the low quality of VHS transcriptions of their episodes being shared online by fans, Monty Python announced in their YouTube channel:

> For 3 years you YouTubers have been ripping us off, taking tens of thousands of our videos and putting them on YouTube. Now the tables are turned. It's time for us to take matters into our own hands. We know who you are, we know where you live and we could come after you in ways too horrible to tell. But being the extraordinarily nice chaps we are, we've figured a better way to get our own back: We've launched our own Monty Python channel on YouTube. No more of those crap quality videos you've been posting. We're giving you the real thing — high quality videos delivered straight from our vault. What's more, we're taking our most viewed clips and uploading brand new high quality versions. And what's even more, we're letting you see absolutely everything for free. So there! But we want something in return. None of your driveling, mindless comments. Instead, we want you to click on the links, buy our movies & TV shows and soften our pain and disgust at being ripped off all these years.

Humour aside, the outcome of this free availability was alleged to be a 23,000% increase in DVD sales on Amazon. This figure did the rounds on social media and further fuelled the debate on the ambivalence of the main arguments posited by media companies.

This Monty Python online masterstroke may have worked as a re-introduction of a classic body of work to a younger generation, and as such may not be readily translated into other creative contexts, let alone be made into an axiom. Yet it reveals both the interest that people have in *owning* creative content (as opposed, or in addition, to simply streaming it online) and the value of a semantic space of proximity and reciprocity with the audience.

SCRAPING, SQUEEZING, RE-PACKAGING

Focusing momentarily on the interest in ownership, it is clear that this has been maximised for profit by major labels in recent years: music classics keep being re-released periodically, and essentially re-sold to a captive audience that will welcome these 'enhanced' versions of the original product as a vicarious opportunity to travel back to their youth. Pink Floyd's 1973 classic 'Dark Side of the Moon' received its latest re-release in 2011 in the shape of a six-disc set with multiple versions of the original 40-odd-minute LP (original, live, various remastered versions, multi-channel), as well as extensive essays, photos, a scarf, drink coasters and a replica of the 1973 tour ticket: it might essentially be described as a fetishisation of the music experience as a carrier of narrative, a freezing in time of the ageing pop fan in its affection for what that music artefact stood for in their own lives, an embalmed and re-touched time capsule that says little beyond the declaration of its own status as a pop monument. This happens not in replacement of, but concurrently with, a 'digital re-packaging' of musical legacies for use in media platforms, and the loyal fan will gladly acquire both.

Back to Monty Python and the ways in which a 'benevolent' online relationship with illegal sharing of their own, copyrighted content ultimately proved beneficial to the authors. One could probably say those VHS transcriptions maintained a transitional inscription of Monty Python within popular culture, just as YouTube has become host to a multitude of pop music videos that would otherwise have vanished for good – via the analogue-to-digital transcription work of music consumers who may have simply wanted to share their own memories of youth.

THE HIJACKING OF OBLIQUITY

In truth, equivalent music documents on YouTube are usually a lo-fi rendition of the original. Grain-infested, low definition transcriptions of home recordings of 1980s MTV specials; reduced frequency spectrum; fourth-generation, hiss-enhanced cassette recordings from 1970s rock gigs that echo the guitar solo in the back while an over-excited fan screams continuously at the forefront; vinyl pops and cracks betraying the age and wearing of the originals. As such, their appeal is intrinsically detached from mainstream taste and expectations. Yet what this scope of acoustic contingencies does is widen the spectrum for the actual listening experience: it trains the ear towards distinct sound palettes and a more continuous weaving of the music artefact into its surroundings, both physical and semantic. This seems particularly relevant in face of contemporary pop production, where the mastering (and cyclic, revisionist re-mastering) of music artefacts is often made to maximise a 'punchier' sound in detriment of subtlety, to the point of codifying specific acoustic effects such as autotune in lieu of a wide exploration of the vast territories afforded by current sound tools. Additionally, the mp3 format is still the medium of choice in digital mainstream music transactions, particularly due to its convenience in data transfer and storage capacity, often at the cost of sacrificing a significant portion of the intrinsic frequencies of the original recording: it is therefore relevant that most online bootleg peer-to-peer communities only allow the sharing of sound recordings in lossless formats.

In face of the above, it may be no less than ironic that this wider acoustic, conceptual and sensorial spectrum is often ensured by the recovery of analogue artefacts, themselves often made in less than ideal circumstances; yet this is simultaneously revealing of a deeper level of the meanings to be unraveled from 'cultural preservation', no longer strictly referring to the artefact itself but also the quality of one's engagement with it: conceptual investment, acoustic flexibility, contextual awareness.

The 'bombastic' approach to sound dynamics of a significant portion of today's mainstream music production finds an echo in the narratives that stem from this pop milieu. Mainstream culture seems fairly stuck in the mode of superstardom, regardless of the widening of the spectrum and the positing (and indeed, evidence) of a 'Long Tail' (Anderson, 2006). The pop superstar as an anachronism re-enacted in new incarnations that are both easier on the ear and harder on the psyche. Michael Jackson as the ultimate pop star embodied this drama, and this is ultimately why Michael Jackson, the persona, cornered itself into a dead end. He was a transitional figure, and his role was woven within an irreconcilable paradox: an outdated mythology of the superior genius, having to prove its own worth in a context that enables the scrutiny of one's own fabrication as if it were real. Person turned persona, sensual turned surgical, grace grown beyond its own embodiment, a 'cancer' of ever-growing public exposure – somehow replicated in the current mass obsession with the aestheticisation of one's daily life and self taking place in social networks.

As Jackson's heir in the role of pop stardom, Justin Bieber can only aspire at being a caricature of this fable, a random YouTube kid whose future can be played backwards from its inception, re-living the Michael Jackson catastrophe: superstardom replaced either by its own predictable pastiche, or the depths of private wisdom. Could it be that the debate on piracy is essentially a way of helping maintain the spotlight on the noise of the first option? In other words: if all we are provided with, in our radar of music possibilities, is the iTunes model versus the demonised, free downloading of the same content, it comes as no surprise that the debate is polarised. Meanwhile, viral phenomena confirm this self-digesting 'culture of pastiche' by fostering both the fan as the pop star in his/her own right (Britney Spears fan Chris Crocker's 2007 YouTube rant 'Leave Britney Alone' once made him, albeit briefly, more celebrated than Britney herself) and the deconstruction of a craze as a craze in itself from its very inception (the music label for Psy's strident online 'turbo-pop' hit 'Gangnam Style' subsequently sues various makers of its online parodies, including a Danish political party). All this somehow feels as the end-point of the popular culture model that flourished in the second half of the twentieth century, and the hardening of the superstar model as epitomised by Psy could well be its supernova.

CONCLUSION

The use of the expression 'soft rescue' is therefore meant to signal not just the discreet ways in which the Sharity networks continue to make an analogue heritage available beyond the radar of mainstream culture, quietly circumventing copyright laws as it would be too expensive for technical copyright holders to sue: 'soft rescue' conveys the ways in which cultural obliquity struggles in face of the pervasiveness of digital consumerism, even if often presented and celebrated as participatory. Similarly, 'magnetic obscurity' may refer to out-of-print sound artefacts committed to tape, but it may justly apply to the need to maintain an investment on the part of the listener as well: the need for a proximity that can only occur when the artefact provides texture – be in contextual, acoustic or narrative. And that texture, surprisingly, is today more readily available throughout various discarded residues of cultural production, both past and present, flourishing on the ambivalence of legality: in the absence of intrinsic monetary interest, other kinds of investment may blossom. If we are to adopt a spiral, be it a psychoanalysis of cultural production, rather than the dead end of cynicism.

REFERENCES

Anderson, C. (2006). *The long tail: Why the future of business is selling less of more.* New York, NY: Hyperion.

Anderson, C. (2009). *Free: The future of a radical price.* New York, NY: Hyperion.

Crocker, C. (2007). *Leave Britney alone. Home-made video.* Retrieved from www.youtube.com/watch?v=kHmvkRoEowc. Accessed on 2 May 2013.

Neylin, C. (2003). *Bootleg! The rise & fall of the secret recording industry.* London: Omnibus Press.

Pink Floyd. (1973). *The dark side of the moon.* London: EMI.

Shirky, C. (2010). *Cognitive surplus: Creativity and connectivity in a connected age.* London: Allen Lane.

FURTHER READING

'Andy'. (2013). *Universal music tells Gangnam Parody Mayors: Pay $42,000 by tomorrow, or else.* Retrieved from http://torrentfreak.com/universal-music-tells-gangnam-parody-mayors-pay-42000-by-tomorrow-or-else-130530. Accessed on 30 May 2013.

Archive.org. (2013). Retrieved from www.archive.org. Accessed on 18 May 2013.

DGM Live. (2007). Retrieved from www.dgmlive.com. Accessed on 18 May 2013.

iTunes. (2013). Retrieved from www.itunes.com. Accessed 2 May 2013.

Megaupload. (2013). www.megaupload.com. Closed 20 January 2012.

Monty Python. (2008). *Monty Python Channel on YouTube. Promotional video.* Retrieved from http://www.youtube.com/watch?f&v=OGqX-tkDXEk#! Accessed on 2 May 2013.

Monty Python YouTube Channel. (2013). Retrieved from http://www.youtube.com/user/MontyPython/about. Accessed on 2 May 2013.

Pink Floyd. (2011). *The dark side of the moon: Immersion edition. Multi-disc box set.* London: EMI.

Psy. (2012). *Gangnam style. Music video.* Retrieved from https://www.youtube.com/watch?v=9bZkp7q19f0. Accessed on 2 May 2013.

Rapidshare. (2013). Retrieved from www.rapidshare.com. Accessed on May 2 2013.

The 365 Days Project. (2013). *Archives.* Retrieved from http://www.ubu.com/outsiders/365/index.shtml; http://wfmu.org/365. Accessed on 18 May 2013.

Ultra-Lounge. (2013). Retrieved from http://www.ultralounge.com. Accessed on 12 May 2013.

PRISON AND POP

Victor P. Corona

ABSTRACT

Purpose – *This chapter examines how prison spaces are depicted in fictional contexts built around icons of popular music. Given that both icons and inmates occupy spaces that the majority of the population does not observe or experience, I am interested in the degree to which prisons serve as stagings for queer expression, even when inhabited by mainstream music stars.*

Design/methodology/approach – *The lyrical content and visual texts of Elvis Presley's "Jailhouse Rock," Michael Jackson's "They Don't Care About Us," Lady Gaga's "Telephone," as well as material from mainstream musicals like Chicago, are closely analyzed and linked to other scholarly work on prison narratives.*

Findings – *In addition to binding the power of pop iconicity to the experience of incarceration, the musical numbers and cultural artifacts examined here also reveal differing manifestations of queer motifs in their visual and lyrical construction. Mainstream representations of prisons' unique and liminal social orders are therefore considered to be open to queer renderings of affection and provocation.*

Originality/value – *Although prison sexuality is intensely studied by human rights organizations and criminologists, the possibilities for queer*

Music and Law
Sociology of Crime, Law and Deviance, Volume 18, 179–195

ISSN: 1521-6136/doi:10.1108/S1521-6136(2013)0000018012

expression within fictional prison contexts have not been explicitly linked to the pop personas of music superstars and their creative projects.

Keywords: Prison; stardom; popular music; Michael Jackson; Elvis Presley; Lady Gaga

INTRODUCTION

Few places frighten and fascinate like the prison, the designated residence for those considered worthy of medium- to long-term separation from society. Modern systems of laws revolve in large part around the use of incarceration to both punish individuals for their infractions and prepare some of them for reintegration into society. The intended "correcting" of those who have deviated from mainstream rules involves a range of sanctioned practices, including drug abuse treatment, spiritual ministry, vocational training, athletic regimens, and guidance for post-release careers.

When prison scenes are depicted in music videos, films, or television, I suspect that reactions may be divided into at least two camps: the responses of those who have spent time in prison as inmates, visitors, or staff, and those who have not. Like the military or nightlife, unless one has had direct contact with these subcultures, it is difficult to fully make sense of their inimitable phenomenological textures. As of the writing of this chapter, I have visited a prison inmate in a maximum-security correctional facility in upstate New York eight times: the first three times in the prison's separate Special Housing Unit, the latter times in the General Population visiting area, filled with young children, girlfriends, parents, and pastors. Compared with the apprehension that attended my first visit, it is almost humorous to consider that my more recent visits to a grim building adorned in razor wire have become routinized. Like any form of social acclimation, one learns where to go and how to comport oneself, how to casually interact with staff members, or when to hold up your hand against the ultraviolet light to display the coded ink stamp given to visitors.

Popular culture's deployment of prison scenes reveals a unique tension between the marginality of incarceration and the mainstream terrains occupied by pop artifacts. Such representations in mainstream films have attracted substantial analysis from scholars (e.g., Alber, 2011; Ciasullo, 2008; Russo, 1987). My preoccupation here is with popular music, since most pop tracks deal with matters of romance, friendship, adventure, sex, individuality, or melancholy, phenomenological environments that are accessible to virtually everyone. Prison visits, however, are not common experiences, much less incarceration itself. The lifespans of most individuals will not include what must be the utter agony of being confined to a small room from which you cannot voluntarily exit, caged alongside others who stand ready to rob or otherwise harm you, and watched over by armed officials thoroughly unsympathetic to your condition. As Michel Foucault, the great theorist and historian of the prison, writes, "Punishment, then, will tend to become the most hidden part of the penal process. This has several consequences: it leaves the domain of more or less everyday perception and enters that of abstract consciousness..." (2012, p. 9). Since prison constitutes a set of experiences unseen and poorly understood by mainstream populations, the contained set of social relations that prisons configure easily lend themselves to abstraction and romanticization.

This tension between isolated reality and external representation is this chapter's point of departure for an examination of the extent to which a prison may be seen as a *queer space*. To be clear, this is not a criminological study of contemporary prison sexuality. Rather, I am interested in how pop music stars' insertion of themselves into fabricated imprisonments enacts a modality of prison life that is open to queer identity-building both for themselves and for the viewer. As a sociologist interested in new cultural formations that are often based on new performances of gender, I am curious about what Alber (2011) examined as "prison metaphors," especially those that appear open to queer expressions of affection, protest, intimacy, and creativity.

The material to be examined consists of Elvis Presley's "Jailhouse Rock" (1957), Michael Jackson's "They Don't Care About Us" (1996), and Lady Gaga's "Telephone" (2010), as well as other relevant cultural objects. What makes these visual texts so compelling is precisely the fact that "The King of Rock and Roll," "The King of Pop," and a would-be "Queen of Pop" are reduced to uniform-wearing, numeral-inscribed inmates in spaces that afford a fantastical exploration of queer sensuality. The uniqueness of prison liminality is mirrored by the fact that fame is as much of a distinctive experience as prison life, albeit one much harder to achieve. The existence of the famous celebrity is usually upheld as rare, glamorous, and highly coveted, while the life of an inmate is accessible to anyone willing to incur the wrath of the law. What is curious, however, is that celebrities enduring their most woeful moments at times compare their lives to being imprisoned, to being jailed in a cage of glitter and gold. For them, the Panopticon of Jeremy Bentham and Michel Foucault is occupied not by watchful agents of the state but by omnipresent paparazzi, reporters, and fans. Given these divergences and congruences between fame and felony, the following analysis will use three mainstream music numbers as visual texts with which to explore how pop icons perform the prison experience for their audiences. Contexts in popular music, I will argue, create levels of aesthetic layering that emphasize the quality of prisons as queer spaces.

PRISON AS CONTAINER AND INCUBATOR

In the social sciences, the great theorist of the prison and its place as a modern instrument of social configuration is of course Michel Foucault. His *Discipline and Punish* offers tremendous insight into prisons, their internal structures and protocols, and their relationship with prevailing social norms, while other writings and interviews expand on his core theses. Although a full engagement with Foucault's history of the prison is beyond the scope of this chapter, I focus on his interest in the relationship between the criminal's punishment and the broader social body. As Foucault argues, "It is the criminal, in fact, that is needed by the press and public opinion. It is he who will be hated, against whom all the passions will be directed, and for whom the penalty and oblivion will be demanded" (1994, p. 432). The prisoner thereby acquires a functional purpose: a subject is configured against which the animosities of a social order may be directed. As Foucault claims elsewhere, "At the end of the eighteenth century, people dreamed of a society without crime. And then the dream evaporated. Crime was too useful for them to dream of anything as crazy – or ultimately as dangerous – as a society without crime. No crime means no police. What makes the presence of and control of the police tolerable for the population, if not fear of the criminal? This institution of the police, which is so recent and oppressive, is only justified by that fear" (1980, p. 47). Such socially useful roles have been famously depicted in literature, for example, the consequences of moral, religious, and political deviance in Nathaniel Hawthorne's *The Scarlet Letter*, Arthur Miller's *The Crucible*, and George Orwell's *1984*, respectively.

The inverse of such an odious social position is occupied by the great cultural icons whose fame serves as a font that invests significance and inspiration in the lives of the masses. Posters of long dead individuals like Marilyn Monroe, Andy Warhol, James Dean, and Audrey Hepburn still populate storefronts, newsstands, and advertisements, perpetuating their iconicity beyond their mortality. As noted by Herwitz (2008), "Rather than acknowledge that suffering is waste, emptiness, lack of meaning, the cult turns to the suffering of the star icon, makes her aura into something transcendent, identifies with that transcendence, and thus practices a view of the world in which reconciliation with suffering becomes imaginable through her, in which the initiates' own suffering becomes mysteriously elevated" (p. 28). If collective hatred is piled onto the condemned prisoner who makes social life dangerous, curiosity and adulation uplift the revered icon that makes existence glisten.

The repeated representations of prison settings in popular culture mean that a certain lore has arisen involving inmates' social order, sexual norms, and the corruption of prison administrators. And the insertion of these contexts into mainstream television is almost inevitable. It is virtually de rigeur for a sitcom to include a jailhouse episode so as to derive comedic fodder from the spectacle of thrusting the shows' protagonists into a fetid jail cell populated by prostitutes or petty thieves. Hit comedies ranging from *The Golden Girls* to *Everybody Loves Raymond* feature episodes where the main characters somehow find themselves in their local jail. The accompanying innuendo around same-sex romance is inevitable. The storylines of other shows like *Orange Is the New Black, Arrested Development, Oz*, and *Prison Break* revolve around movement into and out of prisons, to say nothing of the many reality television shows depicting the lives of inmates, corrections officers, and parolees. But what is the purpose, then, of depicting culture's most admired and applauded pop music stars in the role of inmate? Although attention-grabbing and shock value certainly feeds into the desirability of such spectacle, I will claim that pop's penetration of such a realm of deviance is predicated on the prison's aesthetic power as a fluid and shifting queer space, less constrained by mainstream norms and thereby providing endless fodder for fantastical representations of "deviant" sensualities.

TIME TO RUMINATE: PRISON AS IDENTITY BUILDER

A casual look at television commercials, billboards, or mass transit ads demonstrates that the summer cinema season is now driven largely by films based on superhero franchises from the two primary comic publishers, DC and Marvel. Sequels, prequels, and reboots featuring the latest in computer-generated imaging explore tales of good and evil originating from characters and storylines developed as far back as the 1930s. Among the most successful of these franchises has been Christopher Nolan's Batman trilogy (*Batman Begins* (2005), *The Dark Knight* (2008), *The Dark Knight Rises* (2012)), which aspired to lend a more modern, realistic air to DC's noir detective mythos. Much of Nolan's "legend" revolves around the narrative locus of a prison. We see prisons as contemplative spaces, murky arenas from which new identities can emerge, whether heroic or villainous. The isolation of incarceration and its life-altering quality afford an opportunity for introspective evaluations of past decisions, present circumstances, and prospects for the future. Some prison contemplations yield results that have cast long shadows over political history, for example, Adolf Hitler's authoring of *Mein Kampf* in Landsberg Prison in 1924 or Evita Perón's visits to her imprisoned husband Juan in 1945 before the initiation of his dictatorship. Of course, some prisoners complete their sentences with a strong commitment to a lawful lifestyle while others become repeat offenders who do not radically alter their behavior following their release.

Before turning to my cases, I want to briefly examine how the prison serves as a contemplative space in the wildly popular Nolan trilogy. In the first film of the series, Bruce Wayne leaves behind an affluent life in Gotham after his wealthy parents are murdered and seeks out criminals in order to understand the pathology that feeds his home city's decay. While in Bhutan, "the prince of Gotham" is jailed and visited in his cell by his would-be mentor and eventual nemesis. From this initial encounter in his cell Wayne is recruited into a secret society from which he would later adapt his own vigilante persona. Wayne returns to Gotham with the intent to fight the mob via his new Batman identity.

In the film's sequel, Gotham's mob bosses retaliate by allying with a maniacal terrorist known as the Joker. After an extravagantly explosive sequence that culminates in the Joker's arrest, the subsequent scenes of his jailing and interrogation at the police headquarters' holding cell are arguably the most dramatic, jarring, and expository of all the character's scenes. Caging the villain affords an opportunity to contemplate his twisted pathology as well as a narrative space within the film for him to articulate a nihilistic, anti-social ethos and enact his iconic antagonism with the Batman.

It is, however, in the trilogy's final film that the prison assumes a central place in the mythos. Bane, the film's main villain, acquires his thoroughly brutal fighting prowess and fierce devotion to destruction in an Escher-like foreign prison known as the "worst hell on earth," where Bane claims to have "learned the truth about despair." After a vicious fight, Bane brings a nearly broken Batman back to the prison, which he comes to control years after escaping. During the hero's imprisoned convalescence and ruminations over how to escape, Bane blasts open Gotham's main prison, which Bane claims is a symbol of the city's irreparable corruption. The Dark Knight eventually finds the inspiration with which to "rise" out of the prison pit. As this brief sketch hopefully makes clear, the prison as a container and incubator is an indispensable narrative motor for Nolan's trilogy. With so much time to ruminate, some prisoners begin legendary heroic journeys, others prepare for murderous rampages, and others expose their utter psychosis.

THE KING, NUMBER 47, AND NUMBER 3

The 1957 film *Jailhouse Rock* traces the rise of construction worker-cum-convict Vince Everett played by "The King," Elvis Presley. Everett acquires musical training while serving a prison sentence that he later develops successfully into a career as a recording artist. From the perspective of the sociology of fame, the film illustrates constants in how a celebrity persona is produced that existed in the 1950s and persist even today, for example, cajoling DJs into playing a song or negotiating personal relationships in business contexts. Presley's character must manage his obligations to past compatriots and sift through his own feelings toward his gorgeous business manager.

Other conflicts for the nascent superstar are peculiar to the time period, for example, navigating the transition from gaining airplay on the radio to developing a televisual presence. (The novelty of the TV terrain for recording artists was perhaps analogous to the rise of YouTube and social media today.) Everett sings the film's title track when NBC organizes a "nationwide television extravaganza" and invites him to participate in the broadcast. The number is staged in a stylized and austere cellblock setting with Everett and the other prisoners wearing identical black-and-white stripe shirts underneath black jackets. During the number, dancing to the jailhouse rock song involves twirling around a firepole, sliding down a long cafeteria table, and culminates with even the prison guards joining in as they merrily spin their batons.

Although the performance is fairly straightforward and mundane, some of the lyrics raised eyebrows for the same-sex prison relationship that they cheekily evoke. Presley sings about two inmates that he identifies by their prison numbers, 47 and 3. The first addresses the other as "the cutest jail-bird" ever seen. The prisoner initiating the exchange says that he would be "delighted" with the other's company and invites him to join in the Jailhouse Rock. Given the thoroughly masculine quality of most Presley films and his overall persona, the insertion of a romantically suggestive comment among male inmates, even sung in the third person, is unusual. If it was merely innocuous banter one could imagine Presley employing the first person, but this scenario is largely unthinkable. More importantly, as soon as the verses are sung we see an inmate playfully touch another inmate's face and exchange a caress of hands, followed by joyful dancing alongside Presley.

It is interesting that even in a black-and-white 1957 film the liminal place of the prison affords some space, however brief and constrained, of queer suggestion. Despite the insinuation of same-sex flirtation among inmates, including an invitation to dance and share "company," the intensely masculine reading of the scene and the film in general is not jeopardized by the lyrics. In fact, during a concert aired on CBS in December 2007 called "Movies Rock," recording artist Chris Brown, who attracted vigorous public outrage for his battery of then girlfriend Rihanna, sang the complete "Jailhouse Rock," even pointing to a male backup dancer as he sang the "cutest jailbird" portion.

The lack of access to heterosexual intimacy in prisons and the violently maintained status hierarchies have long been held as viable explanations for male inmates' indulgence of same-sex relations while incarcerated. While the prison social context could afford an opportunity to explore sexual preferences unavailable to them outside prison walls, sex among inmates is more often rape by prisoners seeking to fulfill libidinal desire as well as assert their dominance. As watchdog groups have documented, for example, Human Rights Watch (2001), although violent rape is often at the heart of prison sexual relations, more subtle forms of coercion can also compel sex among inmates. Access to material goods and contraband may be exchanged for sexual acts. According to Human Rights Watch, "…an inmate hierarchy exists by which certain prisoners enjoy a great deal of power over their fellows and other prisoners are exposed to exploitation and abuse" (2001). The implications of the "Jailhouse Rock" flirtation are therefore potentially deviant in a double sense: the initiation of a queer romance that defies the hegemonic masculinity of the King's iconicity as well as a potentially coercive interaction among inmates of unequal status.

Other films like *The Shawshank Redemption* (1994), based on a Stephen King novella, also take on the issue of sexual abuse in prisons. *Shawshank* features a group of male prisoners known as the "Sisters" who repeatedly and violently rape the story's protagonist (see Alber, 2011). Curiously, the film limits deviance from sexual norms to a band of aggressive rogues while largely leaving the main protagonists (played by Tim Robbins and Morgan Freeman) in the sanitized realm of friendly reminiscences, playful heterosexual banter, and personal art projects.

But abuse and homosexual relations are not relegated to Hollywood depictions of male prisons. Ciasullo (2008) offers a rich examination of female inmates' depiction in film. She observes certain constants. For example, "Whereas the straight female protagonist is almost always released from prison, the 'true' lesbian almost always remains – or dies – in prison" (Ciasullo, 2008, p. 205). The 1950 film *Caged* examines the arrival of a young woman in prison who clashes with a domineering butch matron. The image of the masculinized woman presiding over blocks of female prisoners is itself an interesting cultural figure, but other scenes among inmates make clear the extent to which sexual deviance accompanies punishment for unlawful deviance outside of prison. As a much older female inmate advises the newly jailed young woman, "If you stay in here too long you don't think of guys at all. You just get out of the habit." The implications of her remark are stark. The prison is effectively *too much* of a liminal space, such that heterosexual attraction may be elided from a woman's identity over time.

Consider a more lighthearted case in the 2002 film *Chicago* (based on the musical of the same name by Fred Ebb and Bob Fosse), particularly Matron Mama Morton, the so-called "Mistress of Murderers' Row" at Cook County Jail. Her musical number "When You're Good to Mama" is a rather sardonic declaration of the ineluctable law of quid pro quo that characterizes prison life and the informal status hierarchy to which I alluded earlier. The song celebrates what Morton refers to as "reciprocity," an institutional social order in which she manages the traffic of contraband and press access in exchange for payments and favors. Her song suggests that when a basket for contributions is passed around, one should contribute, given that one "putting in" for Morton will mean that she will, in turn, "put out" for them. The double entendre evokes both sexual availability as well as procurement of prison contraband. Given that her colleagues and wards are all females, the queer nature of her power stands in relief. Also, the character is played by Queen Latifah, who has herself been the subject of tabloid speculation about lesbian relationships. Perhaps unsurprisingly, Mama Morton falls in line with the imagery of the masculinized, cunning matron seen in *Caged*. When Morton first meets the film's blonde protagonist, she remarks, "Ain't you the pretty one?" as she caresses her flaxen hair. While leading the new arrival to her cell, Morton is seen distributing contraband, casually slapping the thighs of the female inmates she oversees.

THE KING OF POP CARES ABOUT US

In addition to prisons offering a space for individual contemplation of personal ambitions and failings, I also argue that they can be spaces for an articulation of queer reactions to and provocations of broader social currents. To pursue this line of inquiry, consider Michael Jackson's 1996 album *HIStory: Past, Present and Future, Book I*, which included the controversial "They Don't Care About Us" track that yielded two videos directed by another controversy magnet, Spike Lee. The first video was set in a Brazilian favela with Jackson surrounded by an energetic drum corps and festive local children. The colorful imagery was largely celebratory and meant to tidily fit into Jackson's image as a globetrotting humanitarian at ease with impoverished Third World communities. A second video took on a darker and more strident flavor by placing Jackson in two prison spaces: behind bars in his own cell and in the prison cafeteria amid what appears to be an incipient riot. It is a peculiar context to be inhabited by the "King of Pop," who at times seemed so ensnared by his fame, the demands of his family, and the ambiguities of his racial and gender identities (see Nyong'o, 2011).

The video begins with African-American children in a playground singing behind a chain-link fence, which simulates a kind of urban caging. The video then moves to the prison setting, beginning with a cafeteria filled with prisoners in blue uniforms angrily pounding tables. The viewer then peers into a cell holding Jackson, also dressed in blue prison overalls. Multiple monitors that appear to have burst through the walls flash images of the Rodney King beating, the Tiananmen Square massacre, Klu Klux Klan rallies, and violent protests, all images that have become seared into the public consciousness as symbols of division and conflict. The projections and Jackson's performances are clearly intended to augment a sensation of rage and frustration at an unjust status quo. Using special effects, the video culminates with Jackson's frenzied dances within the panorama of violent projections, literally interweaving himself into the narrative of social pain.

It is important to note how the placement of the track's sung set of statements about social justice amidst incarcerated convicts binds political protest to the country's incarcerated population. Although groups like Human Rights Watch have documented abuse in the so-called "prison-industrial complex," one simply cannot presume that the majority of inmates have been sentenced unjustly. The durability of Jackson's visual association of resistance to the Klan or Chinese Communism with the prison population is neither straightforward nor readily convincing. The video itself appears to be reluctant to fully commit to this interpolation. The inmates' pounding and yelling in the cafeteria never reaches the crescendo of an actual riot. Instead, the video ends as so many of Jackson's appearances finished: with vigorous applause. The fact that the wild gesticulations of Jackson's pale and thin frame are being cheered by a tightly-packed room of muscular male inmates lends the video a curiously queer flavor, particularly given tabloid speculation about Jackson's own sexuality. The video's last image takes yet another visual leap away from the entire locus of the video by finishing with an image from the first "They Don't Care About Us" video: Jackson running up the stairs of a favela.

The track attracted controversy for lyrics construed by some to be anti-Semitic. Jackson responded to the press by claiming, "I am the voice of everyone. I am the skinhead, I am the Jew, I am the black man, I am the white man. I am not the one who was attacking. It is about the injustices to young people and how the system can wrongfully accuse them" (Weinraub, 1995). Of course, it is impossible to know the full extent of Jackson's intentions when writing the song although he did spend much of his career augmenting his role as the "King of Pop" with various humanitarian gestures, perhaps most infamously via his Neverland Ranch in California. Therefore, the desire to inhabit such disparate identities could be read as the hubris of a self-designated savior. Alternatively, it is the plea of a man whose uncertain and clashing identities facilitate a queer will to be everything and nothing all at once.

Other lyrics are also interesting in terms of symbolic postures. Jackson appeals to two left-of-center political icons: Martin Luther King, Jr., and Franklin D. Roosevelt. The MLK appeal makes sense given the racial aspect of the incarceration debate, but to cry out to President Roosevelt seems somewhat tenuous with regard to lyrical and visual composition.

It is also useful to note that the *HIStory* album was released two years after child molestation accusations were leveled against Jackson. Accusations of intimacy with young boys fed rumors about his sexuality that even pulled in his dancing, mannerisms, and voice as "evidence" of homosexuality. Jackson's potentially queer identity was read as strange and unlawful, hence "Wacko Jacko." The album was a clear attempt to recuperate the King of Pop's diminished stardom. From this perspective it is not surprising that the prison video for "They Don't Care About Us" (and some elements of the favela video) is intended to be contemplative, political, and polemic. Whether or not the denunciatory quality of the montage was intended to distract from Jackson's embarrassing litigation, it is clear that his exploration of this semiotic and political terrain is not straightforward, especially given Jackson's ambiguous identities as related to his gender, race, and age. It is nonetheless interesting and important to observe that Jackson and his artistic advisors chose prison settings as the visual context for his contemplation of injustice. It is even more remarkable that even the space in which he challenges some of the most grievous human rights abuses of the twentieth century culminates in his veneration by a mob-cum-audience.

CALLING A NEW QUEEN

During the time that I prepared this chapter, television channels and YouTube regularly aired an advertisement for Boost Mobile in which the multiyear contracts that still dominate cellular telephony were equated with incarceration. A woman is led past panoramas of everyday people who unfortunately find themselves behind bars due to their contracts with phone companies. She begrudgingly signs a "Wireless Contract" and is then jailed. The commercial ends with her apparent tweet: "Cell contracts are lame... I'm on lockdown for a couple years!!!" Cell phones thereby imply prison cells. The absence of the market imperative in which a consumer can freely switch among brands is rendered comparable to long-term incarceration. This is one small example, I believe, of the extent to which prisons repeatedly attract commercial attempts to adopt and adapt its bleak and largely hidden spaces.

As I have discussed, prisons necessarily constrain the availability of heterosexual intimacy, while an informal status hierarchy emerges among inmates according to racial identity, gang affiliation, and sexual domination. This is not to suggest that genuinely strong and affective ties cannot be developed among queer friends and intimate partners, although it is important to note that the nature and variety of prison sexuality, of course, is far too complex to examine properly here. Instead, I wish to further examine the affordances of the prison as a queer space in popular culture via Lady Gaga's "Telephone" (2010) music video. As my discussion of

Elvis Presley's "Jailhouse Rock" and Michael Jackson's polemical prison video for "They Don't Care About Us" indicates, prisons may be spaces that permit queer suggestiveness. As I will claim, answering the call of Gaga's "Telephone" demonstrates the possibilities of new assemblies of queer bodies by a fresh generation of pop icons in the digital age of dense interconnectedness.

I have devoted a significant portion of my teaching and writing to the body of work developed by Lady Gaga since her 2009 album *The Fame Monster* album consolidated her ascendancy into the pop music firmament (Corona, 2011). Her video for the "Bad Romance" single retains its position as one of the most watched YouTube videos with nearly 530,000,000 views as of this writing. Her second *Fame Monster* single "Telephone" further solidified her position as a recording artist whose ambition appeared to go beyond the usual simplistic bubblegum formulae of pop princesses. Since then, several researchers have attempted to more closely examine the nature of her creativity and career, including Deflem (2012, 2013), Gray (2012), and Halberstam (2012).

Gaga's "Telephone" video, which was directed by Jonas Åkerlund and also featured Beyoncé, amounted to a short film at over nine minutes. Perhaps her most Warholian aesthetic statement to date, the video continued the narrative initiated in her 2009 "Paparazzi" video in which a young starlet poisons her abusive boyfriend and confesses to his murder. As a consequence of her crime, the "Telephone" video shows Gaga being escorted to her cell in a "Prison for Bitches" comprised of "gender deviants and unruly women" (Horn, 2012, p. 100), given that even the prison guards are transgender. The music video is appropriate for my discussion given that it is "not a comment on actual prisons so much as on the prison of representation itself and the formulaic sign systems we use to represent otherness" (Halberstam, 2012, p. 62).

Of course, the humorous conceit of the video is that the song's actual lyrics recount the experience of being unable to hear someone on the telephone while at a club but what the viewer actually *sees* consists of prison recreation and leisure time, exit from incarceration, a desert road trip, and mass murder. As Switaj mentions, the video "includes discord between the body that the lyrics indicate and that which the visual information indicates. She starts out with the stigmatized and abused body of a prisoner, stripped by guards who want to confirm her biological sex..." (Switaj, 2012, p. 46). After being stripped by the butch prison guards, the blurred image of Gaga's exposed crotch appears in a visually aggressive effort to end tabloid speculation that she was a hermaphrodite. She later ventures into the prison yard, where she shares a passionate kiss with a masculine, leather-clad female inmate, all while Gaga's body is wrapped by chains that recall the mirror of Venus. She eventually leaves prison accompanied by Beyoncé, whom she affectionately calls "Honey B" in a set of scenes that evoke the Thelma and Louise partnership often claimed as part of queer cinema. Gaga and Honey B go on to commit mass murder by poisoning the patrons of a roadside diner, becoming a kind of queer killer duo in the lineage of Valerie Solanas (Halberstam, 2012), Aileen Wuornos, or even Leopold and Loeb (Schildcrout, 2011).

Various scholars have noted the degree to which "Telephone" represents a visually and sonically rich statement of Gaga's queer, hypermodern provocations. Halberstam, for example, observes that Gaga "manages to harness her ring tones to much deeper concepts, like the fragmentation of connection in the age of cell phones, the creation of new forms of rebellion in a universe of media manipulation, and the emergence of new forms of gender and sexuality in a digital age" (Halberstam, 2012, p. 63). Others point to a harmonious depiction of queer identities. Horn notes that the video's women are "represented in all shapes and sizes and several constellations of power, antagonism, friendship and desire without being devaluated or played off against each other. Rather than using the wardens' nonconforming bodybuilder-physique to divert from Lady Gaga's own rumored sex deviation, the video stresses the connection between these different kinds of women as gender outlaws" (Horn, 2012, p. 97). This is not to say that viewers perceive the depiction and rhythm of queer affect and sensuality in "Telephone" as being devoid of collision with other sets of identities. As Gray-Rosendale, Capaldo, Craig, and Davalos (2012) argue, "The prison scenes also seek to represent an 'authentic' tough, urban, street image," thereby romanticizing a lifestyle that is certainly fraught with violent encounters, as the video demonstrates (p. 229).

Gray-Rosendale et al. also make an argument that is relevant to my Presley and Jackson cases. They claim, "By 'playing' prison inmate and imitating what she understands to be prison behavior, Lady Gaga assumes that she has unlimited access to spaces, or to represent spaces un-commonly held by upper-class white women" (2012, p. 229). Horn's conclusion may be used and adapted as a reaction to Gray-Rosendale, et al.'s critique. But while I wholeheartedly agree with Horn's approval of a powerful and new "constellation of gender outlaws" in the Prison for Bitches, this alone is insufficient to counter Gray-Rosendale et al.'s argument, which essentially claims that "Telephone" appropriates a space to which Gaga should not necessarily have access. While they believe that Gaga's class and race positions may perceivably impede her inhabiting of the prison persona, her own past relationships with women and her avid associations with queer communities mean that she has just as much of an aesthetic claim on the prison space as a white Southern male like Elvis Presley and an African-American male like Michael Jackson. In other words, two of Gaga's "constellations" matter greatly and are at the heart of the video's queering of prison space: the one internal to the video consisting of queer guards and inmates – and, I might add, the pop paraphernalia that adorns the video imagery – and, second, the "constellation" external to the video consisting of her collaborators and queer fan communities.

PAROLE

This chapter has taken as its focus certain representations of prisons by pop music. Operating as same-sex spaces purposefully hidden from mainstream populations, prisons adopt a certain mystique in contemporary culture that I have argued is fundamentally queer in its enactment of gender. Affective and intimate practices that would be vigorously policed as sexual deviances in everyday social life become innocuous. Cases abound in television sitcoms, blockbuster movies, and elsewhere although I have chosen to focus on popular music. In her consideration of comparable representations in cinema, Ciasullo (2008) concludes that the set of cinematic representations of prison lesbianism that she masterfully examines actually "encloses the 'true' lesbian behind prison walls, establishes the limits of desire, and above all, restores the (heterosexual) order" (p. 218). I am more optimistic than Ciasullo. When pop icons whose posters adorn fan walls (and, today, fan screens) playfully and creatively occupy prison spaces with queer expression, the 'limits of desire' may be slowly chipped away at, just as the protagonist of *The Shawshank Redemption* steadily chiseled his way out of confinement over the course of several years.

Queer deviations from mainstream norms are naturalized in the space of the prison. Given that it is a liminal and contemplative space, criminals and celebrities alike are given license to disturb the boundaries of gender performance. To be sure, motivations vary. A felon facing a long sentence will have to make certain decisions about her or his sexual desire as well as be confronted with violent situations threatening sexual aggression. A pop star, by contrast, is operating in the domain of theatricality, although Michael Jackson and Elvis Presley did face arrest (Gaga only simulated a mug shot at the end of "Paparazzi"). The relationship between pop and prison is nonetheless important, however, given that they are spaces into which few enter.

It is likely that fascination with prisons will not diminish whatsoever, to say nothing of curiosity about the endless legal scandals that seem to befall celebrities like Lance Armstrong, Amanda Bynes, Lindsay Lohan, Charlie Sheen, O. J. Simpson, and Reese Witherspoon. The image of the crestfallen celebrity in prison overalls will continue to compel public attention. Pop stars' own fascination with cultural representations of crime and its penal consequences will continue alongside the exploratory, rebellious dynamics of queer expression in all modes of cultural production. The depiction of these queer motifs does not need to be explicit or obvious. Like wild animals that use natural camouflage to survive and propagate, queer expressions in fictional prison spaces may at times masquerade behind the façade of hypermasculinity or humanitarianism or classic Americana. In October 2013, Lady Gaga is set to make her film debut in a crime/outlaw thriller called *Machete Kills*; her character's name is La Chameleón.

ACKNOWLEDGMENT

I thank Alexander Cavaluzzo for partial inspiration of the initial sketch of this chapter as well as conversations with students in my Sociology of Gender courses at Hofstra University that helped to develop my claims.

REFERENCES

Alber, J. (2011). Cinematic carcerality: Prison metaphors in film. *Journal of Popular Culture*, *44*(2), 217–232.

Ciasullo, A. (2008). Containing "deviant" desire: Lesbianism, heterosexuality, and the women-in-prison narrative. *Journal of Popular Culture*, *41*(2), 195–223.

Corona, V. P. (2011). Memory, monsters, and Lady Gaga. *Journal of Popular Culture*, *44*(2), 1–19.

Deflem, M. (2012). The sex of Lady Gaga. In R. J. Gray, II (Ed.), *The performance identities of Lady Gaga: Critical essays*. Jefferson, NC: McFarland & Company, Inc.

Deflem, M. (2013). Professor goes Gaga: Teaching Lady Gaga and the sociology of fame. *The American Sociologist*. Retrieved from http://deflem.blogspot.com/2013/05/teaching ladygaga.html. Accessed on May 8, 2013.

Foucault, M. (1980). In C. Gordon (Ed.), *Power/Knowledge: Selected interview and other writings, 1972–1977*. New York, NY: Pantheon Books.

Foucault, M. (1994). In J. D. Faubion (Ed.), *Power*. New York, NY: The New Press.
Foucault, M. (2012). *Discipline and punish: The birth of the prison*. New York, NY: Random House.
Gray, II, R. J. (Ed.) (2012). *The performance identities of Lady Gaga: Critical essays*. Jefferson, NC: McFarland & Company, Inc.
Gray-Rosendale, L., Capaldo, S., Craig, S., & Davalos, E. (2012). Whiteness and the politics of "post-racial" America. In R. J. Gray, II (Ed.), *The performance identities of Lady Gaga: Critical essays*. Jefferson, NC: McFarland & Company, Inc.
Halberstam, J. J. (2012). *Gaga feminism: Sex, gender, and the end of normal*. Boston, MA: Beacon Press.
Herwitz, D. (2008). *The star as icon: Celebrity in the age of mass consumption*. New York, NY: Columbia University Press.
Horn, K. (2012). Follow the glitter way: Lady Gaga and camp. In R. J. Gray, II (Ed.), *The performance identities of Lady Gaga: Critical essays*. Jefferson, NC: McFarland & Company, Inc.
Human Rights Watch. (2001). *No escape: Male rape in U.S. prisons*. Retrieved from http://www.hrw.org/reports/2001/prison/
Nyong'o, T. (2011). Have you seen his childhood? Song, screen, and the queer culture of the child in Michael Jackson's music. *Journal of Popular Music Studies*, *23*(1), 40–57.
Russo, V. (1987). *The celluloid closet: Homosexuality in the movies*. New York, NY: Harper & Row.
Schildcrout, J. (2011). Queer justice: The retrials of Leopold and Loeb. *Journal of American Culture*, *34*(2), 175–188.
Switaj, E. K. (2012). Lady Gaga's bodies: Buying and selling The Fame Monster. In R. J. Gray, II (Ed.), *The performance identities of Lady Gaga: Critical essays*. Jefferson, NC: McFarland & Company, Inc.
Weinraub, B. (1995). In new lyrics, Jackson uses slurs. *The New York Times*, June 15. Retrieved from http://www.nytimes.com/1995/06/15/arts/in-new-lyrics-jackson-uses-slurs.html. Accessed on December 12, 2008.

PART III
ILLEGALITY AND DEVIANCE

UNDERSTANDING DEVIANT MUSIC

Sara Towe Horsfall

ABSTRACT

Purpose – *The purpose of this chapter is to develop a framework for understanding deviant genres of music. Although it seems destructive, deviant music has positive effects, and can encourage greater socialization into the larger society.*

Design/methodology/approach – *By looking at deviant music of the past, it is possible to see more clearly why such music was created, and what functions it has in society. Three main functions were identified: social criticism, spreading the news, and public catharsis of outstanding events.*

Findings – *These three functions are found in deviant music today. But there are differences. Heavy metal, a counter culture, uses offensive language and images to repel unwanted outsiders and thus avoids commercialization. Grunge, music of a drop out culture, became popular and lost some of its alternative identity. Rap started as a legitimate African American youth art form but was hijacked by the music industry and has expanded beyond a meaningful art world. This has left both artists and listeners vulnerable to a distorted image.*

Music and Law
Sociology of Crime, Law and Deviance, Volume 18, 199–219

ISSN: 1521-6136/doi:10.1108/S1521-6136(2013)0000018013

Originality – *The real value of deviant music is its historical record of the inner world of subcultures.*

Keywords: Deviant music; death metal; rap music; grunge music; commercialism in music; authenticity in music

INTRODUCTION

Music is a thing of pleasure – for most people, most of the time. But some music is dark and disturbing, moody and even hateful. It may have curse words, be graphically violent, or unpleasantly loud with screaming. Parents who discover their children listening to this kind of music worry about its influence. They may even work to restrict sales or concert venues. Sanctioning musical expression, however, runs the risk of violating basic freedoms. As a society, we need more understanding to establish the balance between protecting individual rights and protecting society from harm.

We first look at deviance in early popular music, in particular in nursery rhymes and folk music. The social functions of these more violent and deviant songs are examined. Next, music as art versus music as reality is discussed, leading to Becker's concept of art worlds. The music industry and authenticity comes next. Finally, we examine three current popular music forms that are considered deviant, violent, and/or dangerous – death metal, grunge, and rap.

DEVIANCE IN EARLY POPULAR MUSIC: NURSERY RHYMES AND FOLK MUSIC

My Sociology of Popular Music course always begins with Nursery Rhymes. They are, after all, some of the first popular music available for study. Contrary to common notions, many rhymes were not intended for children and are not appropriate for them. They can be violent. For instance, Jack, in *Jack and Jill*, fell so hard his head was "broken." The farmer's wife in *Three Blind Mice* used a knife to cut tails off mice. *Humpty Dumpty* fell and was never the same again. *Old Mother Hubbard* had no food. *Rock a bye, Baby* describes a tree branch falling on a sleeping baby (Brett, 1968; Delamar, 2001; Eckenstein, 1906; The Real Mother Goose, 1977; The Oxford Dictionary of Nursery Rhymes, 1997).

Nor are rhymes necessarily models of good behavior. The mother (presumably) in *Old Woman in the Shoe* "gave them broth without any bread and whipped them soundly and put them to bed." Johnny, in *O Dear, What can the Matter Be*, made promises he didn't keep. *Peter Peter Pumpkin Eater* couldn't keep his wife, although it's not quite clear why or what he did with her. In *Sing a Song of Six Pence* the king is occupied counting money, while the queen is occupied with eating sweets. And it goes on.

Like Nursery Rhymes, most folk songs were also popular songs at one time. *Greensleeves,* one of the oldest songs still sung today, was first published in 1584 in a collection of songs entitled *A Handefull of pleaseant delites*. The term folk music is a misnomer, however, as they did not develop anonymously among "the folk," as the term implies. They were composed by individual musicians/poets but became popular because they expressed common sentiments. Once in common usage, any song with a familiar, easily sung melody was at risk of being misclassified as folk music – even at the height of its popularity, as happened with *Oh Suzanna*, composed by Stephen Foster in the mid-19th century (Nelson-Burns, n.d.).[1]

It is easy to find deviance in folk music. Here are eleven examples for starters. (All can be found on Nelson-Burns (n.d.) comprehensive and informative site.) In *The Female Highwayman* a woman dressed as a robber, complete with a sword and pistol, tests the love of her betrothed. *Clementine* tells how the daughter of a miner drowned in a raging river. In *The Wife of Usher's Well* a woman who looses her three sons at sea goes mad, and finally sees them as ghosts. *A Fox May Steal your Hen, Sir* (from the Beggar's Opera) complains about the outlandish and ruinous fees charged by lawyers. In *Abdul Abulbul Amir*, a Turkish and a Russian sailor challenge each other and fight to the death. Any sailor who doesn't join in with the drinking and merriment is told to lie *Down among the Dead Men* in the song with that name. The consequences of this overindulgence in drink is discussed in *What do you do with a Drunken Sailor?* In the *Farmer's Curst Wife*, a woman is carted off to hell by the devil, but he brings her back because she's so much trouble. *Barbara Allen* tells of a beautiful young woman who spurns a man dying out of love for her. *Delia's Gone* tells about a man who shot a lady who cursed him. In *Frankie and Johnnie*, Frankie shot her lover for being unfaithful.

FUNCTIONS OF DEVIANT POPULAR MUSIC

Social Criticism

There are three obvious social functions of these deviant, often violent songs. The first is social criticism. Nursery Rhymes were written in an era when it was dangerous to speak clearly. The rhymes are likely about famous or powerful persons. *The Three Blind Mice* is thought to refer to three clergymen who died at the stake because of Queen Mary I. *Rock a Bye Baby* is probably a warning to the ambitious who climb too high – perhaps aimed at the royal line of King James II. *Jack and Jill* may refer to a failed plan to marry Queen Mary I to the King of France. Many of the Nursery Rhymes are so well disguised the original meaning is unclear and there are several plausible interpretations. *Baa Baa Black Sheep,* for instance, may the complaint of farmers when King Edward VI enclosed the land, or it may have been a protest against the wool tax of 1275. *Humpty Dumpty* could be King John at Runneymede who was toppled from power, or it may refer to a cannon mounted on a wall during the English Civil War.

Social commentary is also found in folk music, such as *The Cruel War*. Said to be one of the gentlest protest songs, this popular war tune was revived in the 1960s by Peter, Paul and Mary in protest to the fighting in Vietnam.

> I know you're so gentle When you hold me tight,
> Oh how will they make you Get out there and fight?
> I'm counting the minutes The hours and the days,
> Oh Lord, stop the cruel war, For this, my heart prays.

Pre-Civil War abolitionists gained strength by singing *John Brown's Body* to the tune of *Battle Hymn of the Republic*.

> He captured Harper's Ferry with his nineteen men so true;
> He frightened old Virginia till she trembled through and through.
> They hung him for a traitor, themselves the traitor crew. His soul is marching on.

In the early 20th century, revolutionary socialists or Wobblies (Industrial Workers of the World or IWW) concluded that singing was a more effective way to get their message across than printed pamphlets. These very creative wordsters borrowed melodies (an age-old tradition) for their zany rhymes. An added advantage of singing their message was that music turned out to be a good recruiting tool; they sang at every meeting (Herrmann, 1998, p. 174). *The Preacher and the Slave* is sung to the tune of

Sweet Bye and Bye: "Work and pray, live on hay, You'll get pie in the sky when you die." Another song, *The Big Question* uses the melody from *America*:

> My Job now is no more, The boss has slam'd the door; What shall I do?
> Seems like my end is near, My guts feel awful queer, Where do we go from here?
> This is up to you.

And the second verse:

> No, I've not lost a leg, Why must I starve and beg? What Shall I do?
> Where can the answer lurk? Why am I out of work, Gazing on all this murk?
> This is up to you.

Social criticism is common in today's popular music, as well. Freedom of speech results in fewer hidden metaphors, except when there are threats of legal sanction. Two examples of the latter come from the 1960s, and are supposedly about drugs – *Lucy in the Sky with Diamonds* (LSD) and *Puff the Magic Dragon* (marijuana).

Modern protest music is full of social commentary and criticism. Sung in group settings, the music also creates solidarity – boosting resolve and morale, and breaking down barriers. Oftentimes the morale building is as important, or more so, than the message. This is true of the Civil Rights era song, *We Shall Overcome* (it has a borrowed melody), which became standard fare for protestors.

One of the most powerful protest songs was so controversial it was never played on the radio. *Strange Fruit*, a song about lynching in the South, became a theme song of jazz singer Billie Holliday, and may have contributed to her troubled life. She demanded full attention and a proper atmosphere to sing this song. The words were written by a Jewish communist, Lewis Allan (or Abel Merropol).

> Pastoral scene of the gallant South, The bulging eyes and the twisted mouth.
> Scent of magnolia sweet and fresh, and the sudden smell of burning flesh!
> Here is a fruit for the crows to pluck, For the rain to gather, for the wind to suck,
> For the sun to rot, for a tree to drop, Here is a strange and bitter crop. (Margolick, 2001)

Spreading the News

A second obvious social function of deviant music is spreading the news. Historically, those who couldn't read or write used a melody and/or a rhyme to remember details. Early songs had many verses. In its first known version *Greensleeves* had 18 verses. Froggie Went a Courtin' has 17 or 18 verses. The *Farmer's Curst Wife* has 13. *Delia's Gone* has 11 verses. Barbara Allen has 9 common verses. *Clementine* has at least 6. *Frankie and Johnnie* has 6 or more, and *Jimmy Crack Corn* has at least 7.

Many verses were needed to tell the *whole* story. Today these stories have become truncated, and the details lost. The more standard three verse song is one of America's contributions to popular music (Becker, 2013). But even with fewer verses, music still serves as a means of information. For instance, songs about famous Americans – outlaw *Jesse James*, train engineer *Casey Jones*, steel driver *John Henry* – still tell the story to those unfamiliar.

Public Catharsis

A third obvious social function of deviant music is emotional catharsis for events that are difficult to digest. Retelling the story of violent events over and over in song gives people the time they need to absorb and understand these difficult and shocking events. How else can one explain the popularity of songs like *Frankie and Johnnie,* or *Banks of the Ohio* (a morbid song by a man explaining what he was thinking as he kills a young woman who refuses to marry him). *Blood on the Saddle*, a song on a 1961 Rex Wells album, is so graphic it was sung in a grizzly bear costume to make it humorous (see it on YouTube). It is a reminder of the dangers of working as a cowboy.

> There was blood on the saddle and blood all around,
> And a great big puddle of blood on the ground.
> A cowboy lay in it all covered with gore,
> And he never will ride any broncos no more.
> Oh, pity the cowboy, all bloody and red,
> For the bronco fell on him and bashed in his head.

Songs can both tell a story and provide catharsis. *Casey Jones* was a well-known engineer with a distinctive train whistle who was killed in Mississippi in 1900. When his train collided with a stalled freight train, he made sure no one else died, making him a hero. Similarly, a song about the famous outlaw *Jesse James* killed in Missouri in 1882 portrays him as a Robin Hood – a decent man with a wife and three children who was shot in the back by someone he considered his friend. *Strange Fruit* not only tells about group violence perpetrated on a helpless minority, it stands as a reminder to all of us of awful possibilities of group-think.

Music has other functions, of course – celebration, courtship, comfort, expressions of love, devotion, and patriotism. But such music is less likely to be deviant.

DEVIANT ART

This brings us to the question of music as art. How are we to decide the value of deviant music? Does something have to be beautiful or inspiring to be art, or to be valuable? What value do songs of violence, betrayal, and suffering have?

Beauty versus Reality

Art, in its classical conception, is an expression of truth, goodness and beauty: Rembrandt's Sistine Chapel, Greek sculptures, Monet's flower scenes. In music, the classical conception of art is found in Mozart, Beethoven's *Ninth Symphony*, and *The Moldeau* – compositions that bridge the gap with the divine.

But not all inner worlds are pleasant. People everywhere experience pain, fear, hatred, and violence, so these expressions are as universal as expressions of truth, beauty, and goodness. When art reflects social injustices experienced by minorities or others, it can be a way to increase awareness of the need for change – a form of social criticism, as discussed above. But is it art? Not everyone is happy to include this form of expression as art, and some modern art remains controversial – a crucifix in urine, and paintings depicting rape of slaves. It is the skill involved in its expression and the agreed upon aesthetic that gives it meaning (Becker, 1982).

Classical versus Popular Distinctions in Music

In music, this debate is thornier because of the division between classical and popular music. Some claim classical music as art, but not popular music. More training is required both to produce and appreciate classical music. Further, classical music is less commercial so reflects a genuine artistic aesthetic. Popular music, on the other hand, is created and produced by amateurs and reflects passing fads. Largely vocal, the music can be secondary to the message in pop music.

There is a real problem with dividing music this way. Classical and jazz music make up less than 7% of music sales. Classical sales in 2004 were only 2.9% of the market, and jazz was 3.5% (*Newsweek*, 2004). To regard only classical music as art implies that 93% of the music is not art. This is an elitist viewpoint, likely originating among the aristocracy who wanted to distinguish upper-class compositions from popularly performed music in order to justify classical music as an academic discipline (Clarke, 2001; Nelson-Burns, n.d.; Roy, 2010, p. 54; Seeger, 1972, p. 5). Such a view does not contribute to a sociological understanding of society. For whatever reason, society at large doesn't consume classical music. So to avoid a subgroup bias, other music must be included as art.

The Added Aesthetic of Poetry

One more stumbling block for popular music is the fact that, unlike most other forms of art, it consists of music *and* poetry. The composer of a popular song must be proficient in two different sets of aesthetics. In reality, some songs are more poetic than others – U.S. songs tend to be less poetic. Our society does not value poetic expression like they do in countries where poets are national heros.

Further, a song may have borrowed words, or it may have a borrowed melody, or both. In the case of *Strange Fruit*, the lyrics were borrowed and set to music. Most Wobbly songs, on the other hand, have a borrowed melody – a common practice in earlier times. Hymns writers commonly used existing tunes for a new set of words. Or conversely, wrote a melody for an inspiring poem. It is still common in some music today. Rappers use older popular songs as the foundation for their rhymes. Some musicians consider a song with a borrowed melody less creative, that is, less artistic. A song with an original melody and borrowed words, on the other hand, is considered more creative because borrowed words tend to be more poetic and mated with more sophisticated music.

Art Worlds or Scenes – The Supportive Community for Whom it Speaks

Becker's concept of art worlds provides a solution to this dilemma. To understand and/or appreciate an artwork, we do not need to judge whether or not it is art. That can be left to those in the associated art world, who will be far more critical than those outside the world.

> Art worlds consist of all the people whose activities are necessary to the production of the characteristic works which that world, and perhaps others as well, define as art … .

> Art worlds typically devote considerable attention to trying to decide what is and isn't art, what is and isn't their kind of art, and who is and isn't an artist. By observing how an art world makes those distinctions rather than trying to make them ourselves we can understand much of what goes on in that world. (Becker, 1982)

An outstanding characteristic of today's popular music is the multitude of different genres. There are an endless number of categories and subcategories – rock, rap, jazz, grunge, latino, etc. Every genre of music has its listeners and an associated art world who produce the music, consider it art, and for whom it speaks. This supportive community, or *scene*, as it is also called (e.g., the *jazz scene*, the *rap scene*, the *indie scene*) (Cohen, 1999) is often an identifiable subculture, be they youth, an ethnic group, or from a particular class. Thus, each genre and each associated subculture will have its own standard of what is art, of what is *good.* And what is good for one genre may not hold for another, although one might expect some criteria to be found across the board.

Deviant music, and deviant art so far as it is the product of a subculture, should be taken on its own terms. Rather than judging the artistry, one can look for the collective sentiments, understand the social commentaries, become informed of the inner workings of that particular collective. For the sensitive listener, the music can be a window into another world. Without leaving the state or city, one can be an "ethnographic tourist" (Kotarba & Vannini, 2009, p. 5).

It is possible that a counter culture has malevolent intentions. But it is also possible that a harmless counter culture is misunderstood. Such distinctions should be made prior to any discussion of sanctions.

IMPACT OF THE MUSIC INDUSTRY

This brings us to the most challenging facet of music artistry today, the music industry.

Commercialism versus Authenticity

Commercialism pervades all popular music today. For many, this goes hand in hand with authenticity. Is the music produced an expression of the artist and the artist's art world, or is it a creation of the music moguls who cleverly reproduce salable icons to get rich? Typically, the first song of a genre is original, and then it is copied. The copies are less original, done by lesser artists whose goals are commercial rather than artistic expression. In short, they are not as *authentic*. And while they may be commercially successful, people in that genre's art world recognize that they are not as *good*.

A related issue has to do with consumption. Do the music producers determine the market? That is, do people simply buy what is available? Or do consumer tastes play a role in what is produced? A related question has to do with originality of the musical composition: How original is a song after the sound engineers have doctored it up? One view is that exceptionally talented people can't be kept down. An example is Susan Boyle, an unknown, middle aged British lady with a tremendous voice, who became a sensation after she appeared in a televised singing competition. Soon people were buying her recordings. The other view is that even those who are not talented can be "doctored up" and made to sound good (Fenster & Swiss, 1999; Frith, 1992). (For more on authenticity and commercialism see discussions of Adorno, Horkheimer, and others.)

Evolution of Genres

A related issue concerns changes in a genre's music over time. Reaction by the public plays an important role in how a genre develops. Some music has been so controversial it stimulated active rejection. Jazz, for instance, was considered so scandalous at first that laws were passed banning it. Rock 'n' Roll was also sanctioned, although not as severely as jazz. Elvis was shown only from the waist up on the Ed Sullivan Show.

New forms of music are exciting, and create an energy among the listeners. Sanctions add another layer of excitement. But after some time, the edginess wears off. To recreate energy artists exaggerate the shocking elements. Thus Elvis' shaking pelvis morphed into the antics of Mick Jagger, and then further to Madonna wearing underwear as outerwear. In other cases, what was once regarded as distasteful overtime becomes popular. Tarantism, music of a minority region in Italy that was stigmatized in the past is now a fashionable music (Blackstone, 2013).

Because new music and artists are more commercially risky, they are usually found on independent labels. (Sun Records became famous for its "discovery" of Elvis Presley.) Once a musician, or a genre, is established, it moves to the five or six big companies – the majors – who control the production process, and market their product more aggressively (Fenster & Swiss, 1999).

UNDERSTANDING DEVIANT MUSIC OF THE 21ST CENTURY

Several genres of popular music today are often considered deviant – rap, especially gangsta rap, death metal, and grunge are three that will be examined here. All three have been called dangerous, a model for destructive and unsocial behavior, drug use, and incitement to violence. We will look at each in turn using Becker's art worlds. Examining the community that supports them will give us greater understanding of what the music means to them. We can then identify the impact that listening to this music has on their lives. Approaching it this way also allows us to identify those who use the music for other reasons. An important related issue for all discussion of popular music today is its relations to the music industry.

Violence in Death Metal

Death Metal, it is claimed, leads to antisocial behavior, even violence, and is seen by some as a vehicle of Satan. It comes from heavy metal and Jimi Hendrix type acid rock, but is darker and more abrasive. It is anti-authoritarian, fascinated with evil and the dark side of humanity, using death and violence in the lyrics. It is easy to see why some people find it shocking and objectionable. Even the recording companies refused to produce death metal bands commercially during the 1980s. Instead, listeners traded tapes of favorite bands. Commercial recordings were briefly available later, but then the music went underground again (Jensen, 1996; Purcell, 2003).

Studies of the lyrics of death metal songs reveal them as moody, pessimistic and negative – an expression of anger, sadness, and fear, but also angst and longing (Jensen, 1996).[2] The violent lyrics protest the hypocrisy in current political, religious and legal institutions. Satan is also a common theme, although not necessarily glorified. Love, sex, and life, on the other hand, are not common themes.

> [H]eavy metal deliberately seeks to be uncultured, unrefined, coarse, crude, loud – in a word, vulgar. In the world of heavy metal such adjectives are not insults but praise. To performers and metalheads the vulgarity of heavy metal represents originality, energy, honesty and integrity. ... Ozzy Ozbourne is cultural kin to Andy Warhol and John Cage. In the late 20th century, art is not something that elevates and edifies but is a mirror of the disorder and soullessness of modern life, a gesture of despair. (Jensen, 1996)

Unlike old school death metal, which is more simple and primitive, recent bands have become *more* aggressive, if that is possible, with chunky rhythmic guitar riffs, high speed double bass drumbeats, and gruff, guttural vocals (Purcell, 2003). Even the band names express aggressive rebellion: Death, Morbid Angel, Cannibal Corpse, Suffocation, Internal Bleeding, Pyrexia, Dying Fetus, Skinless, Immolation, Incantation, Mortician. Two main themes of recent death metal songs are blasphemous tirades and pure gore. But listeners insist the words are not to be taken seriously. Like horror movies, they are fantasy. "Puns on words and bastardizations of sanctified songs and phrases often adorn the lyrics of gore bands, adding an extra layer of humor" (Purcell, 2003, p. 45). But the sociopolitical commentary (which may still contain fantasy) is deadly serious – on the environment, social values, drug use, etc. A high value placed on individualism and freedom leads to rejection of mainstream religion and culture. In short, lyrics are intentionally shocking to provide a thrill and repel others who don't share their philosophy of life.

The themes of Hitler and the holocaust in some death metal songs illustrate the genre's fascination with violence, its offensive modus operandi, and social commentary. Most death metal listeners do not embrace Hitler as a model, but use him as a warning against concentration of power in one person: contemporary economic or political Hitlers. The rare song that professes admiration for Hitler is likely to do so because of his antireligious stance. The holocaust is also used as a warning – against a time when good is defeated, "some final glorious Satanic slaughter of humanity and the Christian God; a victory of evil over good" (Mengerink, 2013).

Old school metal heads were more male than female, characterized as sensation seeking, reckless teens who used drugs and alcohol. Many were alienated from their primary groups – families, school, and religion. Most, however, maintained good relationships with their mothers. But they did not contribute to family upkeep, and rejected any restraint as too restrictive (Jensen, 1996). Listening to heavy metal music calmed them and provided a catharsis for their anger. Slam dancing at concerts similarly released stress, aggression, and tension. Concerts were a place where listeners could "get as wild as you can without killing yourself." As such, concerts were a "substitute manhood ritual that fills the social vacuum left by a culture that disdains rituals" (Jensen, 1996, p. 16). In short, it was an important part of growing up for alienated youth who didn't have enough value instruction from families, school or religion.

This is less true of more recent death metal, which is a counterculture of strongly individualistic persons (Purcell, 2003). But the environment within this group is friendly not aggressive or anti-social. For example, if someone falls in the moshpit (a circle of fans jumping and cheering close to the stage at a concert) they are immediately assisted by everyone nearby. The age is 13–33, as older fans tend to drop out. They dress in black and leather with tattoos, but are not particularly depressed. In one study, although they were lower middle class, half finish college (with a 3.2 GPA). Most were close to their families, although 28% came from divorced families. They were not religious, but neither were they against religion. They *were* disillusioned with politics. And most importantly, they don't care what others think of them. Metal fans are intense and their behavior at concerts is intense.

> [M]osh pitting, crowd surfing, head banging, showing the horns hand gesture, yelling, and singing along with the band. These interactive action repertoires are schema driven, which enable many individuals to participate through the ritual in the production of meaning. … These behaviors appear extreme, but they promote positive emotional states that connect participants to the ritual event and create positive associations with other participants. The positive emotional states created by the repetition of rituals generate shared experiences, shared commitments, shared norms, and group cohesion. (Meij, Probstfield, Simpson, & Knottnerus 2013)

Death metal music is "easy to sensationalize," and therefore demonized as promoting fear and prejudice (Purcell, 2003, pp. 81, 82). All the researchers cited here concluded that it is not a major cause of violence and immorality. To the contrary, violence is regarded as a fact of life that is worth pondering. Most metalheads reject anyone who uses the music as an excuse for violence; violence happens when someone comes to a show with violent intent. Similarly, suicide rates are blamed on the attraction this music has for those with such problems. The majority of death metal fans are fairly normal with normal families and friendships. But they are alienated from traditional society, and "metal provides identity, acceptance, emotional release, and a sense of community, or a place for some self-proclaimed misfits to call home" (Meij et al., 2013). The music has a positive impact, giving its listeners a non-hostile environment to release pent up hostilities and aggression.

Death metal art world is best seen as a vulgar counter culture. The music clearly exhibits social criticism and leads to catharsis for its listeners. As to spreading the news, one example is that songs about Hitler inform young listeners about this historical figure and his time. There is one more important function of death metal music. The vulgarity is used as a way to repel outsiders who don't belong in their company. But even if this genre of music is not harmful for the majority of listeners, what about the effect it has on those who are already "at risk" for violence, either to themselves or others. It is hard to legislate against violent images without violating personal freedoms. Industry-level warnings on cds are appropriate, however effective or ineffective they might be.

Drugs and Grunge

Seattle in the late 1980s gave rise to a new genre of music called grunge. For a few years, it was a big seller. *Ten* by Pearl Jam, sold 13 million – one of the top rock sellers of all time; *Nevermind* by Nirvana was a close second. A grunge song, *Man in a Box* was nominated for Best Hard Rock Performance in 1992. Said to be the music of Generation X, grunge music is a combination of heavy metal, punk and indie rock. It is slower and more dissonant than punk, with a "stripped-down" sound. Dressed in torn jeans and flannel shirts, the unkempt musicians rejected what they called "glam metal" – flashy use of performance props and dress.

Almost as well known as the music are the grunge musicians who died. Most notable is Kurt Cobain, 27, the lead singer of Nirvana, who shot himself in 1994 after several previous failed suicide attempts. Four years earlier, just as the genre was getting started, Andrew Wood of the band Mother Love Bone died of a heroin overdose. Two years after Cobain, Layne Staley of the band Alice in Chains overdosed on heroin after his fiancée died. In 2011, Mike Starr, bass player in the same band, also died of heroin overdose.

Grunge music was said to express "frustration, alienation, fears and anomie of an entire generation" (Pecora & Mazzarella, 1995). The lyrics are full of angst, social alienation, apathy, desire for freedom, and general disenchantment with society and with the prejudices of society. Cobain called it a disease – a sickness that pervades society. Grunge fans considered the lack of economic opportunity a protection against excessive consumerism. As they shared Cobain's powerlessness and disappointment in life, the music provided catharsis (Fish, 1995). Some researchers say grunge increases hostility, sadness, tension and fatigue, and reduces caring, relaxation, mental clarity and vigor (McCraty, Barrios-Choplin, Atkinson, & Tomasino, 1998). But fans describe great relief when they first discover this music. It brings a sense of release as they continue to listen – here are people who think and feel like themselves.[3]

The grunge art world found an ally in the independent record companies, who became the last bastion for independence, creativity and anti-authoritarianism in an otherwise corrupt society.

> In many ways indie resembled '80s radical movements, especially in its ingrained conviction that real power over the mainstream was unattainable, so the only workable model for resistance had to be small-scale change and self-transformation – the personal as political. (Shevoy, 1995)

But, independents feed into the mainstream. Majors pick up successful indie musicians, refine them and market them to a larger audience. This transformation of grunge was unsettling for Cobain and others. They didn't like the polish the studio's put on their music. In the end, even grunge style, which started as "a serf's rebellion against aristocratic glamour" became a fashion statement with a fancy pricetag (Shevoy, 1995). For Cobain, it was a loss of his small world, his identity, and his authenticity (Heath & Potter, 2004). His suicide, more than any of the others, raised fears of copycat suicides, although that didn't happen (Jobes, Berman, O'Carroll, Eastgard, & Knickmeyer, 1996).

Some grunge fans attribute the suicides to personal problems of the musicians rather than to the message of the music (Orso, 2013). While Cobain undoubtedly felt the weight of commercialization, that was not the extent of his inner demons. In contrast to Cobain, Eddie Vedder of Pearl Jam (whose popularity is demonstrated by his appearance on the cover of Time Magazine in 1993) took a different route. He refused to give in to the mainstream, and he supported a variety of causes. His "pro-choice" views became known early on when he wrote those words on his arm during a concert. His stand against Ticketmaster's monopoly of concert ticket sales led him to testify before Congress. After taking on the marketing giant, his concerts were smaller, held in alternative venues, but the crowds were more loyal. He maintained his grunge identity, and still sings his soulful songs of depression, suicide, loneliness, murder. He also educates his listeners on social issues. By this unflinching commitment to what he believes in despite a drop in popular appeal a thriving art world is maintained.

In conclusion, the grunge art world can be characterized as a drop out subculture. Fans critical of mainstream society find solace and solidarity in the social commentaries of grunge musicians. Vedder educates his listeners as well. Commercialization destroyed much of the intimate scene and the indigenous art world of the early grunge musicians, although for some it continues.

Morality, Rap, and Hip Hop

Claims against rap and hip hop range from causing and promoting violence, to reflecting a dysfunctional ghetto culture, to charges that its immorality is destroying American values, and that its misogyny is demeaning to women.

Rap started in South Bronx of NY City. DJs "scratched" records to extend a song's rhythmic break as dancers showed off their skill. They made up rhymes about local events and soon became the stars. Recordings of these heroes circulated. Afrika Bambaataa, a former gang member, developed the hip hop style and culture as a means of keeping youth out of trouble. It was several years before people outside Bronx heard rap music. The first popular commercial recording came in 1979 – *Rapper's Delight* by the Sugarhill Gang. Rapping had been common for several years in New York City. The Sugar Hill artists were not the best rappers, nor was theirs the best song. They just happened to be in the right place at the right time (Friedlander, 2006; Greenberg, 1999; Ogg, 2001; Szwed, 1999).

South Bronx was known for its urban decay in the 1970s. One of the poorest Congressional districts in the United States, its residents felt abandoned and fearful they would become victims of crime. Rap was an indigenous response. It articulated black life, expressed the inner struggles and provided a cathartic hope for the future. Rappers "epitomized, revolutionized, and transformed" with their "artistry, image and music" (Reeves, 2008, pp. ix, xi, xii).

> Their art was street poetry, braggadocio rhymes recited over break beats to excite, enthrall, and entertain hip-hop's faithful. Much of their metered speech and tall tales were rooted in black oral traditions of African griots (storytellers and history holders), in toasts (black epical rhyming poetry), in the firey, rhythmic cadence of black Baptist preachers, in the oral acrobatic put-downs of the "dozens." (Reeves, 2008, p. 18)

Once public, rap traveled to the west coast where it became transformed and commercialized. Elements previously not common in it – caricatures of black gangstas, pimps, and hoes – became synonymous with it. Critics claim that the music industry sensationalized lingering racism for greater popular appeal (Rose, 2008). New technological marketing targeted youth, so that mainstream listeners today are largely ignorant of black ghetto life. They take the violence and misogyny as reality. Thus, not only was a legitimate African American artform hijacked, it misleads the public.

> No black musical form before hip hop – no matter how much it 'crossed over' into mainstream American culture – ever attracted the level of corporate attention and

> mainstream media visibility, control, and intervention that characterizes hip hop today. (Rose, 2008, p. 8)

But the music industry was aided by the rap artists themselves, who were eager to make money. ("Nobody's into being a musician. Everybody's getting their mogul on" – Chris Rock in Rose, 2008, p. 219.) Critics, who didn't realize what was happening, contributed to it as well. And even though rap artist are portrayed as uncaring, that is not always the reality; they gave considerable amounts to help Katrina victims.

> Clearly, the corporate takeover of commercial hip hop has also been facilitated, directly or indirectly, by artists (especially those who have become moguls and entrepreneurs) who gleefully rap about guns and bitches, liberal and conservative critics and academics, and journalists who uncritically profile these artists and hip hop fans of all races, classes, and genders. This shift was not inevitable; it was *allowed* to happen. (Rose, 2008, p. 25)

Has it gone too far? Is it still a meaningful art world? Many adamantly claim that rap still speaks for the black community. But even defenders admit that sometimes it goes too far. One feminist rapper wonders if it is "inherently unfeminist" to support rap. In general, the black community is uneasy about the crass language, glorification of gangsta life, and ill treatment of black women (Reeves, 2008, pp. 272, 275). There is anger about the fact that lower class black youth now imitate and adopt the gangsta lifestyle portrayed in rap. Glamorized drug dealing is seen as the only way to survive in the ghetto, encouraging black youth into crime. A one-time fan confesses, "I no longer have the love or connection to rap music I once had; every hip hop fan has a moment when, for them, the music kicked the bucket." (Reeves, 2008, pp. ix, xi, xii).

Some fans, however, have found a way to keep the best of the art form. They distinguish between rap and hip hop. Rap, they say, is commercialized and spontaneous, done by solo artists. Rappers pride themselves on stage presence and free style ability. They have low morals, use extreme profanity, talk about violence and commonly degrade women. Rappers burn out quickly through drugs, violence and other problems. Hip hop, in contrast, is thoughtful and artistic. The songs and shows are of higher quality and have longevity. The albums are created carefully over a longer period of time. This sub-genre is exemplified by Kayne West, Jay-Z, Nas, P. Diddy and Queen Latifa.

> Rap is a tool used to express current events and to tell the stories of people within the local community. Hip hop music is used to express hope for the future and to remember the successes of the past. (Wisegeek, n.d.)

In short, it is popular culture versus street culture, old school versus new school. Either way, the relationship of rap and hip hop to the music industry is very different from that of grunge and heavy metal. Rap never was a rebellion of meaning, it was an objection to lack of opportunities for marginalized youth. The art world was not a counter culture, or a drop out sub culture, but a discriminated minority. Rappers, who had few resources to start with, embraced commercialism with open arms. It is almost as if they fell into a trap. Catharsis was the dream of wealth and power, which for some became reality (with few pangs of conscience over the distortions needed to achieve it). The music informed the rest of society about minority needs.

Hijacked or not, rap has spawned active musical protest environments around the world. In almost every case, the non-U.S. rappers belong to a minority group that is protesting discrimination and disempowerment of some kind (Ogg, 2001).

CONCLUSION

There is a place for deviant music. It is valuable to people in the associated art world. It builds a community of like-minded persons, gives voice to criticisms, and presents alternatives. It informs its listeners, and it informs the rest of society.

Art world listeners discriminate. Songs and artists that are not authentic are rejected. Thus art worlds regulate themselves. As a society, it is important to recognize these subcultures and their associated characteristics. So long as they abide by the laws of the land, they must be given their freedoms.

But listeners who are not part of an art world, who are not fully in a scene, are different. They are vulnerable to the distortion of commercialization. Non-scene listeners are less self-regulating and discriminating. Extreme, dangerous, and violent behaviors are likely to be found in this contingent. In terms of rap, (young) non-African American listeners fall into this category. They are unable to recognize exaggerations and may be negatively influenced. (When I ask my female African American students about the misogynistic language, on the other hand, they generally shrug their shoulders and say, "Everyone knows that's not how they treat their women.") Concern for socialization of children may warrant age restrictions.

Commercialization raises other questions. In some ways, modern gangsta rap is the creation of the music industry rather than a subculture. It reflects very little about the real life. The long range view is that it will probably disappear over time, since it doesn't really speak for anyone. The short term view is that it is a problem, on many fronts.

A related question has to do with subcultures that have malevolent goals (not dealt with here). A small minority, they can still be a threat to targeted individuals. Clearly articulated discrimination as motive for violent crimes in song lyrics should be sanctioned.

Which brings us back to Nursery Rhymes. Threat of sanction brings out hidden metaphors and other literary devices. Once the meaning is obscured, it can be interpreted in many ways, and is no longer a specific threat.

> When artists make what existing institutions cannot assimilate, whether the limits be physical or conventional (the weight of sculpture versus the length of plays), their works are not exhibited or performed. That is not because the managers of those organizations are conservative fuddy-duddies, either, but because their organizations are equipped to handle standard formats and their resources will not permit the substantial expenditures required to accommodate nonstandard items, or to sustain the losses involved in presenting work audiences will not support. (Becker, 1982)

NOTES

1. An excellent source for words, melodies and histories of common folk music of the English speaking world is *The Contemplator's Folk Music Site*, posted by Leslie Nelson-Burns, www.contemplator.com.

2. Songs from three popular mainstream metal bands (Judas Priest, Iron Maiden, Ozzy Ozbourne) and three popular speed thrash metal bands (Metallica, Megadeth, and Slayer) were analyzed by Jeffrey Jensen in *Metalheads: Heavy Metal and Adolescent Alienation*.

3. I am indebted to student Russ Orso, who was involved in the grunge scene in the past. His reflections, experiences, and insights added to the depth of this analysis.

REFERENCES

Becker, H. S. (1982). Art worlds and collective activity. In *Art worlds* (pp. 1–39). Berkeley, CA: University of California Press.

Becker, H. S. (2013). The American song. In S. Towe-Horsfall, J. Meij, & M. Probstfield (Eds.), *Explorations in music sociology: Examining the role of music in social life*. Boulder, CO: Paradigm Publishers.

Blackstone, L. (2013). Painful listening: the musical noise and cultural transcendence of southern Italian tarantism. In S. Towe-Horsfall, J. Meij, & M. Probstfield (Eds.), *Explorations in music sociology: Examining the role of music in social life*. Boulder, CO: Paradigm Publishers.

Brett, H. (1968). *Nursery rhymes and tales – their origin and history*. London: Methuen & Co. Ltd.

Clarke, D. (2001/1994). *The rise and fall of popular music: A narrative history from the renaissance to rock 'n' roll*. Austin, TX: Donald Clarke.

Cohen, S. (1999). Scenes. In B. Horner & T. Swiss (Eds.), *Key terms in popular music and culture* (pp. 113–123). Malden, MA: Blackwell Publishers.

Delamar, G. T. (2001). *Mother goose – from nursery to literature*. Lincoln, NE: iUniverse. com, Inc.

Eckenstein, L. (1906). *Comparative studies in nursery rhymes by*. London: Duckworth & Co.

Fenster, M., & Swiss, T. (1999). Business. In B. Horner & T. Swiss (Eds.), *Key terms in popular music and culture* (pp. 113–123). Malden, MA: Blackwell Publishers.

Fish, D. R. (1995). Serving the servants: an analysis of the music of Kurt Cobain. *Popular Music and Society*, *19*(2), 87–102.

Friedlander, P. (2006). *Rock and roll: A social history*. Cambridge, MA: Westview Press.

Frith, S. (1992). Industrialization of popular music. In J. Lull (Ed.), *Popular music and communication* (pp. 49–74). Thousand Oaks, CA: Sage Publications.

Greenberg, S. (1999). SugarHill records. In A. Light (Ed.), *The VIBE history of hip hop* (pp. 23–33). New York, NY: Three Rivers Press.

Heath, J., & Potter, A. (2004). *Nation of rebels: Why counterculture became consumer culture*. New York, NY: HarperCollins.

Herrmann, D. (1998). *Helen keller*. New York, NY: Alfred A. Knopf.

Jensen, J. (1996). *Metalheads: Heavy metal and adolescent alienation*. Boulder, CO: Arnett Westview Press.

Jobes, D. A., Berman, A. L., O'Carroll, P. W., Eastgard, S., & Knickmeyer, S. (1996). The Kurt Cobain suicide crisis: Perspectives from research, public health, and the news media. *Suicide and Life Threatening Behavior*, *26*(3), 260–271.

Kotarba, J. A., & Vannini, P. (2009). *Understanding society through popular music*. New York, NY: Routledge.

Margolick, D. (2001). *Strange fruit*. New York, NY: HarperCollins.

McCraty, R., Barrios-Choplin, B., Atkinson, M., & Tomasino, D. (1998). The effects of different types of music on mood, tension, and mental clarity. *Alternative Therapies in Health and Medicine*, *4*(1), 75–84.

Meij, J., Probstfield, M. D., Simpson, J. M., & Knottnerus, J. D. (2013). Moving past violence and vulgarity: structural ritualization and constructed meaning in the heavy metal subculture. In S. Towe-Horsfall, J. Meij, & M. Probstfield (Eds.), *Explorations in music sociology: Examining the role of music in social life*. Boulder, CO: Paradigm Publishers.

Mengerink, M. A. (2013). Hitler, the holocaust, and heavy metal music: Holocaust memory and representation in the heavy metal subculture, 1980-Present. In S. Towe-Horsfall, J. Meij, & M. Probstfield (Eds.), *Explorations in music sociology: Examining the role of music in social life*. Boulder, CO: Paradigm Publishers.

Nelson-Burns, L. (n.d.). *The contemplator's folk music site*. Retreived from http://www.contemplator.com

Newsweek. (2004). On the downbeat: The Nora Jones effect. *Newsweek*, Feburary 2, pp. 55–56.

Ogg, A. (2001). *The hip hop years: A history of rap*. New York, NY: Fromm International.

Orso, R. (2013). Personal conversations.

Pecora, N., & Mazzarella, S. R. (1995). Kurt Cobain, generation X and the press: College students respond. *Popular Music and Society*, *19*(2), 3–22.

Purcell, N. J. (2003). *Death metal music: the passion and politics of a subculture*. Jefferson, NC: McFarland & Co. Inc. Publishers.

Reeves, M. (2008). *Somebody scream! Rap music's rise to prominence in the aftershock of black power*. New York, NY: Faber and Faber.

Rose, T. (2008). *The hip hop wars*. New York, NY: Basic Books.

Roy, W. G. (2010). *Reds, whites and blues: Social movements, folk music, and race in America*. Princeton, NJ: Princeton University Press.

Seeger, P. (1972). *The incompleat folksinger*. New York, NY: Simon and Schuster.

Shevoy, T. A. (1995). Bleached resistance: the politics of grunge. *Popular Music and Society*, *19*(2), 23–48.

Szwed, J. (1999). The real old school. In A. Light (Ed.), *The VIBE history of hip hop* (pp. 3–11). New York, NY: Three Rivers Press.

The Real Mother Goose. (1977). Chicago, IL: Rand McNally & Company.

The Oxford Dictionary of Nursery Rhymes. (1997). Oxford: Oxford University Press.

WiseGeek. (n.d.). Retrieved from http://www.wisegeek.com/what-is-the-difference-between-rap-and-hip-hop.htm

STOLEN OR RELEASED MUSIC? THE SOCIAL CONSTRUCTION OF PIRACY IN ITALY

Cecilia Blengino

ABSTRACT

Purpose – *This chapter discusses the criminalization of sharing music on peer-to-peer (p2p) networks. Taking the Italian situation into consideration, it aims to introduce a socio-legal reflection about the processes of construction of this deviance.*

Design methodology/approach – *Adopting a constructionist approach, this chapter first explores the ways in which the social problem of music piracy was built in Italy. The choice of the legislator to place this practice within the category of criminal behaviour was analysed and examined. In the second section, the points of view of other participants involved in the practice of file sharing are taken into account.*

Findings – *Placing file sharing within the jurisdiction of criminal law does not seem to respond to the needs to counter the infringement of a shared social value, but it rather seems to reflect the protagonists' involvement into the process of legislative decision about piracy conception and idea of the damage caused by this phenomenon, promoted and*

Music and Law
Sociology of Crime, Law and Deviance, Volume 18, 221–243

ISSN: 1521-6136/doi:10.1108/S1521-6136(2013)0000018014

conveyed by the music business. The way in which piracy is conceived by Italian legislation emerges here in its partial understanding of the effects of this practice. Sharing music on digital networks appears as a highly conflicted crime, whose harmfulness is scarcely perceived by the society. Furthermore, file sharing repression policy seems to give shape to a new victimless crime, whose harmful effects do not seem to actually fall back on artists or consumers.

Originality/value – *Sharing music on the net and violating copyright is little studied from the perspective of the sociology of crime. Using this approach, this chapter contributes to a better understanding of the phenomenon.*

Keywords: p2p; file sharing; piracy; criminalization process; deviance; construction of crime

INTRODUCTION

Sharing music protected by copyright on peer-to-peer (p2p) networks is a growing phenomenon in Italy (Istat, 2011, 2012). This practice is considered a crime according to the current Italian law. In fact, a pressing succession of restrictive changes made to the first Italian law on copyright[1] led to the inclusion of network sharing as a criminal action, regardless of the purpose with which it is practiced.

Studies that deal with the issue of file sharing often start – consciously or not – from the question 'Why do people who normally refrain from committing illegalities become digital pirates' (Balestrino, 2008, p. 455)? Criminological, legal and economic researches concerning music piracy often tend to tackle this issue from a correctional perspective or attempting an etiological analysis.

Starting from an assumption, which does not undermine the objective nature of the crime in itself, these studies mostly express concern about the emergence of new forms of deviance and aim to develop solutions that enable the effective repression of such behaviours. However, the two fundamental questions remain unanswered: what is music piracy? How it is defined?

The first question concerns the very concept of crime and the perspective through which this phenomenon is observed. While the structural consensus[2] approach considers crimes as a departure from the fundamental values shared within a society, constructionist perspective[3] recognizes the criminal phenomenon as the result of the processes of social and institutional reaction. The first approach sets the aim of sociological inquiry in contributing to the solution of social problems (Hester & Eglin, 1992). If music sharing is considered within the constructionist perspective on crime, shifting the focus on the definition of what crime is becomes fundamental: how does it happen? Who leads it?

These questions make it necessary to analyse passages and characters that concretely contribute to the criminalization process. It is therefore necessary to extend the observation area to the entire 'juridical field' (Bourdieu, 1986),[4] inside which different subjects act with roles, interests and different powers affecting the process of criminalization. Furthermore, the social diffusion of the illegal practice of file sharing suggests to adopt the interpretative tools of the deviant phenomenon, which – even though in different terms – observe deviance and crime as a manifestation of legal pluralism (Becker, 1963; Cohen, 1955).

The second consideration makes one wonder about the collective good justifying the introduction of a new type of criminal offence. It could be useful to start from a structural consensus perspective, which considers crime as an attack to the 'strong states defined by the collective consciousness' (Durkheim, 1999, p. 102) and gives it the task of defining moral boundaries of society (Erikson, 1962). A reflection about the use of the criminal law instrument to protect the copyright on digital global networks leads to wonder if a shared social value and a public interest of such instrument exists and what it is. In order to reflect about the damage produced by music file sharing, this phenomenon could be analysed through Hagan's (1994) theoretical contribution, whose theoretical formulation represents an attempt to integrate the two opposing theoretical perspectives, consensual and constructionist, starting from the idea of crime developed by Sutherland (1949). Therefore, the music sharing phenomenon will be analysed through different crime dimensions, whose simultaneous presence is mistakenly recognized by the consensual conception. Thus, I will make some remarks in relation to the severity of the social response, the public agreement and the perceived harmfulness of the deviance (Hagan, 1994, p. 11).

Such analysis clearly shows how the strictness of the Italian criminal standard reflects the involvement of a specific damage perception experienced by music industry. A glance at the other subjects directly involved in the piracy phenomenon shows the lack of a social agreement about this choice. Stating that piracy is harmful does not take into account the positive effects it can generate for such subjects, putting into question the existence of the general interest which justifies the penal intervention.

SOCIAL REACTION TO PIRACY

Music theft: A Social Construction

A proportion of the social response usually associates crime seriousness to harshness of a measure through which it is punished. It usually represents the indicator of how society regards a particular form of deviance as offensive. The mutability of the forms of social response (Hagan, 1994, p. 8) is the sign of a changing of habits and social norms that rules a phenomenon and makes it clear how the social reaction is somehow independent from the amount of social damage.

The following argument will deal with the file sharing phenomenon distinguishing the proper institutional reaction from the social one.

It may be useful to start from the idea that according to Italian criminal law one risks a greater punishment sharing the CD of a singer rather than insulting him directly (Aliprandi, 2012, p. 38).

On the institutional side, Europe and Italy have witnessed a gradual worsening of copyright laws in the last ten years. As in other countries, Italian researches on the impact of the spread of p2p systems on law showed how the reaction of the legal system to such technological innovation has just resulted in an increase of copyright protection (AGCOM, 2010; Aliprandi, 2012; Blengino, 2009, 2011).

Counter-piracy fits within the current tendency of European 'control crime' policies (Garland, 2001). Extension of the criminalization of the copyright violation to non-profit copying has imposed a sacrifice of other rights, such as the purchasers' proper use of protected works and privacy rights (Ziccardi, 2005; Pagallo & Durante, 2009). This priority has given rise to new forms of situational crime prevention, which control and limit possibilities for action and users' rights. It has also given policy tasks to private subjects, imposing providers' data traffic storage obligations and starting a vivid debate about the possibility of obliging them to report their own users' violations, following the method accepted by the French law enforcement.[5] In fact, the 'Hadopi law' delegates private subjects to check the Internet and imposes the network disconnection for such users who repeatedly violate copyright laws. Similarly, circulating news speak about a new enforcement of the protection of copyright issued by a 'blitzkrieg' that the Italian Communications Authority (AGCOM) would declare against piracy, introducing faster procedures, that will allow to disable the links offering illegal material.

All these strategies to contrast piracy were promoted by 'Copyright Crusaders' (Lessig, 2004) and confirm the success of the rhetorical operation performed by digital contents industry in order to assimilate file sharing to theft.

Before music became digital, nobody would have ever thought that lending or borrowing a record or a cassette could become a crime. We should move our attention away from the problem of the observance of copyright in the digital era to the crucial issue of the characters defining such rights. Speaking of 'over the edge' behaviours could not only mean that a particular behaviour has moved away from a law, but also that such limit has moved away from the previous position, taking a certain unchanged behaviour out from the new moral borders of the society (Erikson, 1962).

Few empirical studies which have applied a constructionist approach to the evolution of the software criminal-law protection (Blengino, 2008, 2009; Sette, 2000) or the criminalization of free fruition of digital content (Blengino, 2009) in Italy have shown that these laws are the result of the activities carried out as moral entrepreneurs (Becker, 1963) by representatives of the major industrial and economic sectors involved in the phenomenon. Contents of these technical legislations are strongly influenced by the choice of characters called to take part into the legislative process. Such processes involved particular stakeholders of the industrial field as 'experts'. The parliamentary debate was absent or scarce, since these laws were generally approved through government orders of implementation of European directives (Blengino, 2008, 2009).

If we turn to the concept of 'juridical field' (Bourdieu, 1986) file sharing criminalization process could be observed as a product of the power relationships, which characterize the relationships among subjects with different interests and powers within that field. File sharing criminalization process therefore represents a good example of construction and public introduction of a 'social problem', whose achievements was carried out by lobbies of the audio-visual industry (Spector & Kitsuse, 2001).

The attribution of the crime label to file sharing practice is the result of the ability of the content industry representatives to convey their particular perception of damage to translate their interests in law recognized rights. Records companies and movie editors have been engaged in the conduction of a media campaign highly played on symbolism since a long time. This campaign aims to spread the idea that music and film downloading represents a growing danger (Blengino, 2009; p. 93 et seq.). Such operation was accompanied by their data and research and it preceded by a strong media campaign aimed to set downloading and sharing within the category of theft (Oliviennes, 2008), first in the collective imagination and then into the legislative agenda (Blengino, 2009, p. 152 et seq.).

The idea that downloading and sharing are synonymous of 'stealing' is confined to the level of a – even though very effective – rhetorical argument in Italy. It does not have a real legal formalization, since Italian Penal Code defines theft as the subtraction of other people's movable objects. However, copyright law sanctions worsening is mainly due to the massive communication campaigns launched by the music and film businesses that, with a clear strain on language, have sent messages that compare the downloading of a song to car theft and pickpocketing (Blengino, 2009, p. 154). Music business has also employed informative campaigns in order to awaken young generations' opinion about this topic, by making use of government support and pop music singers as testimonials. Remembering the 2005 advertisement featuring the famous Italian actor and writer Giorgio Faletti in cooperation with SIAE and Ministers Council Presidency against multimedia piracy, or the campaign 'in Classroom, copyright lesson hour: antipiracy exercises' aimed to schools and carried out by audio-visual business associations under the patronage of the Ministry of Education with the participation of some of the most popular young Italian singers among which Giorgia, Le Vibrazioni and Cesare Cremonini.

The project for criminalization of 'theft' of works of art was created through sharing technologies involving the legislature in 2004 with the approval of the so-called 'Urbani act'.[6]

This law was introduced with the aim of opposing music and movie piracy and it owns its name to Berlusconi's government's Culture Minister of that period. Of course this law shows a clear interest of the Head of the Government about this issue, as he was actually the owner of some of the major Italian film businesses. *European Union Copyright Directive* (EUCD) was urgently changed into law in order to fight the spread of illegal audio-visual material in support of the entertainment activities, since piracy 'is a theft and should be treated as such'. The Minister justified this law with the idea that an excessive Internet freedom would lead to the risk 'of navigating in a network with no contents in the future, a cybernetic Dead Sea dried up of ideas'.[7]

Considering that the original function of the copyright was community benefit coming from the increase of cultural production (Lessig, 2004), it sounds as a paradox to notice that legal decisions processes in this field are highly influenced by majors' requests that deprive public of the possibility of enjoying new communication possibilities freely (Gross, 2006). What is also peculiar is the way in which these decisional processes just give users a definite marginal role. All the processes that led to issue, conversion and subsequent amendment of 'Urbani Act' are the product of continuous readjustments inside a conflict which sees business majors' requests coming from the so-called 'people of the net' as protagonists. Although, opinion movements in defense of digital rights and freedoms were created, users' voices remained almost unheard. 'Urbani act' issue and its conversion to law were, in fact, juxtaposed to reactions of associations in defense of digital rights.

Protests, press releases and petitions, with which these associations have claimed their positions with the support of some opposition politicians (Blengino, 2009, p. 148), induced the parliament to listen to the voices of 'Italian most important Internet representatives'. Parliamentary hearings of the parties have been promoted, during which the law dissent was confirmed by representatives of different organizations,[8] stating that 'exchange of goods is normal in real life while it is considered a crime if performed through digital form'.[9]

However, the final version of the law confirmed copying not for profit as a criminal act, totally reflecting what had been asked from the Italian collecting society of copyright (SIAE), requests of software industries and audio-visual businesses (BSA, FAPAV, FPM), while consumers' associations' opinions were ignored.

Similar developments for the creation of an anti-piracy law can be seen in the institution of the Italian Government Technical Committee against piracy and digital media crimes.[10] It gave rise to several arguments from consumers' associations, because it was composed by representatives of different ministers, the Head of SIAE, but it does not involve any users', industries' or culture representatives.

File Sharing and Social Behaviours

Internet access rate has experienced a significant increase in the last years, in line with European average. In 2012, about 60% of Italians used the Internet (Censis, 2012; Istat, 2012). It is a considerable increase, if we consider that users' share was steady at 38.2% in 2008 (Istat, 2013, p. 237). Among households with at least one minor, 70.8% use a broadband connection (Istat, 2012). Probably because of the delay with which Italy is carrying out the process of digitization and ICT spread, and the low circulation of streaming music, downloading music from p2p web sites is still significantly more widespread than usage of music via streaming and access to online stores (Aliprandi, 2012, p. 118).

Currently available data shows a mismatch between the response of European and Italian institutions to file sharing and the social perception of this phenomenon. Despite increasingly strict penalties, distribution practice and sharing of protected files steadily increase its social diffusion (Schulze & Mochalski, 2009). In 2008, 35% of young Europeans had employed this practice to exchange music and movies (AGCOM, 2010, p. 34). The number of users downloading from p2p channels is continuously growing in Italy. In 2011, this practice involved 24.3% of users (Istat, 2011), while in 2012 Internet was used to download music contents from 31% of users (with peaks of 57% between 18 and 19 years) (Istat, 2012).

The incapability of positive law to perform its function of behaviour orientation is confirmed in some surveys, that verified how p2p networks' volume of traffic have not undergone any influence from the changes of the legal background produced by seizures and interruptions of servers' activity. EDonkey traffic levels did not diminish after many server networks were closed (Ferguson, 2006). In the same way, users seemed to be completely careless about the pronunciation of the sentence, even if they are often very 'spectacularized', as it happened in The Pirate Bay case. In reference to the Grockster case, Oberholzer-Gee & Strumpf (2010) verified how a particular decision of the American Supreme Court did not give origin to any effect changing American users' behaviour.

Network undermines copyright assumptions, which state that perfect copies can only be achieved at an industrial level and that distribution of works only occurs in a controlled and centralized way. With regards to this, someone noticed that illegal file sharing, which was born as a consequence of technological changing, should be recognized as the most important social rule (Cox, Waller, & Drinkwater, 2010; De Poorter, Parisi, & Vanneste, 2005).

The little available data shows that the majority of Italian users does not consider illegal downloading as a deviant act (Aguiar & Martens, 2013; Simmini, 2008) and they do not think that it is correct to pay the information contents which are available on the Internet (CENSIS, 2010, pp. 4–5).

A report dated 2008, of the Italian National Statistical Institute sounds striking since 97.7% of the interviewed claimed that they did not pay for digital contents coming from the Internet and 63.4% claimed that they do not feel inclined to pay for such digital contents, 27% of the interviewed declared that they would be willing to pay for the download if that would allow them to get more choice or easily available contents, which are better than the free ones (Istat, 2008). Therefore, it emerges that files being downloaded from p2p channels takes place because more choice is available on these platforms. (Istat, 2011, 2012).

STEALING, LENDING, DONATING: A SOCIAL DISAGREEMENT ABOUT MUSIC SHARING

Social assessment of legislative transgression represents a key element for the comprehension of this criminal phenomenon. A law which is not shared on a social level, will in fact, not be very effective (Hagan, 1994, p. 13).

Within this perspective, next to the point of view of the institutions and moral entrepreneurs, we must also consider the different perspective of *outsiders* (Becker, 1963), that is those who practice illegal file-sharing.

The existence of a strong social disagreement on the assessment of music file sharing is highlighted by researches carried out by Aliprandi (2012), about the opinion and perception of users on the network. This research has specifically investigated the relationship between *enforcing* of copyright and new ways of using the creative content online and the relationship between *enforcing* of copyright and observance of digital citizenship's rights. Over 70% of the interviewed do not agree with the idea that copyright should be imposed even at the cost of limiting the new forms of contents. The analysis shows a good level of awareness of the legal characterization of this behaviour: 60% do not believe that it is a 'fully lawful behaviour', but 71% disagree with the idea that this phenomenon is 'an absolutely negative behaviour'. Seventy percent of the interviewed, consider music sharing 'a not very legal but now very common and generally accepted behaviour'. There is a generally favourable social perception towards the phenomenon: over 60% of interviewed believe that 'this phenomenon is socially useful as it helps to spread culture'. Over 70% of the interviewed were in disagreement with the legislative decision to criminalize music sharing and compare it to the theft of the physical corresponding object. It is also interesting that 65% said to disagree with the assumption that 'this phenomenon damages the entire economic system', although they agree that the p2p mainly damages manufacturing companies (Aliprandi, pp. 131–32).

The moral tensions generated by music sharing were highlighted by observing the users of the platform p2p 'eMule', which is the most common platform used in Italy (Dei, 2008a). This study focuses on the fact that eMule users are split between two conflicting self-representations of their activities: on one side the theft aspect, on the other the idea of a gift supported by the open source culture which considers network and p2p as the foundation of a new, more democratic structure of social relations. Also, eMule users consider sharing as an ethically dense practice, although it is not free from ambiguities and contradictions. This ethic is made up by rules which define sharing 'good manners'. Among the normative references of the users, the way in which the community of eMule defends itself from fake files from the network, should be taken into account. The community defends itself from files whose actual contents did not match the ones declared. Protection from this practice, which undermines the relationship of trust on which the system is based, is implemented with the 'comments' tool. To take responsibility for this kind of a comment, constitutes a real moral imperative for many eMule users, although it may compromise the anonymous nature of the network (Dei, 2008a).

Why do we Share Music?

The dilemma produced by the various and conflicting norms, that rule the practice of music sharing, clearly emerge from the studies analysing the reasons that have led people to this practice. In a context regulated by legal, social and moral normative references (Pagallo & Durante, 2009; Shang, Chen & Chen, 2008), some investigations on the impact that such laws have had on decisions of individuals, have underlined the definite marginal role of positive anti-piracy rules. Criminal laws have very little ability to influence behaviours (Aliprandi, 2012; Dejean, Thierry, & Raphaël, 2010), since the decision to share musical works on the network lies on a specific ideology of consumers' rights (Shang et al., 2008) and the perception to take part into community based on mutual aid (Dei, 2008a, 2008b). The idea of file sharing as a theft, proposed by representatives of the music business, is opposed to the idea of file sharing as a gift, being a community exchange of cultural contents, a peculiar component of file sharing (Dei, 2008b).

Researches bring out the complexity of the reasons and ethical foundations, of the decisions, of those who are simplistically considered deviant. It seems too easy to bring these reasons to mere economic assessments

(Bennato, 2009; Cooper & Harrison, 2001; Shang et al., 2008). In some cases, file sharing is practiced to test the product before purchase (Aliprandi, 2012; Bhattacharjee, Gopal, Lertwachara, & Marsden, 2006; Bennato, 2007, 2009; Eyun, Chang, & Khang, 2006). Other studies have highlighted the social dimension of this practice as a priority (Dei, 2008a; Shang et al., 2008).

Empirical evidence of the inability of an exclusively econometric perspective to get file sharing social motivations in Italy is offered by some researches. These researchers have identified the reasons of music sharing, especially in changing of consumers' needs by consumers of cultural contents. The reason why users practice file sharing is not only connected to the possibility of acquiring content without paying, but also easy access, and the desire to test products before purchasing them, chance to share, and ability to find everything you are looking for (Bennato, 2007, p. 54). Results confirm that file sharing cannot be considered as another commercial offer and they mostly highlight the role played by p2p systems in spreading cultural contents that are no longer available on the market (Bennato, 2009; Dei, 2008a).

On eMule there is at least a strong core of competent users, who take pleasure in showing their collections, counting on the attention of peers who share the same passions. Recently, eMule's most shared items are 'connoisseur' works (Dei, 2008b), which consist of accurately prepared collections including rare recordings, live concerts, cover images, bootlegs, unofficial recordings and albums which have been out of print for a long time. For example, one can find a broad repertoire of Italian progressive music of the seventies, only available in one or two old vinyl albums owned by few collectors. Moreover, most material available on eMule seems to come from users interested in displaying their skills and tastes. This allows to set the network research on the basis of users' names, who are particularly active and characterized by precise tastes, creating the pre-digital mechanism of the group of friends exploring other friends' collections, lending records, exchanging opinions and offering advice (Dei, 2008a).

The whole p2p mechanism would not work if a predatory and a utilitarian spirit dominated: sharers, but they must be inclined to 'giving', even though they are not asked to deprive themselves of what they offer. Unlike traditional collections, an increase of circulating goods seems to increase their value in this context. The eMule software is programmed in order to follow a mutual exchange philosophy: the more a user makes goods available to the others, the easier and faster he/she will be able to download available goods from the Internet.

WHAT AND WHO PIRACY HURTS?

Arguments put forward by the music industry, in favour of an *enforcement* against music piracy, are built on two assumptions. First, they state that copying is a synonym of stealing and second, they think that an illegally downloaded copy takes the place of one that has not been sold.

Merging file sharing with theft tends to conceal a contradiction: downloading a digital copy does not affect the availability of a certain good to other subjects, but rather the sharing of a certain work on a p2p network multiplies the number of circulating copies, representing a powerful vehicle for the circulation of cultural content.

Even the idea that a downloaded copy imply 'a not sold one' must be questioned.

The request of a legal response to file sharing carried out by the music industry is based on the idea that such a practice represents a detriment to the music market, and thus negatively affecting on production and spread of cultural products. File sharing is proposed as a crime, the harmful action of which would eventually affect consumers. The first question is to consider referring to the responses, with which the legal system deals with the 'problem' of file sharing is then concerned to the real existence of damage to cultural diffusion mentioned by the representatives of the music industry and the connection of such damage to the practice of free files sharing on p2p networks.

In order to understand the social harm produced by music piracy, the following pages will try to examine the question while distinguishing data, perceptions and opinions concerning the various parties involved in the phenomenon, in particular the music industry, artists and consumers.

Does Free Download Damage the Music Market?

The thesis that leads back to the p2p accountability, for a significant damage to the music market, should be checked.

We should first clarify that the chain of the music industry cannot be totally identified with discography. In order to understand the evolution of the music market, we should take a look at the entire chain of the music market (Ardizzone, 2012; Ardizzone & Barbarito, 2009).

A tendency of self-preservation and the inability to adequately respond to the needs of change generated by the spread of new technologies, are the main reasons that explain the position taken by the music industry

(Drew, 2013). Even the European Union Commissioner for the Digital Agenda, invited industries to build creative business models, in order to make art a profitable business, giving up the idea that copyright can be the only business model for the market of cultural contents.[11]

Up-to-date researches about the Italian music market show a steady and indisputable decline in revenues from sales of recorded music (Ardizzone, 2012; Ardizzone & Barbarito, 2009, 2010).

Four majors (SonyBMG, EMI, Warner, Universal), reach a market share of almost 80% of the global market and control the distribution. On the other side, consumption and production are competitive, since there are many authors, composers, performers and consumers. Furthermore, there are about a thousand small independent record labels in Italy. Independent labels have a greater economic efficiency than majors, they act as true innovators because they discover new artists, even though they are usually employed by majors afterwards (Ardizzone, 2012, p. 5)

Time coincidence between the onset of the crisis in CD sales and the broadcast of files free sharing (Zentner, 2005), is used by the recording industry to support the view that the decline in music sales should be connected to such programs. However, the so-called 'Napster hypothesis' neglects the possible existence of other factors in the decline of the contents market (Bennato, 2009, p. 64).

Even researches, identifying file sharing as being responsible for the CD market crisis, acknowledge that the decline of such sales can only be partially attributed to p2p (Michel, 2006; Rob & Waldfogel, 2007; Zentner, 2005). This decrease seems to have been mainly determined by other factors, such as the advent of the MP3 player (Cooper & Harrison, 2001; Waelbroek, 2006) and the diffusion of listening to music on the computer (Boorstin, 2004; Bennato, 2007; Oberholzer-Gee & Strumpf, 2007).

We cannot ignore researches that deny the role and responsibility of file sharing in the decrease of selling music. Some studies assert that the effect of file sharing on music albums sales is statistically insignificant, because (Balducci, 2009; Bhattacharjee et al., 2006; Oberholzer-Gee, & Strumpf, 2007; Tanaka, 2004; Waelbroek, 2006) the damage produced by the missed sale would have been, in fact, counterbalanced by following a decision to purchase the new releases of the product.

Other researches even claim the existence of positive effect of file sharing on copyrighted material sales (Boorstin, 2004). Such investigations affirm that p2p users usually buy more music than those who do not practice files sharing (Bjerkoe & Sorbo, 2010; Frank N. Magid Associated, 2009; Andersen & Frenz, 2010). Similar results from a study commissioned by the Swiss Parliament[12] led this country to give legal recognition to the free sharing of music.

Data from an Italian study on the impact of file sharing on consumption, shows an essential balance between the consumption behaviours of 'downloaders free' and 'downloaders pay'. P2p impacts differently on domestic and non-domestic cultural consumption. In fact, while CD purchases decrease, music events are recording a positive trend. File sharing is a behaviour that affects mainly non-consumers, that is to say, those who would not buy contents in any case, either because they are not interested or because they could not afford such products (Bennato, 2007).

The impact generated by the introduction in Italy of new legal channels, aimed to digital format music listening, must be verified. At the moment, we can just say that the introduction of a platform such as Spotify is recording a great success in Italy. It should be examined whether this method can present a real alternative to illegal use, as has been observed by others (Clement, Rangaswamy, & Vadali, 2012).

Does File Sharing Damage Consumption and Consumers?

Spread of music sharing represents a loss for traditional music industry, but this is not the same for music market in general. Changes in music employment made alternative forms of consumption come out and, consequently, also new market spaces.

Despite the crisis, revenues for the music sector have been growing steadily in OECD area (OECD, 2012, p. 182). Even the latest independent data collected in Italy notes the strength of its system (Ardizzone, 2012; Ardizzone & Barbarito, 2010). Although in 2009, the turnover of the entire sector had fallen by 9% compared to the previous year, this decrease is essentially due to the drastic drop in sales in consumer audio electronics sector (−25%), which must be contextualized in a year marked by the economic crisis and a general reduction of consumption and GDP of 5.1%.

Even though the sales of the digital market still do not compensate for the loss of the physical market, the solidity of the music system is good. Digital music is a promising segment and records the best performance of the whole music system (up 13%). Even live music shows an increase of 3% compared to the previous year.

We should also pay attention to the complementary goods market (Bennato, 2007; Oberholzer-Gee & Strumpf, 2010, p. 39; OECD, 2012).

Dutch studies (TNO, 2009; Van Eijk, Poort, & Rutten, 2010) underline that file sharing economic implications are strongly positive. This practice does not reduce sales of these products: 68% of file sharers purchase music and p2p users spend in merchandise and go to concerts more frequently than those who do not download (Van Eijk et al., 2010, pp. 43–44). The greater propension of illegal downloaders to spend for live music found in France (Brousseau & Feledziak, 2007) seems to be also confirmed in Italy. Concerts market showed good results in the last few years. In particular, pop music grew by 7% in 2008 (Ardizzone & Barbarito, 2009, p. 40) and by 3.4% in 2009 (Ardizzone, 2012). Also, record companies are starting to realize that the music market is changing. Sony and Warner bought two concert organizations, market leaders of Italy, and are focusing on the general management of the artist, taking care of merchandising and live events (Ardizzone, 2012).

Furthermore, several researches show that file sharing is used in order to evaluate a product so that it could represent the advance of legal purchases (Aguiar & Martens, 2013; Aliprandi, 2012; Andersen & Frenz, 2010; Bennato, 2007, 2009; Boorstin, 2004).

The recent research, carried out by Aguiar and Martens (2013) on behalf of the EU Commission, has analysed shopping habits of more than 16,000 European consumers, who use legal online systems for listening to digital music. Using clickstream data, the results of the research suggest that, European users do not think that illegal downloading could replace legal digital music. Every 10% increase of illegal downloads seems to correspond to an increase of legal market sales, even though a small one of 0.2%. In opposition to general opinion, this trend would suggest that the illegal spread of copyrighted material actually increases the revenues for the music company. According to this research, if platforms for the unauthorized distribution of audio-visual content did not exist, the flow of clicks to the legal market sites such as Amazon, iTunes and Spotify would decrease. A research, on behalf of the Authority of English Telecommunications (KantarMedia, 2012), about the perception of English users on infringement of online copyright clearly found out that the use of systems for illegal downloads does not decrease a user's purchase on legal contents.

In particular, about 12% of UK Internet population is a 'hybrid' group, which finds contents on the web both legally and illegally, through file sharing systems. This group of consumers is the one who spends more time on cultural consumption, which is about 3 times more than those who do not use any illegal system.

'*Piracy hurts you too: let us say no*!' is one of the most persistent Italian industry campaigns. The music industry arguments, claiming that piracy ultimately harms users, appear to be rather fragile.

Researchers observed the growth of the phenomenon and identified two main reasons for the decision of illegally downloading material: the first is represented by freedom and accessibility, the second from the ability to test 'new products' to decide whether to purchase them later or not.

Considering copyright protected works and works shared via file sharing as substitute goods may sound too simplistic. Some studies underline that file sharing often plays a *replacement* role, that is, to download a product that would not have been purchased if one had had to pay for it (Aguiar & Martens, 2013; Bennato, 2007; Blackburn, 2004; Boorstin, 2004). This form of consumption highlights the improper simplification made by those who consider every downloaded copy as a missed sale. Networks are used to buying music that would not have been purchased otherwise, for economic reasons (Bennato, 2007; Maffioletti & Ramello, 2004) or because it is out of the commercial circuit (Dei, 2008a).

We cannot ignore that accessibility to an almost unlimited amount of music has also had an impact on one of the key aspects of music consumption that is collecting (Dei, 2008b).

Results from researches show how file sharing could increase consumers' wellness (TNO, 2009), increasing the variety of available content, stimulating the decrease in CD prices and promoting cultural contents spread, thanks to the new circulation of songs, which are out of the market. Furthermore, according to the previous practices of exchange and cooperation among music fans, the large amount and variety of music products available through p2p systems would tend to increase the artistic skills of the users (Dei, 2008a).

Does File Sharing Damage Artists?

One of the most popular arguments used by the audio-visual industry is that 'downloading material protected by copyright is not only a crime, but it prevents artists, those you love the most, to continue expressing themselves. Piracy imprisons creativity' (IMAIE Campaign 2006).

Majors' argument that file sharing disincentives artistic production assumes that copies acquired on p2p networks are substitute goods and that reduction of proceeds constitutes an important motivation for artists to reduce production (Oberholzer-Gee & Strumpf, 2010).

Various researches question the theory that artists would be damaged by file sharing (Blackburn, 2004, 2005; Connolly & Krueger, 2006; Mortimer & Sorensen, 2005; Mortimer, Nosko & Sorensen, 2010; Oberholzer-Gee & Strumpf, 2010). Records sales represent a decreasingly important aspect in the revenues of an artist. Digitization has increased the real enjoyment of music, by changing its mode (Oberholzer-Gee & Strumpf, 2010, p. 25).

Some European researches[13] have noticed a relevant increase in artists' revenue in recent years. Musicians and singers have faced the decrease of records' sales by increasing money coming from live tours and performances. Some studies, however, dispute that artistic production is exclusively linked to the perspective of income growth and observe how the economic component plays a relatively small role in encouraging music production. In a context in which the possibility of becoming a star is law, reasons of artistic production may be different from the economic ambitions, keeping, for example, a passion for their work (Oberholzer-Gee & Strumpf, 2010). Copyright infringement through file sharing can then be beneficial for artists, for increasing their visibility (Ben-Shahar & Jacob, 2004; Waelbroek, 2006). For these very reasons, this practice is considered as an additional source of opportunities, promotion or income, by the artists themselves (Bjerkoe & Sorbo, 2010; Madden, 2004). A study on behalf of Dutch government (SEO, 2011) involved, involving about 4,000 musicians, directors, writers and photographers. More than half of the interviewed artists underlined more than one positive aspect in the free distribution of works, focusing, in particular, on benefits in terms of increased visibility. 22% of Dutch artists have also stated they had illegally downloaded works of others. According to a recent survey (Hammond, 2013), even the most popular artists benefit from the positive advertising of illegal sharing.

In addition to data from researches, we can mention some fortunate cases of business models, which are an alternative to copyright standard system. The most famous is the case of Radiohead, the British band that publishes their albums online for some time before marketing them, allowing users to download freely or by donation. The success of the publication of 'In Rainbows' in 2007 was amazing. The record has sold over 3 million copies earning from voluntary payments, from iTunes, CDs and special boxes. Furthermore, Radiohead's tour, coinciding with the release of 'In Rainbows' had sold more than 1.2 million tickets. The same system was adopted by Coldplay in May 2009. They freely distributed the album 'LeftRightLeftRightLeft', giving origin to the amazing success of the Viva La Vida Tour.

Referring to smaller Italian productions, the lucky case of the singer Paolo Toso can be mentioned: he won an important Italian rock festival in 1995, but he was almost unknown until 2009. Toso has obtained his popularity by releasing his single 'The Prince of Fools' in free download on the platform Rockoff. He is still the only Italian singer who allows free downloads of his songs via a free App.

Another case of success, thanks to the spread of free music, is represented by Gem BOY, an Italian band amending jokingly popular songs. The group promotes itself spreading tracks for free on the Internet and this has made the group very famous in Italy. Despite this, Gem BOY do not appear on official music channels such as MTV and have sold a few records, but their songs are very well known amongst young Italians and thousands of people attend their concerts (Gubitosa, 2005, p. 108).

Lastly, musicians have begun to openly declare their disagreement about the rules that criminalize file sharing of copyrighted works. The former front man of the English rock band, Oasis, Liam Gallagher and Italian singers like Frankie Hi Energy and Elisa stated that they were in favour of file sharing for all benefits that this practice creates in terms of visibility of the artist. Other Italian singers, among which Celentano, Ramazzotti, Ligabue, Bocelli urge to open new mechanisms of management of copyright, which would be better suited to the new patterns of music consumption.[14]

CONCLUSIONS

Music sharing is designed as a highly conflicted crime (Hagan, 1994, p. 16). The placement of file sharing within the limits of the criminal law seems a technological upgrade in the dynamics of social inequity which, according to Hagan (1994, p. 23), lead to the criminalization of vulnerable subjects. Such an operation reflects a partial understanding of the effects produced by free file sharing.

In view of the different meanings given by the social characters, the criminalization of file sharing was not related to the extent of social harm caused by that practice. But it was rather determined by the ability of the content that the industry represents to turn private interests into general ones . Such effects also do not seem to fall back to artists or consumers, who derive some benefits from free file sharing.

File sharing did not spoil, but changed the cultural contents market. Negative effects suffered by the music industry would be paid back through a commercial strategy performed by the music producers. File sharing criminalization is, therefore, suitable to be read as the product of power relationships within the juridical field (Bourdieu, 1986), which characterize the relations between subjects with different interests and a different ability to translate those interests into rights. The high contingency of dynamics inside the legal field, however, leaves hope that in the future the positions in the debate on p2p can somehow find a balance.

NOTES

1. Copyright law 22 april 1941 n. 633 was changed by Law 18 august 2000 n. 248, Law Decree 9 april 2003, n. 68 implementing the directive *2001/29/CE on the harmonization of copyright,* Law 21 may 2004, n. 128 and Law 31 march 2005, n. 43.
2. Durkheim's idea, that crime is a necessary and useful social fact serving to strengthen the collective consciousness supporting regulatory compliance, is the basis for different sociological theories on crime, from Merton (2000), to advance to the Chicago School and theories of deviant subcultures (Cohen, 1955; Sutherland, 1987).
3. Within this theoretical approach, the interactionist perspective stressed that crime doesn't have any objective connotation, since it depends on the meaning assigned to an act (Becker, 1963; Erikson, 1962). For a review of authors and research conducted within this theoretical stand please refer to Hester and Eglin (1992).
4. While recognizing the sophistication of Bourdieu's concept of juridical field, here this metaphor is used specifically to emphasize the plurality of actors and forces that contribute to the displacement of the contours of the penal area (Bourdieu, 1986, p.16).
5. French Law 12 june 2009 n. 669.
6. Italian Decree law 72/2004 transformed in Law 21 may 2004, n. 128.
7. Available at http://punto-informatico.it/452662/PI/News/speciale-decreto-urbani.aspx
8. All these organizations are mentioned by Blengino (2009, p. 149). Some full interventions can be found at http://www.key4biz.it/
9. Intervention of the consumers' association Adiconsum in the Parliament Commitee on Culture (http://www.key4biz.it/download/free/news/Audizione_Decreto_Urbani.pdf). In the same direction see also the intervention of the association Altroconsumo, (http://www.altroconsumo.it/accesso-ai-contenuti/20040520/decreto-urbani-la-nostra-posizione-ATTACH_s48231.pdf)
10. DPCM 15 september 2008 signed by Silvio Berlusconi.
11. www.ilpost.it/2011/11/21/cambiare-copyright-neelie-kroes/
12. Rapport du Conseil fédéral sur les utilisations illicites d'œuvres sur Internet en réponse au postulat 10.3263 Savary, http://www.ejpd.admin.ch/content/dam/data/pressemitteilung/2011/2011-11-30/ber-br-f.pdf

13. In particular see the results of Times Labs Blog's research on http://blog.tntvillage.scambioetico.org/?p=4306, and and the study by BI Norvegian (Bjerkoe & Sorbo 2010).

14. Available at http://www.itespresso.it/i-cantanti-big-contro-la-siae-42380.html

REFERENCES

AGCOM - Autorità per le garanzie nelle comunicazioni (2010). *Il diritto d'autore sulle reti di comunicazione elettronica. Indagine conoscitiva.* Retrieved from http://www.agcom.it/default.aspx?DocID=3790

Aguiar, L., & Martens, B. (2013). *Digital music consumption on the internet.* JRC Technical Reports, Institute for Prospective Technological Studies Digital Economy Working Paper 2013/04, European Commission. Retrieved from http://ftp.jrc.es/EURdoc/JRC79605.pdf

Aliprandi, S. (2012). *Il diritto d'autore nell'era digitale. Una ricerca empirica su comportamenti, percezione sociale e livello di consapevolezza tra gli utenti della rete.* Ph.D thesis. Università di Milano Bicocca. Retrieved from http://boa.unimib.it/bitstream/10281/30053/1/Phd_unimib_724942.pdf

Andersen, B., & Frenz, M. (2010). Don't blame the peer to peer file-sharers. *Journal of Evolutionary Economics, 20*(5), 715–740.

Ardizzone, A. (2012). Filiera dell'industria musicale e nuovi modelli di business in Italia. *Tafter Journal, 51.* Retrieved from http://www.tafterjournal.it/2012/08/31/filiera-dellindustria-musicale-e-nuovi-modelli-di-business-in-italia/

Ardizzone, A., & Barbarito, L. (2009). *Economia della musica in Italia, Rapporto 2009.* Milano: IULM.

Ardizzone, A., & Barbarito, L. (2010). *Economia della musica in Italia, Rapporto 2010.* Milano: IULM.

Balducci, F. (2009). Music or high-tech lovers? Inferring into the determinants of music consumption. In *Rivista Italiana degli Economisti* (Vol. 2, p. 361–394). Available at SSRN: http://ssrn.com/abstract = 1525506

Balestrino, A. (2008). It is a theft but not a crime. *Science Direct, European Journal of Political Economy, 24*, 455–469.

Becker, H. S. (1963). *Studies in the sociology of deviance.* New York, NY: Free Press.

Ben-Shahar, D., & Jacob, A. (2004). Selective enforcement of copyright as an optimal monopolistic behaviour. *Contributions to Economic Analysis & Policy, 3*(I), 1.

Bennato, D. (Ed.), (2007). *I comportamenti di consumo dei contenuti digitali in Italia.* Fondazione Luigi Einaudi.

Bennato, D. (2009). L'utente di file sharing oltre il senso commune. *Sociologia della Comunicazione, 39*, 61–78.

Bhattacharjee, S., Gopal, R., Lertwachara, K., & Marsden, J. R. (2006). Consumer search and retailer strategies in the presence of online music sharing. *Journal of Management Information Systems, 23*(1), 129–159.

Bjerkoe, R., & Sorbo, A. (2010). *The norvergian music industry in the age of digitalization.* BI Norwegian School of Management, thesis.

Blackburn, D. (2004). *On-line piracy and recorded music sales.* Working Paper. Harvard University.

Blackburn, D. (2005). *Developing superstars: The effect of unauthorized copying on investment in musical talent.* Working Paper. Retrieved from http://davidjhblackburn.com/papers/developing_superstars.pdf

Blengino, C. (2008). I reati della rete e la costruzione dei rischi nello spazio digitale. *Antigone, 3*, 104–26.

Blengino, C. (2009). *La devianza informatica tra crimini e diritti: un'analisi socio giuridica.* Roma: Carocci.

Blengino, C. (2011). La condivisione di musica sulle reti peer to peer: Una riflessione sociogiuridica sul crimine. *Sociologia del diritto, 1*, 83–106.

Boorstin, E. (2004). *Music sales in the age of file sharing.* Retrieved from http://www.cs.princeton.edu/~felten/boorstin-thesis.pdf

Bourdieu, P. (1986). La force du droit: Elements per une sociologie du droit. *Actes de la Recherche en Sciences Sociales, 64*, 3–19.

Brusseau, E. (2008). The economics of music production: The narrow paths for record companies to enter the digital era. *Communications & Strategies, 72*, 131–154.

Brousseau, E., & Feledziak, B. (2007). *L'économie des Droits d'Auteurs dans le domaine de la Musique.* Report, Ministère de la Culture et de la Communication.

CENSIS. (2010). *44° Rapporto annuale sulla situazione sociale del Paese.* Retrieved from http://www.censis.it/10?shadow_ricerca=109145

CENSIS. (2012). *46° Rapporto annuale sulla situazione sociale del Paese.* Retrieved from http://www.censis.it/10?shadow_ricerca=118876

Clement, M., Rangaswamy, A., & Vadali, S. (2012). Consumer responses to legal music download services that compete with illegal alternatives. *Service Science March, 4*, 4–23.

Cohen, A. (1955). *Delinquent boys: The culture of the gang.* Glencoe, IL: Free Press.

Connolly, M., & Krueger, A. B. (2006). Rockonomics: The economics of popular music. In V. A. Ginsburgh & D. Throsby (Eds.), *Handbook of the economics of art and culture,* (Vol. 1, pp. 667–719). Amsterdam: Elsevier.

Cooper, J., & Harrison, D. M. (2001). The social organization of audio piracy on the Internet. *Media Culture Society, 23*(1), 71–89.

Cox, J., Collins, A., & Drinkwater, S. (2010). Seeders, leechers and social norms: Evidence from the market for illicit downloading. *Information Economics Policy, 22*(4), 299–305.

Dei, F. (2008a). Tra dono e furto: la condivisione della musica in rete. In M. Santoro (Ed.), *Cultura in Italia. Nuovi media, vecchi media* (pp. 49–74). Bologna, Il Mulino-Istituto Cattaneo.

Dei, F. (2008b). Tra le maglie della rete. In F. Dei (Ed.) *Culture del dono* (pp. 11–41). Roma: Meltemi.

Dejean, S., Thierry, P., & Raphaël, S. (2010) *Une première évaluation des effets de la loi Hadopi sur les pratiques des Internautes français,* M@rsouin, CREM et Université de Rennes 1.

De Poorter, B., Parisi, F., & Vanneste, S. (2005). Problems with the enforcement of copyright law: is there a social norm backlash? *International Journal of Economics of Business, 12*, 361–369.

Drew, R. (2013). *New technologies and the business of music: Lessons from the 1980s home taping hearings, popular music and society.* doi:10.1080/03007766.2013.764613

Durkheim, E. (1999/1895). *La divisione del lavoro sociale.* Milano: Comunità.

Van Eijk, N., Poort, J., & Rutten, P. (2010). Legal, economic and cultural aspects of file sharing. *Communications & Strategies, 77*, 36–54.

Erikson, K. T. (1962). *Wayward puritans*. New York, NY: John Wiley.

Eyun, J. K., Chang, B.-H., & Khang, H. (2006). Exploring influential factors on music piracy across countries. *Journal of Communication*, *56*(2), 406–426.

Frank N. Magid Associated. (2009). *Introducing hollywood's best customers vuze user vs. General Internet*. Retrieved from http://www.magid.com/sites/default/files/pdf/vuze.pdf

Garland, D. (2001). *The culture of control*. Chicago, IL: University of Chicago Press.

Gross, R. (2006). *Tragedy of the commons: Intellectual property rights in the information age*, Mit Press, retrieved from http://www.imaginelaw.com/lawyer-attorney-1181356.html

Gubitosa, C. (2005). *Elogio della pirateria*. Altreconomia.

Hagan, J. (1994). *Crime and disrepute*. London: Pine Forge Press.

Hammond, R. (2013). *Profit leak? Pre-release file sharing and the music industry*. Retrieved from http://www4.ncsu.edu/~rghammon/Hammond_File_Sharing_Leak.pdf

Hester, S., & Eglin, P. (1992). *A sociology of crime*. London & New York: Routledge.

ISTAT. (2008). Rapporto annuale. La situazione nel Paese nel 2008, Roma.

ISTAT. (2011). *Cittadini e nuove tecnologie*. Retrieved from http://www.istat.it/it/archivio/48388

ISTAT. (2012). *Cittadini e nuove tecnologie*. Retrieved from http://www.istat.it/it/archivio/78166

ISTAT. (2013). *BES. Il benessere equo e sostenibile in Italia*. Retrieved from http://www.istat.it/it/files/2013/03/bes_2013.pdf

KantarMedia. (2012). *OCI tracker benchmark study Q3 2012*. Retrieved from http://stakeholders.ofcom.org.uk/binaries/research/telecoms-research/online-copyright/Kantar-Media.pdf

Lessig, L. (2004). *Free culture*. New York, NY: The Penguin Press.

Madden, M. (2004). *Artists, musicians and the Internet. Artists and musicians are enthusiastic internet users and they believe the internet helps them make and sell their work*. PewInternet. Retrieved from http://www.pewinternet.org/Reports/2004/Artists-Musicians-and-the-Internet.aspx

Maffioletti, A., & Ramello, G. (2004). Should we put them in jail? Copyright infringement, penalties and consumer behavior. *Review of Economic Research on Copyright Issues*, *1*(2), 81–95.

Merton, R. K. (2000/1949). *Teoria e struttura sociale*. Bologna, Mulino.

Michel, N. J. (2006). The impact of digital file sharing on the music industry: An empirical analysis. *Topics in Economic Analysis & Policy*, *6*(1), art.18, bepress.

Mortimer, J. H., Nosko, C., & Sorensen, A. (2010). *Supply responses to digital distribution: recorded music and live performances*. NBER Working Paper. Retrieved from http://www.nber.org/papers/w16507

Mortimer, J. H., & Sorensen, A. (2005). Supply responses to digital distribution: Recorded music and live performances, working paper. Harvard and Stanford University.

Oberholzer-Gee, F., & Strumpf, K. (2007). The effect of file sharing on record sales: An empirical analysis. *Journal of Political Economy*, *115*(1), 1–42.

Oberholzer-Gee, F., & Strumpf, K. (2010). File sharing and copyright. *Innovation Policy and the Economy*, *10*, 19–55.

OECD. (2012). *OECD internet economy outlook 2012*. OECD Publishing.

Oliviennes, D. (2008). *La gratuità è un furto. Quando la pirateria uccide la cultura*. Milano: Scheiwiller.

Pagallo, U., & Durante, M. (2009). Three roads to p2p systems and their impact on business practices and ethics. *Journal of Business Ethics*, *90*(4), 551–564.

Rob, R., & Waldfogel, J. (2007). Piracy on the silver screen. *Journal of Industrial Economics*, *55*(3), 379–395.

Shang, R.-A., Chen, Y.-C., & Chen, P.-C. (2008). Ethical Decisions about sharing music files in the P2P environment. *Journal of Business Ethics*, *80*, 349–365.

Schulze, H., & Mochalski, K. (2009). *Internet study 2008/2009*. Retrieved on http://www.ipoque.com/sites/default/files/mediafiles/documents/internet-study-2008-2009.pdf

SEO. (2011). *Wat er speelt De positie van makers en uitvoerend kunstenaars in de digitale Omgeving*. Retrieved from http://www.rijksoverheid.nl/documenten-en-publicaties/rapporten/2011/04/11/rapport-wat-er-speelt.html

Sette, R. (2000). *Criminalità informatica*. Bologna: Clueb.

Simmini, R. (2008). *Il download illegale di musica e film da internet e la devianza minorile, discorso pubblico e discorso giuridico*. Retrieved from http://files.splinder.com/ce10d8cfd5aa19f7f012dc55c85bda96.pdf

Spector, M., & Kitsuse, J. (2001). *Constructing social problems*. London: Transaction Publishers.

Sutherland, E. (1949). *White collar crime*. New York, NY: Dryden Press.

Tanaka, T. (2004). *Does file sharing reduce music CD sales?* 13 december. Retrieved from http://hermes-ir.lib.hit-u.ac.jp/rs/bitstream/10086/15965/1/070iirWP05-08.pdf

TNO. (2009). *Economic and culture effects of file sharing of music, film and games*. Retrieved from http://www.ivir.nl/publicaties/vaneijk/Ups_And_Downs_authorised_translation.pdf

Waelbroek, P. (2006). Evolution du marchè de la musique préenregistrée à l'ère numérique. *Reflets et Perspectives*, *XLV*(4), 83–92.

Zentner, A. (2005). File sharing and international sales of copyrighted music. *Topics in Economic Analysis & Policy*, *5*(1), 21.

Ziccardi, G. (2005). *Informatica, diritti e libertà*. Modena: Mucchi.

EMPIRICAL INSIGHTS INTO RECORDED MUSIC CONSUMER BEHAVIOR AND COPYRIGHT INFRINGEMENT

Juan D. Montoro-Pons and
Manuel Cuadrado-García

ABSTRACT

Purpose – *Despite an abundance of literature on the effects of copyright infringement on music consumption, empirical evidence remains ambiguous. The aim of this chapter is to quantify the effect of copyright infringement on recorded music purchases and live music attendance for Spanish frequent music consumers, and to measure its effect on participation for all music consumers.*

Design/methodology approach – *We rely on survey data for the Spanish population as our main information source and use propensity score matching to estimate the average effect of copyright infringement on music consumption. In order to do so, the methodology aims at estimating the difference between actual outcomes (record purchases or*

Music and Law
Sociology of Crime, Law and Deviance, Volume 18, 245–267

ISSN: 1521-6136/doi:10.1108/S1521-6136(2013)0000018015

attendance to live concerts) for copyright infringers and the (counterfactual) outcome would they had not been infringers.

Findings – *Two findings stand out. First, and with regards to recorded music consumption, we find a net positive effect of copyright infringement on full album purchases although a nonsignificant one for tracks. Second, there is a positive and significant effect on live attendance, which is consistent with an indirect appropriation effect across products. These results are robust when participation is considered, but some interesting differences arise between recorded music purchasers and live concerts attenders.*

Originality/value – *First, the use of a counterfactual control group provides an additional approach to the assessment of copyright infringement. Second, within the same framework we investigate the effects of copyright infringement on recorded and live music, an approach that sheds some light on the degree of complementarity between both markets.*

Keywords: Piracy; music consumption; sampling effect; substitution effect; propensity score matching

INTRODUCTION

The consumption of digital goods has been in the center of an active debate over the effective protection of copyright. The music industry, the demand of which has been significantly affected since the turn of the century, is a good example. To illustrate this point and using data from Spain, sales of – physical and digital – recorded music between 2001 and 2011 have declined by an average annual rate of 10.21%, going down from 449 to 160 million euros. The industry claims that the Internet and other technological advances that have weakened copyright protection, allowing the potentially infinite reproduction of information goods at a virtually zero marginal cost which, in turn, creates incentives for the substitution in consumption, is the main cause for the reported fall in sales and revenue worldwide. By contrast, consumers and Internet user groups single out alternative causes for the decline in sales, such as the end of a cycle in which consumers substituted their music collections from analog to digital media; tougher competition from other leisure activities such as video-gaming and the Internet;

the possibility of purchasing individual tracks – brought about music digital platforms such as *iTunes*, *Spotify*, or *Amazon* – instead of full albums; or even the lack of creativity or innovation by the industry.

From a theoretical standpoint it remains ambiguous whether copyright infringement can be the ultimate cause of the observed decline in the sector. Consider the case of digital goods that can be easily reproduced and distributed in a market for copies. Two main effects can be identified. First, a negative *substitution effect* that allows consumers to substitute between alternative goods. If the market for copies is a close substitute for originals, then one would expect the former crowding-out the latter. This negative impact on the consumption of originals arises from the fact that originals and copies are competing. Second, a positive effect can stem from the exposure to the market itself (no matter whether it is the market for originals or copies). If the Internet increases accessibility to sampling, by lowering its cost, then copyright infringement can have positive effects in the consumption of recorded music via a greater exposure to and awareness of recorded music, and firms can capture part of the increased demand. Note that in this setup consumers face an asymmetric information setup being music an experience good the quality of which can only be assessed after consumption, in this case after sampling.

Substitution and sampling are not the only effects of copyright infringement on music demand. The economic literature on intellectual property rights shows that other factors play a role in explaining the final effect of copyright infringement on sales. Peitz and Waelbroeck (2006a) survey the theoretical literature on piracy of digital products and identify four main strands: basic models of piracy (where substitution effects prevail), models with indirect appropriation, models with network effects, and models with asymmetric information (in which sampling effects are present).

While the substitution effect is inherent to any model of the demand for information goods under piracy, the main question is to what extent it is offset by other (potentially) positive effects on demand. One way of tackling this is by means of the concept of indirect appropriation. Under indirect appropriability firms can benefit from copyright infringing behavior via price-discrimination for a given product, that is, charging a higher price to those who are more likely to copy more, or by selling goods or services that are complements to the original product. While the former is an example of indirect appropriation across consumers, the latter is an example of indirect appropriation across products (see Peitz & Waelbroeck, 2006a).

In this vein, Varian (2000) models a market for information goods and shows that a seller profits can increase under weak copyright enforcement. The structural parameters of the model (transaction costs of copying, the marginal cost of production, and the ability of the firm to discriminate between different demand segments) determine the outcomes of the model and the likelihood of piracy increasing profits. Boldrin and Levine (2002, 2005) show that markets – in the absence of copyright – allow innovators to appropriate a significant share of the social surplus of their creation, enough to compensate them for the opportunity cost. However, the authors point out that this revenue stream is less than the monopoly rent from copyright. Different scholars critic Boldrin and Levine's conclusions by targeting their underlying assumptions: if demand is not inelastic and/or the seller cannot price-discriminate then copyright still is a second best (see (Klein, Lerner, & Murphy, 2002; Liebowitz, 2006).

If music involves social interaction then network effects enter the model. Network effects or consumption externalities emerge when the utility of one consumer depends on the consumption decision of other consumers. If this is the case, a weak copyright enforcement, leading to an enlargement of the market via copies, may increase firms' profits. Considering the case of music, if piracy increases the level of awareness of a band and its reputation it can, ultimately, be economically profitable.

Examples of network effects in theoretical models are given by Takeyama, (1994, 1997) and Shy and Thisse (1999). In all these cases a regime in which both a market for originals and copies coexist imply a larger demand for originals relative to the case where there is no copying. In contrast Herings, Peeters, and Yang (2010) focus on direct externalities of P2P networks – compared with the previous indirect consumption externalities of file-sharing and copying. They conclude that the effect of increased consumer participation on such networks which leads to decreasing search costs, download time, and increased availability, unambiguously decrease firms' profits.

The enlargement of markets due to the effect of piracy is also the main focus of Minniti and Vergari (2010) who show that, in emerging markets, the activity of file-sharing allows firms to reach a larger share of consumers that would not otherwise buy, while this effect could be negligible in mature markets. In their model firms can profit from piracy by partially serving an emerging market – in this case firms would not be interested in fighting piracy – while profits decrease in covered markets, that is, mature ones – hence the tougher stance against piracy of firms in these.

As it has been mentioned, information asymmetries make sampling a valuable tool for consumers when dealing with experience goods (Peitz & Waelbroeck, 2006b). When consumers do not hold enough information to assess the quality of a good, then copyright infringement can help spread valuable information and increase the demand for information goods. In this line, it can be shown that piracy can increase profits if this leads to consumers reducing the amount of uncertainty about the final product. As the authors put it, under sampling "consumers are willing to pay more because the match between product characteristics and buyer's tastes is improved".

One widespread argument used by the recording industry is the negative impact of piracy on creativity in the long run. The argument states that piracy threatens the career prospects of new artists as the industry reduces its investment on promoting new talents given the dire profits prospects. However, at least theoretically, it need not be this way. In a recent chapter (Alcalá & González-Maestre, 2010), an asymmetric impact of piracy is considered, helping to raise the awareness of young and niche artists and reducing earnings to superstars. This, in turn, reduces the concentration of sales in the market increasing the market share of young artists hence leading to a greater artistic diversity. Moreover, and contrary to industry's claims, by increasing the chances of new artists in the short run, piracy may enhance creativity in the long run.

The previous discussion shows that the theoretical literature leads to ambiguous outcomes about the effect, if any, of copyright infringement. This chapter aims at finding additional evidence to this research question by using data from the 2010/2011 Survey on Habits and Cultural Practices in Spain (HSCP). We do so by primarily focusing on a segment of the population, that of frequent music consumers. While results only apply to this subgroup it is worth mentioning that they make up 61% of all recorded music buyers that purchased at least one album over the year before the survey was taken. Moreover they do not only represent a significant share of annual recorded music purchases but also are more involved in music in many other ways, which allows us to conjecture that they make up the most significant, and maybe profitable, part of the market. However, and to check for the robustness of these results, we also analyze the impact on participation for all music consumers.

We start with a short review of the empirical literature on copyright infringement in the recorded music sector. Next we describe the dataset, the quantitative analysis, and show the main results. We close with a discussion of the main results.

MUSIC CONSUMPTION AND COPYRIGHT INFRINGEMENT: THE EMPIRICAL EVIDENCE

Looking at the empirical literature, the evidence of copyright infringement on music demand is as varied as the theoretical one, which mostly has dealt with the extent of the net effect. In order to attain this goal, different scholars use different approaches. These can be grouped depending on the type of data used: cross-section or longitudinal country-level data; survey data in microeconometric analysis; and specific data for downloads and legal sales for albums.

Using aggregate country-level data, Hui and Png (2003) analyze the impact of physical piracy on legal demand, and find a net substitution effect such that a unit increase in piracy reduces legal sales in 0.42 units. Peitz and Waelbroeck (2004) use a panel of 16 countries over 1998–2003 to test the effect of Internet piracy. The authors proxy it using the percentage of adult Internet users that downloaded MP3 files at least once; their findings show a CD-sales reduction of 20% over the period of 1998–2002. From a different perspective, Montoro-Pons and Cuadrado-García (2008) use a panel of OECD countries to analyze the relative effectiveness of the legal system in enforcing copyright protection. By testing the sensitivity of the legal demand to the (shadow) cost of copies in countries classified according to their different legal origins, the authors find that the common law system reduces the extent of copyright infringement. This in turns means that the magnitude of the substitution effect depends on the legal framework.

Other authors use individual-level data. Michel (2006), using US household data, concludes that file-sharing, proxyed by PC users, has reduced recorded music expenditure by a 13%. Rob and Waldfogel (2006) use a survey of US college students and show that file-sharing reduced music purchases between 10% and 20% in their sample. Waldfogel (2010) replicates the 2006 analysis by using two surveys undertaken in 2009 and 2010. The interest of repeating this exercise lies in assessing the effects of piracy under a new market arrangement in which individual tracks can be purchased from digital platforms such as iTunes. He finds that the rate of sales' displacement is between 0.15 and 0.30, a value that, surprisingly, is rather similar to the previous findings. Zentner (2006) uses a European survey among 15,000 consumers in year 2001. Using two dummies that control music purchases and Internet downloads, the chapter concludes that file-sharing networking reduce the probability of purchasing music by 30%. Gopal, Bhattacharjee, and Sanders (2006) use an intentions survey to test different hypothesis related to sampling. They find that the reduction of sampling costs has a positive effect on the amount of sampling and sales for unknown music.

Andersen and Frenz (2010) use a survey on the Canadian population and regress CD purchases on a set of covariates and the reported number of downloads. The authors account for the endogeneity of number of downloads by regressing it on instruments of Internet skills. Their main conclusion is that the effect of downloads is not statistically different from zero. Although not being the main focus of the chapter, Montoro-Pons and Cuadrado-García (2011) use a representative survey of cultural consumption of the Spanish population over 15 and find that file-sharing does not significantly affect the probability of prerecorded music purchases for frequent purchasers but has a clear negative effect on it for casual consumers. Finally Montoro-Pons, Cuadrado-García, and Casasús-Estellés (2013) find that copyright infringement increases the frequency of attendance to live performances, an outcome that is consistent with the hypothesis of indirect appropriation across different products.

A third avenue of research relies on individual album (or concert) sales to look at the effects of downloads. Oberholzer-Gee and Strumpf (2007) combine a sample of album sales in the United States in year 2002 and music file downloads and show that piracy has no statistically significant effect on sales. More recently McKenzie (2013) uses time series data on ranks for songs and a proxy for illegal downloads (number of people who have a particular song available for download at any point in time) and finds similar results to the previous study, that is, there is no significant effect on sales. Similarly Battacharjee, Gopal, Lertwachara, Marsden, and Telang (2007) use Billboard charts and file-sharing data to conclude with a negative asymmetric effect of file-sharing on survival in the charts: file-sharing does not affect high-ranked albums although it increases the risk of those at the bottom of the charts. Finally Mortimer, Nosko, and Sorensen (2012) use a dataset of concerts and album sales to analyze the impact of piracy of digital goods on complementary nondigital goods, that is, concerts. They find that while piracy decreases album sales, it increases the demand for concerts. However, this effect is asymmetric, it is more pronounced for smaller artists due to the increased awareness.

As the previous review shows, findings are ambiguous with regards to the effect of infringement on recorded music, while the (limited) evidence for live music points to a positive effect. However, and due to the variety of data sources used, this evidence is at best fragmented. Our empirical work aims at analyzing, using the same dataset, three distinct effects of piracy: on album sales, on track sales, and on attendance to music concerts. By using a matching algorithm we try to overcome the potential problems of selection bias in this kind of studies. Next, we develop the empirical research.

AN EMPIRICAL RESEARCH OF COPYRIGHT INFRINGEMENT IN SPAIN

The Dataset

This research relies on secondary data provided by the 2010/2011 Survey on Habits and Cultural Practices in Spain (SHCP2010). The SHCP2010 is a survey-based research that samples approximately 14,500 individuals. Its main objective is to describe participation and habits in activities related to the different cultural sectors and the arts for the Spanish population over 15. The survey is carried out by the Spanish Ministry of Culture – as part of the National Statistics Planning – and complies with the guidelines by the EUROSTAT's working group on Cultural Statistics. The National Statistics Agency (INE) collaborates in the methodological underpinnings of the sampling design, which is a two stage sampling method with stratified primary sampling units. The theoretical sample size was set to 16,400 second stage units, that is, individuals and the final number of individuals surveyed is 14,486. The survey was conducted using personal interviews between March 2010 and February 2011.

As for its scope, the survey covers individuals' involvement with heritage, reading, performing arts, classical and popular music concerts, cinema and video, prerecorded music, television and radio, computer and the Internet, and other practices related to culture and/or leisure. It also provides information about attitudes toward and opinions on these activities and their practice; cultural equipment of Spanish households; educational attainment; and other sociodemographic factors.

Interestingly, and related to our research question, it includes information about participation through the media for the cultural industries. In these cases the survey asks the respondents to point out whether she/he has engaged in some sort of copyright infringing activity (framing it in a neutral language) by copying or downloading from the Internet copyrighted materials.

The Spanish Music Consumer

As for recorded popular music consumption (either digital or physical) survey-takers are classified according to their frequency of participation. By asking when was the last time the respondent purchased recorded music, four categories of consumers are formed: those that purchased music over the past three months; between three months and one year; more than a year; and never. We label the first class as frequent consumers and the second class as casual consumers. Based on this, roughly 11.4% and 7% of the whole sample is classified as frequent and casual consumers respectively while the remaining 81.6% are rare or no consumers at all. The latter category is the largest one and includes roughly 62% of the sample. Focusing on consumers that purchase over a year, frequent consumers represent 61% of the sample and casual consumers the remaining 39%.

Next, the survey asks how many records and/or tracks the respondent purchased over the past three months. In this case only frequent consumers have a nontrivial answer. Table 1 summarizes the main descriptive statistics for purchases of full albums and tracks. On average, consumers purchased 0.37 albums, however this value is affected by the excess of zeros, that is, nonfrequent consumers, in the sample. If we remove these, the average frequent purchaser bought 3.3 albums, with a median of 2 albums. For track purchases, results show greater dispersion: the overall mean is 0.51 tracks, although frequent purchasers buy 4.45 tracks on average. The fact that even the third quartile of the distribution equals zero means that most frequent consumers are not inclined to buy individual tracks at all.

Finally, we include information about live concerts attendance over the past three months for frequent and casual consumers and the sample as a whole in Table 2. The differences in live consumption between recorded music buyers and the rest of the sample are not as large as those seen in the

Table 1. Descriptive Statistics for Album and Track Purchases.

Recorded Music	Mean	SD	Q1	Median	Q3
Albums					
Frequent consumers	3.29	6.11	1	2	3
Sample	0.37	2.31	0	0	0
Tracks					
Frequent consumers	4.45	80.18	0	0	0
Sample	0.51	27.07	0	0	0

Key: SD = Standard Deviation, Q1 = First Quartile, Q3 = Third Quartile.

Table 2. Descriptive Statistics for Live Attendance.

Live	Mean	SD	Q1	Median	Q3
Frequent consumers	0.6826456	2.152507	0	0	1
Casual consumers	0.3480826	1.181709	0	0	0
Sample	0.2594919	1.176973	0	0	0

Key: SD = Standard Deviation, Q1 = First Quartile, Q3 = Third Quartile.

Table 3. Cross Tabulation for Music Purchases and Copyright Infringement.

		Copyright Infringement		Total
		N	*Y*	
Recorded music purchase	*N*	10,606	2,232	12,838
		73.22%	*15.41*	*88.62%*
	Y	1,082	566	1,648
		7.47%	*3.91%*	*11.38%*
	Total	11,688	2,798	14,486
		80.68%	*19.32%*	*100%*

previous table. This can be explained if we look at them as two different cultural practices; in this case attenders are in any category of recorded music consumption in the sample. Data show that while frequent recorded music purchasers still attend above the average at the sample level – 0.68 times over past three months compared to 0.26 for the population as a whole – this difference is smaller than that observed for recorded music. This can be explained by noting that only 26% of frequent purchasers were also concert attenders, and that 53% of live concert attenders are recorded music purchasers, either frequent or casual. Overall, it seems that there is some correlation between recorded music and live music consumption although not a strong one.

Regarding copyright infringement, the survey asks whether the respondent copied or downloaded from the Internet over the past three months and the last year. The former case includes 19.3% of the respondents, while increasing the time frame to one year slightly increases that percentage to a 22%, which implies that most copyright infringers are rather active. Table 3 shows the cross-tabulation of the population based on both consumption and copyright infringement of recorded music over the past three months. The two categories overlap for roughly the 4% of the sample,

Table 4. Cross Tabulation for Live Concerts Attendance and Copyright Infringement.

		Copyright Infringement		Total
		N	*Y*	
Attendance	*N*	10,707 *73.91%*	2,045 *14.12%*	12,752 *88.03%*
	Y	981 *6.77%*	753 *5.2%*	1,734 *11.97%*
	Total	11,688 *80.68%*	2,798 *19.32%*	14,486 *100%*

which represents over a third (34%) of frequent recorded music purchasers. When we include those that copied or downloaded over the past year the overlap increases slightly by a 0.5%.

Table 4 shows the cross-tabulation between live attendance and copyright infringement. Here 5.2% of the sample is involved in both activities. Interestingly the percentage of attenders that infringe copyright is 43%, almost 10% more than the percentage for recorded music purchasers.

To sum up, data for Spain show that frequent recorded music consumers are also the majority of recorded music consumers over a year, and that a significant share of these (over one third) are active in copyright infringement. Two interesting features on music consumption arise from the previous data analysis: first, attendance to live concerts by recorded music frequent consumers is greater than the average, suggesting some complementarity between both forms of music consumption; second, while both live attenders and recorded music consumers are involved in copyright infringement, the former are slightly more active. While descriptive data suggest an association between copyright infringement and music consumption, either recorded or live, that does not imply a causal link, as we need to discard other factors that could affect both copyright infringement and music consumption. To do so, we discuss next an empirical framework to find the evidence linking both.

The Impact of Copyright Infringement on Recorded Music Purchases: A Propensity Score Matching Approach

The evaluation of the causal effect of piracy on consumption can be a tricky one. Usual statistical techniques, such as regression, will provide a biased observed effect if there are confounding factors that affect both the outcome (in this case music purchases) and the exposure (copyright infringement). An instrumental variables approach could address this issue but that would require the availability of good instruments. To illustrate the problem, let us think in the simplest setup: to compare reported music purchases in the sample for copyright infringers and non-infringers. The mean album purchases for non-infringers is 0.31 and that of non-infringers is 0.66, leading to a difference of 0.35 albums more in the latter case. This could be interpreted as the positive effect of copyright infringement on the number of albums purchased. However, this would miss the fact that there could be a selection bias if individuals that buy more music are also more likely to infringe copyright, for instance if strong preferences for music imply that individuals are both more likely of purchasing and copying/downloading. Note that this problem is absent in randomized trials, as individuals are exposed to the treatment (in our case copyright infringement) on a random basis. In this case one can compare the outcomes of exposed and unexposed individuals directly to analyze the causal impact.

Using the program evaluation terminology, let us define Y_i as the outcome for individual i, that is, number of purchases or attendance. Let D_i be copyright infringement (either $D_i = 0$ or $D_i = 1$) by individual i. Then we can make the outcome dependent on the exposure of i to copyright infringement: $Y_i(D_i)$. In this setup, copyright infringement is defined as the treatment and the ultimate goal is to determine its effect on some output (in this case music consumption). The effect of copyright infringement for individual i would be equal $Y_i(1) - Y_i(0)$, and the average effect at the population level would be its expected value, that is,

$$E[Y_i(1)|D = 1 - Y_i(0)|D = 1] = E[Y_i(1)|D = 1] - E[Y_i(0)|D = 1]$$

From the discussion above, it is clear that we would like to observe a counterfactual. Assume that individual i is a copyright infringer, hence $Y_i(1)$. Note that the effect on i of copyright is defined as $Y_i(1) - Y_i(0)$. But given that i is an infringer we do not observe the realization $Y_i(0)$. Indeed the problem of trying to compute the average effect at the population level equals to finding this counterfactual outcome: what would the purchases for those infringing copyright had been in case they had not been involved in copyright infringement. In other words, we would like to compare the outcomes for those exposed to piracy with and without the exposure. While the former are actual outcomes (observed data) the latter are not.

Propensity score matching is a way to overcome this difficulty by using treated and untreated (i.e., control) subjects that are as similar as possible – Caliendo and Kopeinig (2008) provide a practically oriented survey, while Dehejia and Wahba (2002) or Smith and Todd (2005) provide evidence suggesting that matching methods contribute to overcome selection bias. The key is to find a large group of non-treated individuals, that is, non-infringers, who are similar in a set of preexposure characteristics X. However, instead of defining similarity based on the observed characteristics X, a propensity score or the probability of participation is used. In this research the propensity score is the probability of copyright infringement by one individual given a set of observed characteristics X. Computing the propensity score involves the estimation of a binary dependent variable model for copyright infringement and check that some properties are met. Then a matching algorithm is used to match treated (copyright infringers) and untreated individuals. Finally a sensitivity analysis is performed to assess the causal effect of interest. Next, we follow these steps.

Computing the Propensity Score

The estimation of a probit model for copyright infringement implies modeling the probability of infringing copyright p in terms of a set of explanatory variables X:

$$p = \text{Prob}(D = 1|X) = F(X, \beta)$$

where $F(\ )$ is the cumulative distribution function for a standard normal distribution. The choice of covariates X for the model is done such that these are independent on treatment conditional on the propensity score. The main assumption is that X determines the probability of treatment, in other words, that the selection process that explains the treatment, that is, copyright infringement, is based on observables. In our case, the choice of covariates to explain treatment can be grouped in five blocks.

First, sociodemographic characteristics. In this group we include gender as a dummy variable, age, – and its square to account for nonlinearities – marital status (measured as a dummy for singles) and a dummy that informs whether the survey-taker is responsible for children under the age of 18 living in their same household. We also account for the size of the household (number of members).

Second, economic variables. One drawback of the SHCP2010 is that it does not include information about the survey-taker income. Therefore, we use indirect income indicators, such as labor market situation (dummy variables for being student, employee, unemployed, retired, and househusband) and the level of education attainment (dummy variables for attaining a high school degree, vocational training, and university education).

Third, geographical variables. We include a set of dummy variables measuring the city size of the survey-taker. This provides the following classification for cities: province capitals; cities with population over 100,000; cities with population between 50,000 and 100,000; and cities between 10,000 and 50,000 inhabitants (with the reference value being cities below 10,000 inhabitants that are not province capitals).

Fourth, we also include variables that measure households' physical capital. The survey includes information for music related equipment (music instruments, radio sets, CD players, portable disc players, MP3 players, tape players, turntables, and the like) and other cultural and IT equipment in the household (TV sets, cameras and videocams, videogame consoles, ebook reader, number of books, computers, smartphone, broadband, and mobile broadband mainly). However, the large number of variables in this group calls for a dimension reduction for estimation purposes. To do so, we summarize all the information about music equipment and physical capital by using a principal components analysis. This reduces the number of variables from 19 to 6: 3 for music related equipment and 3 for other physical capital. Yet these still capture over 50% of the total variance of the individual components.

Finally, a dummy for the term in which the survey was taken is included. Note that in the estimation some interactions terms between some of variables are included. The inclusion of these is suggested in the literature as a means to guarantee that the balancing condition is met. Specifically, the following interaction terms were included: age and age to the square and student; age and the three phisycal capital variables; and physical and music capital among them.

Note that survey weights were not used in the estimation as once we obtain the treatment and control groups some observations (those not in the common support) are removed from the sample, which leads to meaningless survey weights. Finally, it is important to mention that all the control variables pass the standard balancing tests required to guarantee that conditioning on the propensity score provides the same information as conditioning on the set of covariates X. In other words, when the balancing hypothesis holds, observations within the same propensity score must have

Table 5. Distribution of the Propensity Score.

Propensity score Inferior	Copyright Infringement		
	0	1	Total
0.0035	1,092	13	1,105
0.0125	755	17	772
0.0250	1,025	39	1,064
0.0500	1,376	112	1,488
0.1000	1,035	127	1,162
0.1500	855	161	1,016
0.2000	1,048	384	1,432
0.3000	634	323	957
0.4000	435	339	774
0.5000	314	443	757
0.6000	273	500	773
0.7000	117	298	415
0.8000	12	42	54
Total	8,971	2,798	11,769

the same distribution of observable characteristics with independence of the treatment status (i.e., whether individuals engage in copyright infringement or not).

Table 5 shows the final distribution of treated (copyright infringement=1) and controls (copyright infringement=0) across blocks of the propensity score. Note that some observations are discarded, reducing the sample size form 14,486 to 11,769, as they do not fall within the common support given by 0.0035, 0.9961.

Matching and Computation of the Average Effects for Frequent Consumers

In order to compute average effects we need to compare the outcome of treated and untreated. This implies matching each treated individual within the common support of the propensity score with a control. Matching can be undertaken by two main strategies: either by choosing an individual in the control which is most similar to the treated observation, or by building a weighted average of the controls where the weight for each control is determined by the closeness to the treated individual. The main difference between both strategies is the number of control individuals used, with the former discarding individuals in the control group and the latter using all of them.

We consider two matching methods in our empirical work. First, nearest neighbor matching (a method within the former matching strategy) is performed, in which a control is chosen for each treated individual such that it has the closest propensity score. Second, kernel matching (within the latter strategy) is used, where all controls form the counterfactual and weights are inversely proportional to the distance to the propensity score of the treated individual. In this case two kernel functions are used: the Gaussian kernel estimator and the Epanechnikov kernel estimator. Asymptotically different methods yield the same result, although for finite samples this is not the case. We opt to use the three of them in order to check the robustness of the results.

A second issue in the practical implementation of a matching procedure is that of estimating the standard error of the average treatment effect. We use analytical errors for nearest neighbor matching and bootstraped standard errors for the kernel estimator, using 400 replications.

Table 6 shows the results of the estimated average effects. For each method five columns are included. First and second with the number of treated individuals and controls used in computing the average treatment

Table 6. Estimated Average Treatment Effect for Album and Track Purchases and Live Attendance for Frequent Consumers.

	Treated	Controls	Difference	Standard Error	t
Albums					
Unmatched			0.349		
Kernel (Epan.)	2798	8971	0.125	0.068	1.833
Kernel (Gauss.)	2798	8971	0.133	0.074	1.809
Nearest Neigh.	2798	1676	0.119	0.089	1.338
Tracks					
Unmatched			0.864		
Kerner (Epan.)	2798	8971	−0.157	1.202	−0.130
Kernel (Gauss.)	2798	8971	−0.172	1.288	−0.134
Nearest Neigh.	2798	1676	−1.165	2.299	−0.507
Attendance					
Unmatched			0.488		
Kerner (Epan.)	2798	8971	0.192	0.050	3.877
Kernel (Gauss.)	2798	8971	0.215	0.047	4.570
Nearest Neigh.	2798	1676	0.186	0.053	3.504

effect. Next the estimate of the effect, its bootstrapped (or analytical for nearest neighbor matching) standard error and the test statistic for the statistical significance of the estimated effect. An additional row on top of each block shows the average treatment effect at the sample (unmatched) level, that is, the result of computing the difference between mean average consumption for infringers and non-infringers. The difference between this and the matching estimators is positive and large in all cases, pointing to a significant selection bias that is alleviated by matching.

In all cases results show that the number of controls used in nearest neighbor matching is significantly less than kernel matching, making the estimated average effect more imprecise. The advantage of kernel matching is that it uses the whole subsample of controls compared to the selection process implied in the nearest neighbor method. Nevertheless, point estimates are relatively similar in magnitude. Measured by the average effect, copyright infringement increases album purchases by a magnitude that is between 0.119 and 0.133, a significant but yet smaller effect than the unmatched result (which suggests an increase of 0.35 albums). Note that the average purchase is 0.37 albums for the whole population (although 3.29 for the subsample of frequent purchasers), this means a 33% increase in purchases (or a more modest 3.28% if we restrict the analysis to frequent purchasers).

As expected, the standard error in nearest neighbor matching is significantly greater than those based on kernel matching. Frölich (2004) shows that using a Monte Carlo simulation kernel estimators, under certain conditions, tend to be more efficient that nearest neighbor methods, that is have less variance. The effect of this greater standard error is that the result for album purchases becomes marginally nonsignificant (although a lower tail test would support the existence of a positive effect), with only the kernel estimates pointing to a significant and positive effect.

Looking at track purchases we see the greatest difference between the unmatched average effect (an increase of 0.864 tracks due to piracy) and the estimated average effects that are all negative although none of them significant. In this case we cannot conclude with copyright infringement having a clear effect on the purchase of individual tracks by frequent consumers.

The third block of results, shown in Table 6, is on the effect of copyright infringement on attendance to live performances. In this case all the results are statistically significant and support an increase of attendance between 0.186 and 0.215, compared to the unmatched effect equal to 0.488. To frame the result in relative terms, note that frequent music consumers attend to 0.68 music concerts over the past three months. In this case, an increase of 0.2 concerts per three months represents approximately a 30% increase in attendance.

Matching and Computation of the Average Effects on Participation

Results so far support a positive effect (null for tracks) of copyright infringement on music consumption by frequent consumers. However, this need not hold at the population level. Furthermore, the net effect could be negative if copyright significantly reduces purchases for casual consumers. Although unlikely, given that frequent consumers represent almost two thirds of all music consumers, it would be unwise to rule it out without further evidence. Unfortunately, the SHCP2010 only provides information about recorded music purchases for frequent consumers, hence the need to find this evidence using alternative ways. As a second best, we proceed to estimate the average effect of copyright infringement on participation as a binary variable for all music consumers over a year. By doing so we are measuring the effect of infringement on the probability of purchasing music (now without distinguishing between albums and tracks) or attending to a concert.

Table 7 presents the main results. In order to compare participation among different groups in the sample we include the participation effect on all consumers and on frequent consumers only. Some results are consistent with those shown in the previous section, as the size of the computed standard errors, and the estimated unmatched average effect that is greater in all cases than the estimated matched ones. However, the fact that the unmatched effect is greater in the sample of all consumers than in that of frequent consumers suggests a stronger selection bias in the former.

Looking at the results in detail gives some interesting insights. The effect on purchases is slightly greater for frequent purchasers (and the smaller standard errors make these more precise). Overall in both cases results point to a slight increase in recorded music participation (2.3–3.4% for all consumers and 3–4.2% for frequent consumers) due to copyright infringement.

The previous effect is reversed for attendance. Here we find a stronger effect of copyright on participation for the full sample of consumers. While infringement increases frequent music purchasers attendance by roughly 6%, it increases the participation of all music consumers by roughly 9–10%. This points to two related issues. First, supporting previous empirical work, there is a nonnegligible indirect effect of piracy on the

Table 7. Estimated Average Treatment Effect for Participation (Purchases and Live Attendance) for All Consumers.

	Treated	Controls	Difference	Standard Error	*t*
Purchases (all)					
Unmatched			0.140		
Kernel (Epan.)	2798	8971	0.029	0.013	2.345
Kernel (Gauss.)	2798	8971	0.034	0.012	2.759
Nearest Neigh.	2798	1676	0.023	0.016	1.393
Purchases (frequent)					
Unmatched			0.110		
Kerner (Epan.)	2798	8971	0.039	0.010	3.821
Kernel (Gauss.)	2798	8971	0.042	0.011	3.948
Nearest Neigh.	2798	1676	0.030	0.014	2.148
Attendance (all)					
Unmatched			0.327		
Kerner (Epan.)	2798	8971	0.091	0.013	6.875
Kernel (Gauss.)	2798	8971	0.099	0.013	7.629
Nearest Neigh.	2798	1676	0.088	0.018	4.934
Attendance (frequent)					
Unmatched			0.185		
Kerner (Epan.)	2798	8971	0.061	0.012	5.319
Kernel (Gauss.)	2798	8971	0.067	0.012	5.767
Nearest Neigh.	2798	1676	0.062	0.014	4.364

attendance to live concerts. Second, this effect is greater when we consider the whole population of music consumers suggesting that the link between recorded music and live music consumers is not a strong one. This could be consistent with a weakened complementarity between both markets (live and prerecorded) where frequent consumers in one market are not necessarily the most active in the other.

Finally, it should be noted that we have performed a sensitivity analysis for hidden selection bias on all the presented results by computing the Mantel-Haenszel bounds for the binary outcome variable (purchases of albums and tracks and attendance for frequent consumers and purchases and attendance for all consumers). From it we derived the robustness of the results on participation, that is, whether copyright infringement increases the likelihood of buying or attending. Overall it supports the robustness of the above results under different assumptions about the (over/under) estimation of the treatment effect.

DISCUSSION

Based on the previous empirical evidence we find some statistically significant effects of copyright infringement on recorded music consumption. These results are robust to various specifications and allow us to conclude that copyright infringement is, at worst, neutral in that it does not affect, on average, consumer behavior. More interestingly, most of the findings point to small but nevertheless significant positive effects. We next discuss the main findings and their implications.

First, we find a significant and positive effect of copyright infringement on album purchases by frequent consumers. This increased consumption could be linked to the increased awareness that recorded music gets from the exposure of individuals to it and/or a positive consumption external effect. Nevertheless, whether this effect is due to network or sampling effects is not as relevant as the existence of the effect itself.

This same effect is found to be nonsignificant for track purchases. To understand this we need to look at the data from which two interesting facts arise: only 7.6% of frequent consumers do purchase tracks, and 30% of those who purchase tracks are exclusively involved in recorded music through tracks purchasing. In other words, tracks purchasing is still a marginal activity in the sample and a significant share of those who buy tracks do not buy albums. This suggests that, to some extent, the underlying behavior driving tracks and albums purchases can be different: while buying an album individuals are revealing strong preferences about a band, picking individual songs only reveals preferences for that track and a weaker link to the artist. In the former case piracy would be expected to have a different effect than in the latter, with sampling playing a stronger role for full albums purchasers.

The third result in our chapter refers to the effect of copyright infringement on live music performances. Here, we see a significant positive effect in all estimates, a finding that supports the hypothesis of indirect appropriation across products. However this effect, measured in terms of the increase in the participation rate, is stronger for all music consumers than for frequent ones. That casual consumers who infringe copyright exhibit a greater increase in attendance than frequent ones suggests that while live performances and recorded music consumption are complements, the degree of this complementarity is not necessarily a strong one. While in the past live performances helped to sell records, nowadays albums can be considered as a way of promoting concerts. Over time, the degree of complementarity between both markets has diminished.

Table 8. Descriptive Statistics for Different Recorded Music Consumption Profiles.

Recorded Music Consumer	Age	Female	University	Live	Copyright	Broad
No	49.31	0.528	0.153	0.205	0.174	0.545
Albums	40.05	0.457	0.301	0.681	0.325	0.764
Tracks	33.56	0.564	0.282	0.564	0.667	0.846
Tracks/Albums	36.28	0.448	0.379	0.770	0.529	0.770
Total	48.22	0.520	0.170	0.259	0.193	0.571

To gain a descriptive insight on the behavior that could be driving these results we present some summary statistics by different music consumer profiles. Table 8 shows consumers classified according to music purchases in four classes: no media buyers (those who did not buy in the past three months), only albums, only tracks, and finally, tracks and albums. It also includes the mean at the overall sample level, that is, total. Note that, except for age and live (number of live performances attended over the past three months), all the means are to be interpreted as a sample proportion, for instance 45.7% of album purchasers are female and 30.1% have a university degree.

As it emerges, there are some clear similarities between different music consumers. Music consumers are younger than the average (with track only consumers being the youngest) and more educated (the proportion of university graduates is significantly greater). However, there are also differences between them: track only buyers have a greater share of women, are more actively involved in copyright infringement (almost twice the proportion for albums only), and have a greater broadband penetration (roughly 85% compared to approximately 76% for other recorded music consumers). Overall differences in average consumer profiles could help explaining differences in the effects of copyright infringement on consumption.

In a similar vein, Table 9 classifies consumers by recorded and live music consumption habits. From it we see that live attenders are younger, and more educated than the mean (specially when combined with prerecorded consumption) and also more likely to infringe copyright (more than the average but also than prerecorded music only users). Again, this is consistent with live and recorded music consumption being driven by different motivations that, ultimately, yield the different observed outcomes.

Finally, we should note that even though the precise effects apply only to frequent consumers, the analysis on participation suggests that these

Table 9. Descriptive Statistics for Different Music Consumption Profiles.

Music Consumer	Age	Female	University	Live	Copyright	Broad
No	50.96	0.533	0.145	0.000	0.146	0.522
Only recorded	41.40	0.473	0.294	0.000	0.297	0.740
Only live	34.75	0.482	0.221	2.015	0.421	0.757
Live/Recorded	34.85	0.419	0.335	2.635	0.475	0.841
Total	48.22	0.520	0.170	0.259	0.193	0.571

effects could hold also when we consider both casual and frequent consumers. From it we conjecture that the effect of copyright infringement could be asymmetric. Participation estimates suggest that the effect on recorded music for casual consumers will be smaller than that of frequent consumers, while the effect on attendance will be greater. In any case we have found no evidence of a decrease in participation, a result that reinforces our previous conclusions.

REFERENCES

Alcalá, F., & González-Maestre, M. (2010). Copying, superstars, and artistic creation. *Information Economics and Policy*, *22*, 365–378.

Andersen, B., & Frenz, M. (2010). Don't blame the P2P file-sharers: The impact of free music downloads on the purchase of music CDs in Canada. *Journal of Evolutionary Economics*, *20*, 715–740.

Battacharjee, S., Gopal, R. D., Lertwachara, K., Marsden, J. R., & Telang, R. (2007). The effect of digital sharing technologies on music markets: A survival analysis of albums on ranking charts. *Management Science*, *53*, 1359–1374.

Boldrin, M., & Levine, D. (2002). The case against intellectual property. *American Economic Review*, *92*, 209–212.

Boldrin, M., & Levine, D. (2005). Intellectual property and the efficient allocation from social surplus from creation. *Review of Economic Research on Copyright Issues*, *2*, 45–67.

Caliendo, M., & Kopeinig, S. (2008). Some practical guidance for the implementation of propensity score matching. *Journal of Economic Surveys*, *22*, 31–72.

Dehejia, R. H., & Wahba, S. (2002). Propensity score-matching methods for nonexperimental causal studies. *Review of Economics and Statistics*, *84*, 151–161.

Frölich, M. (2004). Finite-sample properties of propensity-score matching and weighting estimators. *Review of Economics and Statistics*, *86*, 77–90.

Gopal, R. D., Bhattacharjee, S., & Sanders, G. L. (2006). Do artists benefit from online music sharing? *Journal of Business*, *79*, 1503–1533.

Herings, P. J., Peeters, R., & Yang, M. S. (2010). Competition against peer-to-peer networks. *Information Economics and Policy*, *22*(4), 315–331.

Hui, K., & Png, I. (2003). Piracy and the legitimate demand for recorded music. *Contributions to Economic Analysis and Policy*, *2*(1). (Article 11).

Klein, B., Lerner, A., & Murphy, K. (2002). The economics of copyright fair use in a networked world. *American Economic Review*, *92*, 2005–2208.

Liebowitz, S. J. (2006). File-sharing: Creative destruction or just plain destruction? *Journal of Law and Economics*, *49*, 1–28.

McKenzie, J. (2013). P2P file-sharing: How does music file-sharing affect recorded music sales in Australia? In P. Tschmuck, P. L. Pearce, & S. Pearce (Eds.), *Music business and the experience economy*. Berlin: Springer-Verlag.

Michel, N. J. (2006). The impact of digital file sharing on the music industry: An empirical analysis. *The B.E. Journal of Economic Analysis & Policy*, *6*(1). (Article 18).

Minniti, A., & Vergari, C. (2010). Turning piracy into profits: A theoretical investigation. *Information Economics and Policy*, *22*, 379–390.

Montoro-Pons, J. D., & Cuadrado-García, M. (2008). Legal origin and intellectual property rights: An empirical study in the prerecorded music sector. *European Journal of Law and Economics*, *26*, 153–173.

Montoro-Pons, J. D., & Cuadrado-García, M. (2011). Live and prerecorded popular music consumption. *Journal of Cultural Economics*, *35*, 19–48.

Montoro-Pons, J. D., Cuadrado-García, M., & Casasús-Estellés, T. (2013). Analyzing the popular music audience: Determinants of participation and frequency of attendance. *International Journal of Music Business Research*, *2*, 35–62.

Mortimer, J. H., Nosko, C., & Sorensen, A. (2012). Supply responses to digital distribution: Recorded music and live performances. *Information Economics and Policy*, *24*, 3–14.

Oberholzer-Gee, F., & Strumpf, K. (2007). The effect of file sharing on record sales: An empirical analysis. *Journal of Political Economy*, *115*, 1–42.

Peitz, M., & Waelbroeck, P. (2004). The effect of Internet piracy on music sales: Cross-section evidence. *Review of Economic Research on Copyright Issues*, *2004*, 71–79.

Peitz, M., & Waelbroeck, P. (2006a). Piracy of digital products: A critical review of the theoretical literature. *Information Economics and Policy*, *18*, 449–476.

Peitz, M., & Waelbroeck, P. (2006b). Why the music industry may gain from free downloading? The role of sampling. *International Journal of Industrial Organization*, *24*, 907–913.

Rob, R., & Waldfogel, J. (2006). Piracy on the high Cs: Music downloading, sales displacement and social welfare in a sample of college students. *Journal of Law and Economics*, *49*, 29–62.

Shy, O., & Thisse, J. F. (1999). A strategic approach to software protection. *Journal of Economics and Management Strategy*, *8*, 163–190.

Smith, J. A., & Todd, P. E. (2005). Does matching overcome LaLonde's critique of nonexperimental estimators? *Journal of Econometrics*, *125*, 305–353.

Takeyama, L. N. (1994). The welfare implications of unauthorized reproduction of intellectual property in the presence of demand network externalities. *Journal of Industrial Economics*, *42*, 155–166.

Takeyama, L. N. (1997). The intertemporal consequences of unauthorized reproduction of intellectual property. *Journal of Law and Economics*, *40*, 511–522.

Varian, H. R. (2000). Buying, sharing and renting information goods. *Journal of Industrial Economics*, *48*, 473–488.

Waldfogel, J. (2010). Music file sharing and sales displacement in the iTunes era. *Information Economics and Policy*, *22*, 306–314.

Zentner, A. (2006). Measuring the effect of file sharing on music purchases. *Journal of Law and Economics*, *49*, 63–90.